Believing Thinking, Bounded Theology

Believing Thinking, Bounded Theology

The Theological Methodology
of Emil Brunner

CYNTHIA BENNETT BROWN

☞PICKWICK *Publications* · Eugene, Oregon

BELIEVING THINKING, BOUNDED THEOLOGY
The Theological Methodology of Emil Brunner

Copyright © 2015 Cynthia Bennett Brown. All rights reserved. Except for brief quotations in critical publications or reviews, no part of this book may be reproduced in any manner without prior written permission from the publisher. Write: Permissions, Wipf and Stock Publishers, 199 W. 8th Ave., Suite 3, Eugene, OR 97401.

Pickwick Publications
An imprint of Wipf and Stock Publishers
199 W. 8th Ave., Suite 3
Eugene, OR 97401

www.wipfandstock.com

ISBN: 978-1-4982-0457-6

Cataloging-in-Publication data:

Brown, Cynthia Bennett.

Believing thinking, bounded theology : the theological methodology of Emil Brunner / Cynthia Bennett Brown.

xii + 194 p. ; 23 cm. Includes bibliographical references.

1. Brunner, Emil, 1889–1966. 2. Theology. 3. Neo-orthodoxy. 4. God—History of doctrines. 5. Barth, Karl, 1886–1968. 6. Kierkegaard, Søren, 1813–1855. I. Title.

ISBN: 978-1-4982-0457-6

BT98 Z25 2015

Manufactured in the U.S.A.   07/17/2015

All Scripture quotations are from the ESV® Bible (The Holy Bible, English Standard Version®), copyright © 2001 by Crossway, a publishing ministry of Good News Publishers. Used by permission. All rights reserved.

"The source and norm of all Christian theology is the Bible. Its subject matter is the secret and, at the same time, manifest meaning of the Bible: the God who inclines Himself toward man and makes Himself present to man: Jesus Christ and His Kingdom."

—EMIL BRUNNER, *THE DIVINE-HUMAN ENCOUNTER*, 30

Contents

Preface | ix
Acknowledgments | xi
Abbreviations | xii

1 Introduction | 1

Part I: Believing Thinking
2 The Task of Dogmatic Theology | 11
3 Case Studies in *Dogmatics* | 35

Part II: Bounded Theology
4 Beyond *Dogmatics* | 77
5 Beside Brunner—Karl Barth | 104

Part III: Transformed Being
6 Behind Brunner—Søren Kierkegaard | 141
7 Conclusion | 182

Bibliography | 189

Preface

"...the mystery hidden for ages and generations but now revealed to his saints. To them God chose to make known how great among the Gentiles are the riches of the glory of this mystery, which is Christ in you, the hope of glory."
—Colossians 1:26–27[1]

How clearly I recall the feeling when I first learned that the doctrine of the Trinity was not found in Scripture. It was a mix of bewilderment and shame that I had been a Christian for some twenty-five years yet never knew this. A shadow of mild betrayal: Why had no one ever told me? A sense of uncertainty: What do I do now? I am a disciple of Jesus Christ who ardently pursues truth (I was in graduate school at the time), and I have believed something that is *not in the Bible*? If I have been so mistaken for so long about this, what else do I believe that isn't actually biblical?

And that wasn't the only discovery I made during that study stint. I also discovered theology. I was thirty years old, had been going to church since I was five, had been a cross-cultural missionary for six years, and it was only in a systematics module that I came to discover theology. I finally had a language to explore and express my faith. Oh, happy day!

My story is not the point of this book but this episode serves to illustrate the significance of the *doing* of theology. I do not mean the sitting in class and writing papers, but rather the ancient task of moving from the text of Old and New Testaments and into explication and application of revelation to faith and life. This "how" of theology is my preoccupation in the pages that follow. *How* do we engage Scripture according to its own

[1]. All Bible citations are from The Holy Bible (English Standard Version).

Preface

measure, in terms that necessarily go beyond its own language, context, and terminology but still remain faithful to God's self-unveiling in it? *How* do we explicate the Christian faith in such a way that it makes transformative sense to every person who encounters it? *How* do we submit ourselves as theologians, pastors, scholars, parents, teachers, learners to its ancient wisdom in ways that impact twenty-first century life in a revolutionary manner?

My purpose in the following pages is to explore and answer these and other questions through the lens of twentieth century theologian Emil Brunner. In a first instance I seek to hear Brunner on his own terms, in order to distill the pattern he establishes for believing thinking, teaching, and preaching. As a result of this listening I then aim to outline the pattern of his work—his methodology. My conclusion can be summed up thusly: Emil Brunner's theology is thoroughly biblical (if non-biblicist), warmly pastoral, carefully intellectual, and insistently Christocentric, offering an exposition of the Christian faith that is truly worth our time. The "how" of his theology deserves renewed attention, as does a renewed look at the broader content of his work from this angle.

Brunner has influenced significantly my own theological work over the past decade. When I recently realized this fact, I had a moment of grave concern. Brunner has been out of fashion for some decades in the UK and this is where I happily live and work. Would I find any allies, or would I be defining myself as outdated and irrelevant for the rest of my career? Furthermore, Brunner for much longer has been branded a liberal of sorts by certain evangelical scholars, in the United States in particular, and my faith-heritage is rooted in such a context in New England where I was raised. Would I be alienating myself forever from loved and valued dialogue partners by writing about a man who has been so censured? You can perhaps understand my anxieties about the impact—of the impact—of Brunner on my own thinking, praying, and doing of theology. If you undertake to engage with this book, I hope you too will be at the least intrigued about what has been neglected in recent decades in this disciple of Jesus Christ from Zurich. I trust that you will find something of his work that draws you closer in heart and mind to the unveiling of God's glory in Christ . . . and the hope of that glory in us.

Acknowledgments

My thanks for this particular text traverse a decade but space restricts my named appreciation to a few people. Professor Stephen N. Williams is first among that number for his supervision of my doctoral work on Brunner and also for his continued example as a colleague of what it means to *be* a Christian theologian. Previous to my PhD studies, professors at both Regent College (Vancouver) and Taylor University (Indiana) left an indelible imprint on my mind and heart that I still gratefully carry today, though I cannot name each individual here. Students over the past five years, both undergraduate and postgraduate, have engaged with me in the process of putting Brunner's methodology to the test—whether they knew it or not; I am grateful to and for them.

Recent months have brought me the consistently pleasant and constructive engagement with folk at Wipf and Stock, whom I thank. I would also like to acknowledge *Scottish Journal of Theology* for the use of ideas first published in 2012 in my article "The Personal Imperative of Revelation: Emil Brunner, Dogmatics and Theological Existence."

To my husband Martin I owe great gratitude. He has supported in numerous practical ways by corralling uncooperative Word documents, proofreading again and again, undertaking extra tasks of all kinds so that I could meet deadlines, and generally encouraging me to press ahead step by step. Finally, thanks are due to the two people to whom this book is dedicated, who have supported me unswervingly for two score years plus a few: my parents, Edward and Susan Bennett.

Abbreviations

CD   Karl Barth, *Church Dogmatics*
SD   Søren Kierkegaard, *The Sickness Unto Death*
CUP Søren Kierkegaard, *Concluding Unscientific Postscript*
PF   Søren Kierkegaard, *Philosophical Fragments*

1

Introduction

"Real theology is not only for experts, but it is for all to whom religious questions are also problems for thought."

—BRUNNER, *MAN IN REVOLT*, 12

WHAT IS THE PURPOSE OF THIS BOOK?

ONE CANNOT EXPLORE THE landscape of theology for too long before discovering a field surrounding the topic of methodology that has been growing for some decades. The twentieth century Swiss theologian Emil Brunner is of special interest on this subject, in particular, his view of the theological task and the boundaries that he places on the work of dogmatics. His perspective on the "how" of theology merits serious attention, although his theological method has yet to receive critical assessment in the same way that the thought of some of his contemporaries has. In this light, the purpose of this book is to state the nature of and the limits to theological inquiry established by Emil Brunner and, further, to illustrate the claim that his approach deserves careful consideration for theology today.

The dearth of recent investigative work on Brunner, with the notable exception of Alister McGrath's *Emil Brunner: A Reappraisal*, means that substantial primary source study must be done before evaluation can be proposed or conclusions drawn. Because my goal is to outline Brunner's methodology, within that narrow scope I am most concerned with his mature thought. All of the primary sources considered here were penned during or after what might be called Brunner's eristic-dogmatic period (1928–1960), save two that were published one year before.[1]

The book unfolds in the following manner. Part I establishes Brunner's foundational conviction that theology is "believing thinking." In chapter 2 I start by establishing what we might call Brunner's methodological first principles. Brunner asserts that truth as encounter, reflected in the apostolic witness, defines the nature of and is the criterion for theological inquiry. God has revealed himself in the historic event of Jesus Christ and the apostles' testimony to this event is the seedbed in which we do our theological digging. Out of this earth theology grows from its roots of exegesis, catechesis, and polemics. All theological endeavors must emerge from and be consistent with the biblical narrative of the apostolic witness. The doctrine of the Trinity serves as our first case study for the purpose of testing Brunner's paradigm in his own work. Chapter 3 continues with further case studies as I survey Brunner's three-volume *Dogmatics*. Particular attention is lent to subjects such as the divine nature and will, the *imago Dei* and redemption, the church as *ekklesia*, and the role of faith. Because of Brunner's emphasis on the historical event of Jesus Christ, a few words must be said about both the demythologizing task and the place of *Heilsgeschichte*.

Part II focusses on the "bounded theology" that results from Brunner's schema. I expand the focus in chapter 4 beyond *Dogmatics* to other published works. To what extent does Brunner respect the boundaries he establishes, and how effectively is he able to deal with the heart of the Christian faith in so doing? The theme of revelation dominates this chapter and illuminates the particular shape and nature of God's self-communication, as well as Brunner's critical rejection of the doctrine of infallibility. Chapter 5 carries on in the same direction but by a parallel route. Recalling the outline of Brunner's view of the doctrine of the Trinity in chapter 2, I turn to the

---

1. See Johnson, "Soteriology as a Function of Epistemology," 7–9. Johnson draws our attention to three periods: the predialectical (1914–1920), the dialectical (1921–1927), and the eristic-dogmatic. The last period is the context of this study, given that the works we will examine were written during this period or just after, with the exception of two that were penned in 1927, being *The Philosophy of Religion from the Standpoint of Protestant Theology* and *The Mediator*.

INTRODUCTION

work of Karl Barth, Brunner's contemporary, and his own methodological approach to the same doctrine. Here we learn not only about Barth's methodology but also a bit more of the "why" and "how" of Brunner's approach, including his rejection of the virgin birth as dogma.

"Transformed being" is the focus of Part III. It builds on the first two parts of the book by exploring the *effect* that theology should have on the one's whole existence. To round out our understanding of personal encounter, I explore in chapter 6 the influence of Søren Kierkegaard on Brunner's understanding of truth.[2] Unsurprisingly for anyone who knows Kierkegaard's work, questions of truth, paradox, existence, and subjectivity are some of the themes explored. Finally, in chapter 7 I posit some concrete contributions to the life and work of the Christian theologian today. When theology is done in response to God's loving personal encounter with us, two things occur: transformation happens within the individual who responds in faith and submission to the Lordship of Christ, and empowered engagement with the church and the world follows. Without this kind of transformation, theology has not been effectively worked out in the Christian. Courageous, believing, and boundaried thinking is required.

WHO WAS EMIL BRUNNER?

When compared with the raft of books and theses dedicated to the likes of Barth, Bonhoeffer, and Bultmann, only scant biographical details on Brunner have seen printed form. The following particulars are worth summarizing here.[3] The Zurich region was the place both of his birth in 1889 and of most of his education through his Doctor of Theology degree in 1913. The few years that followed found Brunner in various successive roles: as a language teacher in England; as a member of the Swiss militia; and as a vicar intern back in Zurich. In 1916 he took the pastorate of a small village congregation in Obstalden, and a year later he took a wife, Margrit Lauterburg. This rural pastorate would be his primary work until 1924, save a year of study at Union Theological Seminary in New York (1920).

---

2. It should be noted that the inclusion of both Kierkegaard and Barth springs from their immediate relevance to Brunner's thought and is undertaken for the elucidation gained by exploring their work alongside his.

3. A source which summarizes biographical information is Humphrey, *Brunner*, 15–20. A more comprehensive book published in 2006 is Jehle, *Emil Brunner*, and McGrath picks up on numerous points from Jehle in his own volume.

3

A significant move in 1924 ushered him to the University of Zurich, where he held the Chair of Systematic and Practical Theology until 1955. A second sojourn in the United States took place during these decades (1938–1939), this time as visiting professor at Princeton Theological Seminary. Brunner's later influence extended even further afield than North America, as he spent 1953–1955 in Tokyo, contributing to the fledging International Christian University and earning him the title of "missionary theologian."[4] Though suffering from measured physical limitation after a brain hemorrhage in 1955, Brunner remained an active theologian and churchman, continuing to publish books and articles until his death in 1966.

It is difficult to add to this thumbnail sketch an equally concise synopsis of the various factors contributing to his personal and theological development, including the historical era in which Brunner and his colleagues lived and worked.[5] It is evident from a variety of factors throughout his life that Brunner was made sensitive to, and remained concerned about, the crossroads between faith and life, between the gospel and what it means to be human, between the church and culture. Early influences include Hermann Kutter, Christoph Blumhardt, and Leonhard Ragaz who encouraged his family's engagement in the Religious Socialist Movement, awakening Brunner to the struggle of many for social justice. Alongside this sociological formation, Brunner identifies an internal "search for a scientifically satisfying formulation of my faith," for which he chose Kant and Husserl as his guides. It was his questions about the reality and certainty of God, however, that led him to immerse himself in Luther and Kierkegaard, two figures who feature time and again throughout his writings.[6]

It is not only intellectual questions that influenced his concern for the application of the Christian faith, though. During the years of his professional life, Brunner's travels affected his theology as much as did his pastoral and teaching work in Switzerland. He reflects that, amidst the variety of experiences during his career, "scholarly work in theological and philosophical areas was and still is strictly subordinated to the proclamation of the Gospel . . . The question of the relation of faith to philosophy was and still is a fascinating question for me but, nevertheless, basically a secondary problem. I was and am above all a preacher of the Good News."[7]

---

4. See editorial "Emil Brunner and the Wide-open Spaces," 255.
5. See Burnier, "Protestant Theology in Wartime Switzerland."
6. Kegley and Bretall, eds., *Theology of Brunner*, 4–11.
7. Ibid., 8.

INTRODUCTION

His passion for people to grasp the gospel as much with their lives as with their minds led him to a series of questions that shaped his writings. The first conclusion he came to about the problem of "the proclamation of the Gospel in a secularized society and to the peoples of the world" was one of anthropology and apologetics. This investigation led to a second priority in his thinking, "namely a reformulation of the biblical concept of truth . . . Since then, all of my work in dogmatics has been done in the light of this aspect: the God who communicates himself." Lest we get the wrong idea, however, Brunner regards his apologetic concern as secondary to the main task of theology, which he describes as "the struggle for the right understanding of faith in Christ."[8] It is this struggle, above any other, that dominates the focus of the following pages.

WHY STUDY BRUNNER?

"It is not unusual in any field of scholarship to find a true giant overshadowed by the colossi. Emil Brunner's stature and influence in twentieth century theology would be indisputable were it not for Barth and Bultmann who overshadowed him."[9] In this way Stanley Grenz and Roger Olson begin their introduction to the man and thought of Emil Brunner. It is not only in comparison with other recent theologians that the lack of material on Brunner is evidenced; the texts dedicated solely to his theology are few in number, whereas his contemporaries such as Barth and Bonhoeffer, and subsequent theologians the likes of Moltmann and Pannenberg, are thoroughly studied still. McKim identifies a different reason for Brunner's obscurity. He suggests that "Brunner's vanishing resulted, at least in part, from his effort to communicate effectively the ancient faith to modern Western society. In that attempt, Brunner tried to remain faithful to the biblical witness while simultaneously recognizing the sea of change that had occurred at the Enlightenment. His efforts often placed him in the theological center, where there is precious little room in contemporary Protestant thought."[10]

Given the absence of recent attention, why is the present project either necessary or beneficial? Firstly, it is profitable because Brunner still is afforded consistent, if passing, mention in introductory texts to modern theology. Schwarz's 2005 masterpiece is one such example in which he

---

8. Ibid., 11–15.
9. Grenz and Olson, *Twentieth-century Theology*, 77–78.
10. McKim, "Brunner the Ecumenist," 91.

draws attention to the mixed geographical attraction that Brunner held. "Since Barth's influence on the European continent was so overwhelming, however, Brunner's more dialogical approach was more appreciated in the British Isles and above all in Asia and America,"[11] where his voice is still heard in both Reformed and modern theology studies. The fact that he was more popular in American circles and that his influence is still perceptible in Japanese theology[12] indicates Brunner's commitment to live the personal encounter of faith about which he writes, even at the potential cost of prestige in his homeland.

McEnhill and Newlands comment that although Brunner's work has faded into the background since his death, the impact of his work continues to be acknowledged. Sometimes it is "as a footnote in the development of dialectical theology or as a useful foil in explaining Barth's rejection of natural theology," but "this was not always so; Brunner received a far earlier and far wider reception in the English-speaking world than Barth. However, he has since suffered considerably in comparison with Barth who is generally thought to be more creative, more radical and more insightful. All this may be true but it is to be hoped that Brunner's more open and apologetic style, along with his avowal of certain key themes of Reformed theology that Barth may have too readily neglected, will one day merit a return to prominence for this important thinker."[13] In my view, that day is near.

This brings us to a second reason Brunner's work merits study: to be heard on his own terms, not only in comparison with his Basel counterpart. It is undeniable that "Brunner made his own distinctive contribution to the break with nineteenth century liberalism that dialectical theology represented."[14] As a result, it is not only possible but also valuable to appraise Brunner's work for itself, without having to pit him against Barth or Barth against him. Despite, or perhaps because of, their differences, both men have something significant to bring to the theological table, and to disregard Brunner because of Barth's uncommon stature is to be unnecessarily

11. Schwarz, *Theology in a Global Context*, 316. Hebblethwaite concurs, suggesting that Brunner was appreciated as "more balanced" than some of his colleagues: Hebblethwaite, *The Christian Hope*, 136.

12. Personal correspondence with Dr. Nozomu Miyahira, a Japanese theologian from Seinan Gakuin University in southwest Japan, yields a list of sources that references this claim (25 February 2009).

13. McEnhill and Newlands, *Fifty Key Christian Thinkers*, 84.

14. Ibid., 80.

short-sighted. As Jewett states, "Though he has not written so voluminously as his compatriot, Karl Barth, he has shown a versatility, amplitude, and balance of thought not found in the man at Basel."[15] Brunner's impact on twentieth century theology was important, and neo-orthodoxy, especially in its Anglo-Saxon expression, was due in large part to Brunner's work of translation and propagation. Nelson goes as far as to say, "One could safely risk the generalization . . . that in the years 1935–55 no single theologian had more influence upon British and American Protestant ministers and teachers."[16] Reymond's view extends to the contemporary context when he writes, "a knowledge of Brunner's basic theological thought is absolutely essential . . . to an intelligent understanding of the contemporary theological scene in America for . . . [his ideas] have done much to determine the direction of American theology today."[17]

Still and all it must be asked, does the absence of more recent, focused study of Brunner mean that his relative obscurity is deserved and that he is side-lined in modern theology for the good reason that he is just not worth studying? This is certainly one possible interpretation of the data. It is equally possible, however, that Grenz and Olson are correct in their assessment and that Brunner truly is a giant worthy of deliberation. Indeed, that is a premise of this book, that he remains valuable into the twenty-first century. In this I share McGrath's view: "Brunner needs to be reconsidered and rehabilitated—not in his totality, but certainly in relation to some of his methods and approaches, which retain validity and significance, especially in the theological and cultural climate which has developed in the west in the twenty-first century."[18] My proposition is not that Brunner offers a methodology to end all methodologies, but that his understanding of the nature and limits of theological inquiry deserves to be heard more clearly than it has been and that it remains relevant to today's theological task. We will see that his approach is not entirely unique, for commonalities with other historical and twentieth century theologians are numerous. If, however, theology at its best is conversation, then Brunner's voice is worth listening to, either again or for the first time.

---

15. Jewett, *Brunner's Concept of Revelation*, 139.

16. Nelson, "The Final Encounter," 486. See also Dorrien, *Barthian Revolt*, particularly 1–10, 106–19. McGrath concurs: *Reappraisal*, 177.

17. Reymond, *Contending for the Faith*, 210.

18. McGrath, *Reappraisal*, 226.

PART I

Believing Thinking

2

The Task of Dogmatic Theology

"The God of the Bible is a God who speaks, and the Word of the Bible is the Word of this God."

—Brunner, *The Divine-Human Encounter*, 31

Theology for Brunner, first and foremost, is believing thinking. Faith is both preliminary and simultaneous to knowing and speaking about God. How does a modern Swiss-German theologian arrive at such a conclusion in a post war to end all wars world? How does theology retain any shred of legitimacy or trustworthiness at all? In what way can theologians remain optimistic about their task when so much has gone so wrong, and that on a Christian continent? With this context in mind, the purpose of this chapter is to offer an overview of Emil Brunner's approach to the task of dogmatic theology during his as the eristic-dogmatic period (1928–1960). Central to this task is to identify and outline his key paradigms and defining terms that have significant influence on the method and content of his work. As McGrath notes, the core elements of Brunner's theology were in place by 1929 so this time frame will allow us to evaluate how his method works itself out in cooperation with his theology.[1]

---

1. McGrath, *Reappraisal*, 72.

Part I: Believing Thinking

PART ONE: BRUNNER'S METHODOLOGY OUTLINED

The Divine-Human Encounter is a compilation of lectures that Brunner delivered at the University of Uppsala, Sweden, in 1937 on the subject of the Christian understanding of truth.[2] Succinct yet incisive, it serves as a valuable introduction to the motivation that lies behind Brunner's methodology by offering insight into the context guiding Brunner's explanation of Christian knowledge of God. His purpose in this particular study is two-fold: one, to show the compromising and pervasive impact that the object-subject antithesis has had on Christian faith; two, to redefine truth according to a biblical conception and to indicate its implications for theology. For the purpose of dogmatics he rephrases the age-old question, What is truth and how do we come to know it? as How is knowing related to being? Let it be clear at the outset that Brunner is not jettisoning the object-subject correlation in all areas of truth-seeking; quite the contrary. His particular focus is the work of theology and the proclamation of God's word that, given the nature of revelation, requires a unique approach. As McGrath observes, these lectures "represent one of the most significant attempts to develop a theological understanding of the relationship of revelation and faith which avoids the problematic notions of 'subject' and 'object' arising from the Enlightenment, particularly in relation to the Kantian tradition. Yet they also provide an understanding of human identity as a 'Thou'—rather than an 'It'—which resists commodificationist and collectivist reductions of human individuality."[3]

Truth as Encounter

Illustrating the impact of the object-subject antithesis on Christianity can be done effectively in an historical synopsis. As Brunner represents it, the Christian community in its early years was irreversibly influenced by the Greek philosophical worldview as it sought to understand, teach, and convert others to the gospel. As time distanced the church from the historical event of Jesus Christ, God's definitive self-revelation in the God-man lost its decisiveness for faith. The perception of God's word was altered as a result. It became popular belief, says Brunner, that "the divine revelation

---

2. The lectures are alternatively known under a subsequent publication titled *Truth as Encounter*.

3. McGrath, *Reappraisal*, 160–61.

The Task of Dogmatic Theology

in the Bible had to do with the communication of those doctrinal truths which were inaccessible by themselves to human reason; and correspondingly that faith consisted in holding these supernaturally revealed doctrines for truth."[4] This change, alongside the elevation of truth as something objectively obtained, resulted in the antithesis between so-called objective truth, expressed in the church's *Credo*, and faith's subjective acceptance of God's revelation (*credo*). This calamitous divorce between the truth of God's revelation and a faith response to it is what Brunner laments and seeks to rectify in his call to return to a biblical understanding of truth.

Brunner's survey of the impact of this antithesis on the church is as compelling as the story is tragic.[5] He contends that, by and large, the Christian community throughout the centuries has propagated, however unknowingly, this misrepresentation of the gospel. Pressed by the powers of history, ecclesial turmoil, and corrupt human nature, the church has swung between the poles of subjectivism and objectivism, with both extremes misconstruing the nature of truth and faith. Brunner highlights a notable exception to this flux in the Reformers, to whom he often returns in his writing. Sadly, however, the point at which the church had arrived by the nineteenth century was nothing short of the "subjective dissolution of theology," which he would inherit in his own day.[6]

Brunner and his contemporaries, therefore, found themselves no longer dealing with believing discourse about God's gracious interface with humankind in Christ but with a religion that judged belief in special revelation as *passé* and truth as stagnant and quantified. The church needed above all else a new foundation for its knowledge of the truth as the basis for its commission on earth—to know God and to make him known. This fresh source was not to be anything new at all, though; "the truth of the salvation and revelation clearly discoverable and available in the words of the Bible" was the original root to which to return.[7] The critical difference lay in the approach to truth, no longer as an object to be possessed but as the gift of God's active, personal self-communication.

Foundational to this shift is an altered understanding of revelation. With the Reformers, Brunner understands the divine self-communication

---

4. Brunner, *Encounter*, 12. Further discussion of the influence of Hellenism on Christianity is found in Brunner, "The Significance of the Old Testament," 247–49.

5. Brunner, *Encounter*, 14–29.

6. Ibid., 25.

7. Ibid., 20.

Part I: Believing Thinking

as both present tense and inextricably entwined with the historical event of Christ: "the Word of the living, present Spirit of God, wherewith the Incarnate Word, Jesus Christ Himself, takes possession of our hearts and Himself makes His home there."[8] He maintains that the knowledge of faith is not an enterprise by which the knower possesses the thing known, but rather a process that transforms the knower. Here Brunner answers the question posed at the beginning of *The Divine–Human Encounter*: the relation of the knower to the known is personal encounter. In this light, Brunner's thesis "truth as encounter" becomes the only viable starting point for the particular kind of knowledge that dogmatics is concerned with, that of knowing God personally. His claim is a battle cry to twentieth century theology to bring the study of God back to its absolute subject.

How does truth as encounter differ from truth as defined by the object-subject antithesis, particularly as it pertains to dogmatics? The influence of the latter leads to a definition of faith as intellectual assent to fixed statements of "truth" established by the self-appointed authority of the church. Brunner insists that biblical faith is markedly different. It is belief in the risen Lord whom we know through personal relationship. As a result, truth as encounter is distinguished from the antithesis in that it is personal instead of objective, and it is active rather than static.

Brunner firstly emphasizes God's self-revelation as personal, as historical event, and as unique. Based on this, he traces the divine–human encounter in the following way. God first reveals himself to persons through Jesus Christ, the risen Lord, who discloses in human form the fullness of the divine being. Relationship is thereby established between the individual and God. To this divine communication the individual is invited to respond in obedience-in-trust (*pistis*), thus completing the encounter in fellowship. Scripture is replete with examples of such events between God and individuals, the quintessential encounters being those of the apostles with the risen Christ. This is the biblical description of faith that Brunner establishes as the foundation of theological inquiry.

Secondly, this decisive experience with God is what Brunner calls the event of *personal correspondence*. The specific connection between the event and knowledge that occurs therein is described thusly: "Knowledge and act, knowing and *happening*, are in this instance a single process. God communicates Himself in love: and this happens in the fullest sense only

---

8. Ibid.

The Task of Dogmatic Theology

when His love is known in responding love."[9] This is where Brunner arrives at a renewed conception of faith. Instead of passive assent to objective statements about God, faith becomes the positive participation in relationship with God through Christ, leading to transformation of the knower. What does Brunner's depiction of personal correspondence tell us about how we know God? Most importantly it affirms that God is the self-revealing God who initiates relationship with human beings. He communicates himself out of love for his creation, and the partnership created by his love impacts the human person who responds in faith. Otherwise stated, knowing occurs when human beings lovingly respond to God's revelation in the living dynamic of "I-Thou" interface.[10]

A further question immediately follows. What significance does this portrayal of truth have for the work of theological inquiry? Brunner explains that "we are beginning to suspect why in the Bible the word 'truth' appears in what is for us a strange context with the words 'doing' and 'becoming.' Faith, which appropriates God's self-revelation in His Word, is an event, an act and that a two-sided act—an act of God and an act of man. *An encounter takes place between God and man*."[11] Truth, then, is personal encounter.

With good reason Brunner addresses the question of how such a first-person, divine–human relation could be possible if God is holy and humankind is permeated with sin. How does this understanding of truth as encounter relate to justification?[12] Brunner's response is singular: Jesus Christ. He explains at length how the person and work of Jesus in salvation history constitute God's self-revelation and effectuate humankind's reconciliation with its creator. In the person of Jesus Christ we encounter God and enjoy union with God. "God's quality of being Person, revealed in Jesus

---

9. Ibid., 45. God as love is indicative of his movement towards us, of his self-giving in revelation, his forgiveness and reconciliation, and the movement of the kingdom of God among us. See Brunner, *Word and World*, 50; Brunner, *Theology of Crisis*, 13, 11; Brunner, *Mediator*, 313.

10. Brunner, *Dogmatics II*, v. This reference to the "Copernican turning point" in philosophy by Ebner and Buber is brief in space but its influence is evident throughout Brunner's work. See also Brunner, *Word and World*, 64. McGrath also identifies this influence; see *Reappraisal*, 157–160. Hynson helpfully points out the correlation between Buber's use of the German for "meeting" or "encounter"—*Begegnung*—and Brunner's title for *Truth as Encounter* which turns on the same term—*Warheit als Begegnung* in "Theological Encounter: Brunner and Buber," 352.

11. Brunner, *Encounter*, 53.

12. Ibid., 56–75.

Christ, is itself of such a nature that it establishes fellowship. Being person [*Person-sein*] and being in fellowship [*In-Gemeinschaft-Sein*] are identical. Such is the Biblical concept of the Personality of God."[13] This is the constant message of Scripture, and it is the on-going experience of salvation for the people of God.

How does Brunner come to such a confident conclusion about how we know God? Divine revelation in Jesus Christ is again his answer. Before we explore the specifics of the incarnation attested to in the apostolic witness, though, Brunner's definition of the nature of theological inquiry must be addressed.

Encounter and Theological Inquiry

Brunner reminds his readers of the character of theology when he states, "dogmatic thinking is not only thinking about the Faith, it is believing thinking."[14] Because personal encounter with God cannot occur apart from faith, dogmatics—that is, believing reflection about that encounter—is only possible where intellectual inquiry about God transpires within the context of belief. It is clear from this that the proper context for theology is the community of faith. Dogmatics is the responsibility of the teaching church as it measures the experience of personal encounter against the witness of God's self-disclosure in Jesus Christ.

Dogmatics has three purposes, or roots, within the history of the church: exegesis, catechesis, and polemics.[15] Brunner identifies the first impetus as the need for careful interpretation of Scripture, which is required for Christian discipleship. Inherent in this responsibility is the need to hear what the whole Bible says about daily life and faith, a message that is not always readily accessible on a surface reading of individual texts. Catechesis, theology's second purpose, has as its goal the instruction of believers concerning the Christian confession of "Jesus is Lord," traditionally in preparation for baptism but also in doctrinal matters. Finally, as the church is faced with questions from within its own community, the work of theology must engage in a careful defense of the gospel to counter heresy and to return the

---

13. Ibid., 101.

14. Brunner, *Dogmatics I*, 5.

15. Brunner offers a summary of these "roots" in *Encounter*, 11. A more thorough description is found in *Dogmatics I*, Prolegomena.

Christian community to the point of truth, that is, personal encounter with God through Christ.

The impact of this understanding of truth as personal encounter and theological inquiry as believing thinking about that encounter is that the knower enjoys fellowship with God through Christ as well as fellowship with others in the church. As real and tangible as this transformation is, Brunner reminds his readers that we do not yet know and see God in the fullness of his being. We only see in part what will one day be fully revealed when we encounter God face to face. The church labors in the interim to know God through the witness he has left in the written word. Brunner's view of Scripture is central to his methodology, so the relationship between encounter and the apostolic witness must be understood correctly. What is the nature of the scriptural kerygma, and how does it communicate God's self-revelation? How can dogmatics respect that nature in order to best hear God's word in it?

Brunner insists that absent in the biblical witness is a doctrine of God as he is in himself (*Gott-an-sich*), as well as a doctrine of man in himself (*Menschen-an-sich*). The biblical testimony instead speaks in terms of "God as the God who approaches man [*Gott-zum Menschen-hin*] and of man as the man who comes from God [*Menschen-von-Gott-her*]." In other words, God reveals himself only in the context of the warp and weft of human history. Such encounter "is not a timeless or static relation, arising from the world of ideas . . . [R]ather the relation is an event, and hence narration is the proper form to describe it . . . God 'steps' into the world, into relation with men: He deals with them, for them, and in a certain sense also against them; but He acts always in relation to them, and He always acts."[16]

Hence the nature of the biblical testimony as Brunner describes it possesses significant implications for how we do theology. His main contention is that the word of God is characterized by action and encounter, communicated in narrative and verbal language. God does not offer ontological statements about himself abstracted from experience. Instead, the people God addresses in the Old and New Testaments experience his work in their lives and only as a result do they affirm God's character as loving, just, jealous, and merciful. It is this dynamic quality of the written word that must be respected and imitated by theological inquiry, hence avoiding the compromise of objective and subjective religion while fostering the personal encounter of faith.

16. Brunner, *Encounter*, 31–32.

Part I: Believing Thinking

In contrast to mysticism, rationalism, and metaphysics, Brunner identifies the context of history as one of the defining features of Scripture that distinguishes it as special revelation. Regarding the event of Jesus Christ as the center and culmination of this salvation history, he observes, "God's relation to the world and to mankind is not something timeless, but it is action in history. Its historicity is as unconditional as the relation itself: hence this event is unique; it happened 'once for all.' Its uniqueness is as essential to this Good Friday event as the unconditioned will to Lordship and fellowship of that love which is disclosed in this unique event."[17]

The heart of the early church proclamation—the kerygma—is the reconciliation that God brings about through Jesus Christ. The risen Lord is preached as the good news that makes us his sons and daughters. For the apostles, the vision was not limited to their time, nor is it so limited for us. The church believes that the kingdom of God draws closer to its final consummation as the word is preached, as Christ's lordship is recognized, and as fellowship is established in the I-Thou encounter of faith.

Until Christ's return, though, we accept that our knowledge is partial, veiled, obscured by sin. For this reason Brunner points out that the revelation of God in Christ does not "*exhaust* the whole mystery of God . . . The Mystery of God stands at the beginning and at the end of revelation."[18] Mystery is not just the result of what we do not know; it is that which determines what we cannot know and should not seek to know. Mystery is, in fact, the first characteristic Brunner treats in his discussion of the divine nature and attributes, and it remains a significant element in his methodology, as we will continue to see.

Encounter and the Apostolic Witness

What could our encounter with the risen Lord possibly share in common with that of the apostles since Christ long ago ascended to the right hand of the Father? Brunner pinpoints in the New Testament the apostolic witness and the preaching of the Christian community as the particular means of divine revelation. The significance of the life, death, and resurrection of the God-man to which the law and prophets point cannot be overstated, for it is in this very event that personal correspondence occurs. It is the apostles' message that through Christ, in his very body, God reconciles rebellious

---

17. Ibid., 106–7.
18. Brunner, *Dogmatics I*, 225–26.

The Task of Dogmatic Theology

humankind to himself, in love, lordship, and fellowship. Brunner argues that only those who responded to it in faith by believing that Jesus is the Son of God register the event of the resurrection. Their witness, above and beyond any others, is set apart because it is *believing* testimony.

As such the apostolic witness serves as the standard by which we gauge what is central to personal encounter and therefore true, and what is peripheral to faith and thus not theology's priority. This measure is what Brunner calls the *principle of contiguity* according to which all doctrine is to be weighed. This principle facilitates such questions as, How closely related is X doctrine to the word of God in Christ? To what extent does the doctrine guide our attention to God and away from itself as the truth? The purpose of the principle is that "the more . . . the testimony about God enables one to hear His address, so much more immediate is the something, the doctrine, connected with the primary concern of the Holy Scriptures."[19]

That said, we must keep in mind that even as the criterion by which our thinking is judged, the apostles' witness is only the *means* to faith; the life, death, and resurrection of Christ alone is the object. One important correlation between the biblical witness and ourselves is that belief in the resurrection is the first point of commonality that we share with the apostles. As the words of Scripture become God's active self-communication to us, the same divine testimony to Christ that took place as God revealed himself to the apostles becomes reality.[20] As a result, Brunner contends that post-apostolic Christians have the same knowledge of Jesus that the apostles had, differing only in the manner in which it is received. We are enabled to encounter God through the word enlivened by the Spirit, "to learn to know Him as they saw Him and knew Him."[21]

Having thus established the reality of personal correspondence, Brunner more precisely describes the connection between encounter and theological inquiry. Revelation alone remains the source of God's self-communication, and we know God only as the Holy Spirit births in us believing hearts. This is the primary concern of faith. Doctrine, on the other hand, retains a secondary role in the life of the Christian community

---

19. Brunner, *Encounter*, 83.

20. Brunner says it this way in *I Believe in the Living God*, 93: "you believe in the resurrection, not because it is reported by the apostles but because the resurrected One himself encounters you in a living way as he unites you with God."

21. Brunner, *Dogmatics II*, 371.

as it illuminates and safeguards that to which faith has attested over the centuries. As necessary and constructive as dogma is, it is never a substitute for faith.

Danger dawns, warns Brunner, when Scripture as special revelation is traded for philosophical, moral, and rational sources of truth that are concerned more with the ideal absolute than with personal encounter. It is especially the work of polemics that can lead in this direction because preoccupation with heterodoxy, which it is meant to counter, can result "in the statement of questions and concepts which are strange to the simple believer and even to the Bible itself."[22] In this context it could be said that Brunner's attitude shifts beyond suspicion into antipathy for any dogmatic expression that is foreign to the biblical testimony and that moves away from narrative into the realm of metaphysics.[23] He suggests that revelation has very little to do with metaphysics because the word of God does not tell us the *how* of God or of his ways, but rather is concerned with an affirmation of *who* he is. It is not theology's purpose to dissolve mystery but to affirm God's revelation in Christ.

Brunner is ultimately concerned with keeping the word, who is Jesus Christ, central to faith. It is this word of God that is of final consequence; all other words we use in theology are means to the end of communicating this one word. This is his primary preoccupation in placing careful boundaries on the work of theological inquiry, to keep it harnessed not only to the content of Christ but also to the personal encounter that facilitates knowledge of him. This is fundamental to the discussion about the nature and limits of theological inquiry. There remains, though, a burr of discomfort. While one might agree that Jesus is determinative for knowledge of God, and while one might accept that human words are instrumental without being the truth themselves, a question follows. What kind of value does theological language possess for knowing God?

Brunner's response is to affirm the role of doctrine for faith, although the approach to the relation between truth as encounter, special revelation, and the written word is complex. He writes, "We continue to maintain that an abyss lies between what happens in the meeting between God and man in revelation and faith, what happens in this occurrence in the second person and everything that has the form of discussion about 'something true'

---

22. Brunner, *Encounter*, 11.

23. Brunner, *Mediator*, 35. For further discussion, see Brunner, *Theology of Crisis*, 25; Brunner, *Word and World*, 14–18, 32.

in the third person."[24] We will see that Brunner does acknowledge a limited place for dogma in the larger context of Christian theology, while he warns that the believer must respect doctrine as much for what it does not say as for what it affirms. Depending on how we deal with the Trinity or any other doctrine, equating dogma with faith can become distracting at best, and, at worst, diametrically opposed to revelation.

Encounter and Doctrine

The difference between doctrine and the word of God depicted by Brunner is not as categorical as it might seem; for, he admits, can we not say that God does communicate something about himself? "Can this faith (*pistis*) be consummated in any other way except that we believe 'something' 'which' God says to us?" Accordingly Brunner acknowledges a substantial difference between the first-person language of personal encounter and third-person commentary on that encounter in doctrine. He continues, "The question is whether this abyss is not bridged after all, whether in the act of God's speaking and man's thus being enabled in faith to hear and think the positive relation between Word and doctrine is not already also established."[25]

This is the vital connection for Brunner between Jesus Christ as the word and theological language: the content of God's self-revelation is only communicated and understood within the context of our language about him. As a result, "we can never separate the abstract framework from the personal Presence contained in it, although certainly we must differentiate them . . . Doctrine is certainly related instrumentally to the Word of God as token and framework, serving in relation to the reality—actual personal fellowship with God; but doctrine is indissolubly connected with the reality it represents."[26] Doctrine, therefore, is not something accidental, but it is the necessary means by which God's communication is accessible to us.

Herein Brunner acknowledges an inherent connection between the something said about God and the divine person we seek to know by faith. The order must be kept straight as the former is there to serve the greater reality of the latter.

---

24. Brunner, *Encounter*, 77.
25. Ibid.
26. Ibid., 79.

> Faith, in other words, is in the final analysis not faith in something—something true, a doctrine; it is not "thinking something," but personal encounter, trust, obedience and love; but this personal happening is indissolubly linked with conceptual content, with truth in the general sense of the word, truth as doctrine, knowledge as perception of facts. God gives Himself to us in no other way than that He says something to us, namely, the truth about Himself; and we cannot enter into fellowship with Him, we cannot give ourselves to Him in trustful obedience, otherwise than by believing "what" He says to us. Since, therefore, this conjunction of token and reality, of signification and what is signified, is already given in the act of divine revelation, we call the connection not only instrumental but sacramental.[27]

To restate it, the something we come to know about God in divine revelation directly corresponds to the person of God that we know through faith-obedience.

A final comment is needed. How is a proper relation between conceptual content and personal encounter maintained in the work of theological inquiry? "It must suffice to recognize that an abysmal difference, and yet at the same time a necessary connection lies between the two . . . The Reformation insight remains valid: Word of Scripture and Word of Spirit, personal directness in doctrinal indirectness, even as Jesus Christ must fulfill the law in order to free us from it."[28] This is the insight and tension that dogmatics must maintain.

PART TWO: THE DOCTRINE OF THE TRINITY

Barth's voice, among others, can be heard in Brunner's appreciation of dogmatics, and the reader is right to make such connections, as far as they go. Nevertheless, it is as we approach the doctrine of the Trinity that the unique character of Brunner's methodology comes to the forefront. McGrath's assessment is appreciative: "Brunner is an important . . . contributor to the twentieth century theological debate over the place and function of the doctrine of the Trinity in a Christian dogmatics. The divergences over the place of the dogmatic location and function of the doctrine of the Trinity within the 'dialectical theology' movement of the mid-1920s have not been

---

27. Ibid., 80.
28. Ibid., 86.

given due attention, and remain an important point of debate in theology. Brunner's position and voice need to be heard."[29] To this doctrine we now turn.

Concern for consistency between the word of God and our words about him is precisely what motivates Brunner to treat the doctrine of the Trinity as he does in *Dogmatics I*. We begin our study by examining the relation between the doctrine and the apostolic witness, followed by Brunner's analysis of the doctrine itself. In his first comments on the subject in the introduction to chapter 16, "The Triune God," Brunner makes what some would take to be a self-evident statement. He asserts that the doctrine of the Trinity is not biblical proclamation and therefore is not considered part of the church's kerygma, but it nevertheless is the doctrine that defends the faith of the church and of Scripture. How can it be that the doctrine of the Trinity is not part of the gospel message but endures as fundamental to the work of theology? This is a difficulty from which he finds no easy escape given his insistence on the centrality of Scripture.

The New Testament Witness

Brunner's methodology requires him first of all to establish the measure of contiguity between the doctrine of the Trinity and the apostolic witness. How closely does the doctrine lie to New Testament data about divine triunity? How does the apostolic witness present the God who reveals himself in human history? We are interested in the movement Brunner makes from the apostolic witness as the source and criterion of theology to the doctrine Trinity as the fruit of theological inquiry. When Brunner speaks of the doctrine of the Trinity, he has in mind specifically the formula *una substantia—tres personae* as the decisive statement crafted and defended by the church fathers. His problem with the dogma is not the veiled divine reality to which it points but the mystery it is often used to dispel.

Brunner's starting point for consideration of the biblical witness is the person of the Father, specifically the "Father in heaven" as the name Jesus taught his disciples. He is not just any father of Old Testament faith or of ancient religion or of a timeless ideal. The Father we know by faith is only revealed as such in the New Testament through the Son. Human beings can know God because through Christ we too become children of God.

---

29. McGrath, *Reappraisal*, 54.

It is through this intimate, first-person relationship that the Father makes himself known as both holy and loving.

The Father communicates himself in history in two ways: in the incarnation of the Son, and through the witness of the Spirit who testifies in human hearts that Jesus is the Christ. As such it is Jesus who makes the Father known in a unique manner, in a way in which nothing in all of creation or salvation history does. Furthermore, it is the Holy Spirit who reveals Jesus as the Son to human hearts, so that with the apostles we declare, "You are the Christ." The divine–human relation does not end there, though; the Spirit renders the Father and Son present today in the church. Brunner summarizes the relations: "If the Name 'Father' designates the origin and content of the revelation, the Name of the 'Son' designates the historic Mediator, and the 'Holy Spirit' the present reality of this revelation."[30]

The issue of the Son is at the heart of the question of the Trinity even more than the identity of the Father, though the two must be presented together. What did the title 'Son' signify for Jesus' disciples in light of their Jewish heritage? Brunner returns to Pss 2 and 110, which indicate that the Son is the one who reveals the authority of the Father-King through his action, thus expressing the same authority as the one he represents. What is consequently significant for revelation is Jesus' action as the Son, for it is in the context of his doing that his being is disclosed.

Brunner emphasizes how the titles attributed to Christ are intended to underscore his work. The title of Messiah tells us that Jesus is the one who was promised, who fulfils the old covenant. As Revealer he discloses the Father, and as Redeemer he liberates humankind from sin. The titles of Prophet, Priest, and King are similar: Christ is Prophet because he possesses in his person the authority of the divine word; he is Priest because he achieves in his own person reconciliation through the cross; he is King because the rule of God is uniquely inaugurated in time and space during his thirty-three years in the flesh.[31] "All this expresses the fact that Jesus is first of all understood by the Church through His work, His function, His significance for salvation. The Christology of the New Testament . . . is determined throughout by *saving history* (*Heilsgeschichte*) and not by metaphysics."[32] For this reason the identity of Christ cannot be separated from his ministry because it is through his work that we come to know his

---

30. Brunner, *Dogmatics I*, 206–7.
31. For a more detailed discussion of these titles see Brunner, *Dogmatics II*, 271–307.
32. Ibid., 273.

person and the person of the Father who sent him.³³ The conclusion with which the apostles present us is that the Son is God himself.

Whereas the Son receives attention as the historical revelation of God, the Spirit is identified as the experiential testimony to Christ and the inward presence of God. It is only by his work that one recognizes Jesus as the Son. This relationship is central to Brunner's understanding of on-going revelation. "The self-communication of God is not only accomplished in the Historical and the Objective; He seeks us, our very self, our heart . . . The Spirit who dwells within us is indeed the Spirit of God, and what He effects can therefore be nothing less than the manifestation of the life which is his own."³⁴

Analysis of the Doctrine

Brunner acknowledges that the problem with the Trinity for the post-apostolic church was not that there are three names around which the New Testament witness turns, but what the relationship is among them. As Christianity spread and encountered various threats from within and without, the issue of a triune Lord could not be left unresolved; so arose the task of the doctrine of the Trinity, the story of which is familiar. During some two hundred years of heterodoxical winds blowing from various directions, the church's response was initially expressed in the Creed of Nicaea with its emphasis on the only begotten Son, followed by the Athanasian Creed emphasizing the triune nature of God. Soon, though, questions were asked about the eternal origin of the Son and the transcendent sphere of the Father and Spirit with him, and the creeds were found wanting in their capacity to respond. Hence, theology's necessary labor led to the tumultuous debate about the Trinity. Brunner appreciates the patristic priority given to Scripture at this point but laments the use of philosophical conjecture in the process that he deems irrelevant to genuine biblical reflection. He has in view the introduction of the term *substantia* that enters the creed and Christian thought and that "has had a particularly disastrous influence . . . To conceive God as Substance is the very sharpest contrast to the Biblical idea of the Absolute Subject." Equally problematic for him is the use of language of *personae*, which cannot escape "an uncertain vacillation

---

33. For elucidation on the inseparability of work and person, see particularly in chapter XV, 'The Person and Work of Christ," in *Mediator*, 399–415.

34. Brunner, *Dogmatics I*, 215.

between Tritheism and Monotheism."[35] Thus he asks, "Is this formula of the Trinity, of the *'tres personae'* and the *'una substantia,'* really in accordance with the center of the message of revelation, the unity of God's Nature and His Revelation?"[36]

From this perspective, it would seem that more harm than good has come from the doctrine's formulation, and that it has side-lined, however inadvertently, the salvation history of biblical revelation. Attention instead was turned to the intra-triune relations and the life of the Trinity itself. Brunner goes on to assert that, besides distracting from that which is revealed in human history to what remains hidden in divine transcendence, there was a further distortion. "The ecclesiastical doctrine of the Trinity aided the growth of the mistaken understanding of *Agape*, the confusion between *Agape* and *Eros*. Since the life of God within the Trinity was severed from the history of Salvation, the *Agape* of God came to be understood as His love for Himself."[37] On one hand, such misunderstandings distract from the work of reconciliation in salvation history, which for Brunner is both the stage and the drama of divine revelation. On the other hand, a positive and central conclusion of the doctrine is that the revealer and the revealed are one. This is the extent to which he affirms the doctrine: God discloses himself in Jesus Christ and is himself the one who loves us from eternity. God is the loving one from eternity because he loves the Son from all eternity. No created order is needed for him to be thus, but rather the created order is an expression of his being love.

With this material in mind it must be asked, to what extent does the doctrine of the triune God reflect Scripture's concern with God's activity to reconcile creation to himself? In other words, where is divine triunity articulated in Scripture as one being in three persons? Brunner affirms that salvation history points to all three names as integral to God's self-revelation and to redemption, reconciliation, and the fulfilment of the kingdom of God. We can say fairly, then, that the New Testament witness reveals God as triune. In so far as the doctrine of the Trinity was meant to affirm and safeguard this revelation, it has value, however limited, for Christian discipleship.

Beyond this restricted use, though, Brunner considers the doctrine unessential for faith. He maintains that, as a metaphysical statement of the

35. Ibid., 239.
36. Ibid., 222.
37. Ibid., 239.

divine being, the doctrine is peripheral to the biblical kerygma and therefore tangential for theology because it fails to reflect God in the event of his drawing near in the God-man. "This rightful attitude of reverent silence before the mystery of God is not served by inventing, by the use of concepts of this kind, a *'mysterium logicum,'*" argues Brunner, "but rather by renouncing the attempt to penetrate into a sphere which is too high for us, and in which our thinking can only lead to dangerous illusions."[38] The difference is critical: faith is preoccupied by the Father's love expressed through Christ and the Holy Spirit in the human story, but the doctrine of the Trinity as a philosophical statement separates who God is from what he does among us.

Brunner distinguishes the doctrine's utility for catechesis from its nonessential role for personal encounter by acknowledging that it is not in conflict with the absolute subject of faith. In other words, the doctrine of the Trinity is differentiated from the event of encounter because no doctrine is prerequisite to faith; at the same time it is not in contradiction to faith (and thereby has relevance for Christian education) in that it safeguards the reality of the divine being as three in one. Moreover, although this doctrine expresses something essential to the Christian message, this message is always given us in the context of God's activity in salvation history. The doctrine consequently should never be considered an invitation to explain the *how* of the intra-triune relations. The role of the doctrine is to preserve the *what* of the biblical revelation—God as Father, Son, and Spirit—and to invite us to worship God in the mystery of faith.

This case study serves to illustrate what Brunner perceives to be the respective natures of, and right relationship between, revelation and doctrine. He maintains that the apostolic witness abides as the hard and fast boundary beyond which theological investigation dares not wander. It would not be too strong a statement to say that, from Brunner's perspective, dogmatics never has need to move beyond God's self-revelation in the historic event of Jesus Christ into the realm of abstract conjecture.[39] If truth is personal encounter, then every formulation of truth must lead towards I-Thou relation with God. In contrast, when we speak of knowing God as adherence to dogmatic statements, we inevitably move in the direction of intellectual speculation and away from fellowship.

---

38. Ibid., 227.
39. For example, see Brunner, *Encounter*, 87–88.

Part I: Believing Thinking

CONCLUSION

Contributions

Thus far we see that Brunner not only assesses what had become a propositionally-bound Protestantism but also suggests an alternative vision of faith in God. His insistence on truth as encounter indicates a dynamic relationship between the knower and the known that more accurately denotes the eternal life of which Jesus spoke when he said, "that they may know you the only true God, and Jesus Christ whom you have sent" (John 17:3). Brunner's schema establishes knowledge of God as an event that has begun in the here-and-now and anticipates its fulfillment in the consummation of the kingdom. This view is in stark contrast to the Christian faith as a standard set of dogma that paralyzes the on-going nature of revelation. Brunner's approach reestablishes our understanding of the present-tense character of God's self-revelation and invites us to participate in his reconciliatory activity as his children. Three principles ground the "how" of his work: theology is believing thinking; theology is boundaried by the apostolic witness; and theology bears the fruit of transformed being.

The first contribution of Brunner's schema is that theological inquiry itself is freed to be a relational event. If the goal of theology is believing thinking within the context of Christian community and for the purpose of discipleship, then it is and should remain an inherently relational activity. In other words, theology happens best in relationship with other believers. In sharing our personal encounter with the living Christ, we come to a deeper understanding of who this God is whom we meet in the pages of Scripture. This is the dynamic nature of theological inquiry within the community of faith.

A second strength is Brunner's perspective on Scripture as *God's* word, through which *God* speaks. God is the one who determines the meaning of his self-expression in the written and living word. Audible in this insistence is the resounding clash of special revelation with modern theology's experiential, human-centered truth. It is with Brunner in mind that Jürgen Moltmann comments, "In this 'word' God is not only the object of human discourse; for God is not an object of experience like the objects in the world which human understanding can know, define and control. If God himself is taken seriously as the Lord, he must be perceived and thought of as the subject who utters his word. Thus theology as *speaking about God*

The Task of Dogmatic Theology

is possible only on the basis of *what God himself says*."[40] Brunner's method keeps the biblical revelation central to faith and to theological inquiry, making the word both the means and measure of our believing thinking. When we let the Spirit of God speak to us on his own terms, the biblical revelation has as much to say to us today as it did to the early church.

A final point pertains to ethics, a subject always in the background of Brunner's reflections. *The Theology of Crisis* in particular is interested, not in the question of "how one may rightly conceive reality, but how one may rightly exist in the midst of that reality. [These pages] are concerned solely with the ethical problem; and therefore they are concerned with Christian faith and nothing else."[41] It is clear that Brunner's approach to theological inquiry allows for and even insists on integration between dogmatics and ethics.[42] We have seen that the person of Christ cannot be separated from his work, and that the apostolic witness emphasizes how Jesus preached and ministered as God-man. In the same way Jesus' disciples are called to live and to work out of their identity as God's children. This is entirely consistent with Brunner's view of theological inquiry as a task of Christian community. As we talk about God and test our experiences against his word, we are simultaneously constrained and empowered to love our neighbor. A lesser interpretation of the biblical proclamation would have a weaker correlation between theology and ethics, for when faith is defined as intellectual assent to a set of revealed truths, our engagement with the world does not have to conform to those propositions in the same way that faith requires. In contrast, when truth is personal we are accountable to the divine person who deals with us in every area of our lives, working with us to welcome his kingdom as he transforms us individually and communally into the image of Jesus. For Brunner, just as this theme of redemption was the good news of the apostolic message, it remains the singular passion of God's word and work in the world.

40. Moltmann, *The Crucified God*, 66 n57.

41. Brunner, *Theology of Crisis*, xiii. See also chapter IV, "The Problem of Ethics," 68–91.

42. Barth and Bonhoeffer are likewise committed to the same theology-ethics interface: see Lovin, *Christian Faith and Public Choices*. McGrath helpfully directs attention to the historical situation in Switzerland during this period that had a profound influence on both theologians' ethical imperative. "Karl Barth and Brunner alike regarded ethics as grounded in theology, and interpreted the *ethical* failure of the German churches in encouraging war through a *Kriegstheologie* (which often seemed to reflect pagan rather than Christian themes) as ultimately a theological failure, demanding a radical theological correction." McGrath, *Reappraisal*, 8.

Part I: Believing Thinking

Questions

Exactly where does Brunner draw the line? Is he averse to moving beyond the exact words of Scripture, or is his concern to protect the broader categories of biblical thought? He comments in *Encounter*, "since thinking is easier for us than practical obedience in faith and love, the danger of willful speculative developments is always with us, and these lead all too readily and in unforeseen ways to transformations in the Gospel."[43] He continues his assessment of the dangers of unbounded theology. "Indeed willful speculative theology, whose particular intellectual interests have led it ever farther away from the essential Biblical message, has brought heavy losses to the Church both in ancient and modern times. Hence the mistrust of all ideas which are not derived directly from the Biblical world is readily understood and entirely justified."[44]

In the context of *The Divine–Human Encounter* he refers to that kind of thinking the impetus of which is to define and control knowledge of God as the object-subject antithesis does, and to offer answers sourced outside of God's revelation in salvation history. Is it a threat to faith that when revelation is transmuted into objective truth the knower thinks he can master knowledge about God and thereby hold sway over God? In this case the danger of divorcing Christian living from belief is very real; the believer can assent to a body of propositions and say "I believe" without ever being transformed by personal encounter with the Lord. This is a risk that Brunner acutely feels, leading him to reject any source of knowledge of God apart from that which is reflected in Christ.

This leads to an important question that arises at the interface between exegesis, dogmatics, and discipleship. How is the believer to respond when, inspired by what he has encountered in Scripture, he prayerfully inquires as to how he is to live the kind of love that Jesus requires? If the love of the Father, Son, and Spirit is to show believers the kind of agape that is to characterize their own relationships, do they not need to know more about this trinitarian existence? Although this line of thought admittedly leads beyond the event of the apostolic witness, such a plausible case can suggest not the detachment of ethics from theology through willful speculation but their integration.

---

43. Brunner, *Encounter*, 11.
44. Ibid., 11–12.

The Task of Dogmatic Theology

How does this hypothetical example stand up to the contiguity principle? In other words, to what extent does the love expressed in the intratriune relations illustrate the love of the body of Christ, hence reflecting the glory of God's self-revelation and reconciliation of humankind to himself in Christ? Brunner's methodology does not allow our thinking to get even this far. He maintains that that which has been shown in the life of Christ is enough to show us how to love: the Father's love for the Son, the Son's loving obedience to the Father, and the Spirit's loving shepherding of the church.

I am in sympathy with Brunner here, but one might still press the issue and say that the interface between dogmatics and discipleship can legitimately lead to subjects of consideration that surpass the margins of the historical narrative. Brunner's response to such an argument is enlightening. "Unfortunately it remains necessary to ask these questions which at first seem alien to the immediate interests of faith, most especially at those points where the proclamation and present faith of the Church have already been molded and transformed, even though unconsciously and in unnoticed ways, by categories of thought to which the Bible itself stands opposed."[45] This concession begins with the necessity of addressing issues that appear contrary to the concerns of Scripture, but concludes by censuring it as a regrettable and even dangerous business and certainly not one we can pursue with confidence. What the church has made of certain doctrines over the centuries, having been seduced by the object-subject antithesis, creates the abiding obstacle for Brunner.

An issue for our study is that without a better understanding of his methodology, the way Brunner appears to restrict the work of theological inquiry could risk suppressing Spirit-breathed and life-giving reflection about encounter. On a practical level, how would the first two roots of dogmatic theology—exegesis and catechesis—be achieved if confined to ideas and language from the biblical world? It is easy to agree with Brunner that salvation history must be taken seriously because it is in specific temporal contexts that God speaks to us; but the message of Christ is true for all times and places, and thus subsequently requires translation. This translation is part of the work of theology, and Brunner's secondary emphasis on eristics and apologetics affirms this necessity.[46] To say that we are living in

---

45. Ibid., 12.

46. Eristic theology, Brunner explains, "is the intellectual discussion of the Christian Faith in the light of the ideologies of the present day which are opposed to the Christian

a world where the effects of sin include ill-fated categories of thought even in theology gets close to the heart of Brunner's concern.

At the end of this chapter, let us summarize the limits that Brunner suggests for the theological task. Firstly, a clear understanding of Brunner's context, specifically of the pervasive effects of modern Protestantism's pressure to locate knowledge of God in all that is human, underlines the anxiety he has to reestablish theology in divine revelation. Furthermore, by the twentieth century modern theology had so thoroughly replaced the historical categories of the event of Jesus Christ with metaphysical language about universal truths that the very definition of revelation had been subverted. Brunner addresses this clearly in the first part of *The Mediator* and there robustly defends the gospel as God's special revelation in human history. The nuanced contextual impetus behind this choice shows this to be a positive boundary meant to protect revelation, as opposed to a negative one intended to restrict the kind of conversation at the heart of dogmatics. Without this safeguard, theology loses the truth it seeks.

Alongside this contextual issue lies a second point: the role of the Holy Spirit in revelation. In the event of personal encounter, the Holy Spirit takes the place of the "something" of the object-subject antithesis. "God [wills to exist] . . . as a personal, and therefore not a strange, Other," explains Brunner, "as One living within the hearts of believers, through the Holy Spirit testifying to Himself as Father within themselves."[47] This third person of the Trinity, active in the word, is the personal presence of God. When he meets with faith in the believer, the process of revelation takes place, which is the testimony of the Holy Spirit in one's inner being.

Brunner goes on to explain that the event of revelation through the Holy Spirit simultaneously signifies and is subordinate to the revelation of Jesus Christ, its content. In this way personal encounter is continually created by the living presence of the Holy Spirit as the "present reality" of the God-man. What is the relation between this dynamic event and Scripture? Otherwise stated, "How does legitimate human speech about Jesus, about God, arise out of the revelation, which is Jesus Christ Himself, and

---

Message." This apologetics program is extensively debated but, since it is not critical to the focus of this book, I simply note its connection to natural theology. Brunner maintains that, even though it is only through personal encounter with Jesus Christ that we come to know God, one element in that relation can be the awareness of God that exists within the human being because he is a responsible and free person. *Dogmatics I*, 98.

47. Brunner, *Encounter*, 69.

therefore is not a spoken word?"[48] It is the witness of the Holy Spirit that produces this translation from written word to living encounter. As Brunner points out, one would not be able to know Jesus as the only begotten of the Father if one were left to interpret it solely from the events of his earthly life. Yet through the activity of the Spirit Jesus is revealed as the Son. The third person of the Trinity enables believers to confess *Kyrios Christos* and to enjoy fellowship with God in I-Thou relationship. Just as the Spirit renders the written word a living word, he also makes the Father and Son real to the church. He offers testimony to Christ and is the inward presence of God that animates his people. Brunner suggests that while the Son receives attention as God's historical self-communication, the Holy Spirit is God's on-going, experiential revelation.[49] Consequently, although the Spirit possesses a less significant role than the Son in the historic discussion of the Trinity, the Spirit is still just as important.

In the next chapter we will test Brunner's work by his own criteria through some specific case studies in his *Dogmatics*. Outlined below are four statements that summarize Brunner's methodology in a manner that will facilitate our investigation.

1. *The historical event of Jesus Christ is God's conclusive self-revelation to humankind.*[50] The foundation of all knowledge of God is revealed in the person of Jesus, testified to in the apostolic witness of Scripture. Jesus Christ is the measure and means of God's revelation, through whom God initiates personal relationship with human beings. The event of Jesus Christ is the only viable starting point for theology. In this light Brunner does not speak of knowledge of God as if God were an object to be intellectually possessed, but of personal encounter with God through Jesus Christ.

---

48. Brunner, *Dogmatics I*, 29.

49. Ibid., 206–15.

50. Does Brunner include the post-resurrection and pre-ascension life of Christ in this phrase, or does he mean the life and death of Jesus up to the resurrection? He indicates in *Dogmatics II* a reluctance to affirm a physical ascension of Jesus for a variety of reasons. "While the exaltation of Christ and His session at the Right Hand of God belong to the fundamental *kerygma* of the witnesses in the New Testament, the exaltation as 'Ascension' plays no part in the teaching of the Apostles." In this light, Brunner not only dismisses the doctrine of the ascension, but it would appear that Jesus' post-resurrection appearances are not the focus of his concept of the historical event of Christ. See *Dogmatics II*, 373.

2. *Theology is believing thinking about truth as encounter.* Dogmatics is the work of intellectual investigation within the community of faith. It is how believers think and speak about I-Thou relationship with God. The goal of this believing thinking is personal discipleship, facilitated through the work of biblical exegesis and catechetical instruction. Dogmatics evaluates the consistency of faith language according to the apostolic testimony *Kyrios Christos* and to God's on-going revelation in personal encounter.

3. *The boundaries to God's self-revelation define the limits of theological inquiry.* In so far as Scripture is the measuring stick of that consistency, the subject matter addressed in the apostolic witness, alongside the nature of its testimony, form the primary boundary for dogmatics. God's revelation in Christ, including his mystery, determines both the content and character of theological inquiry. Theological investigation that is consonant with faith must respect the lordship of God as its absolute subject: he determines what we know about himself by what he has unveiled in the historical event of his Son.

4. *The doctrine of the Trinity is the stepchild of dogmatic theology and is not essential to our understanding of God's revelation.* Because the historical event of Christ does not reveal the relations of the Father, Son, and Spirit beyond their manifestations in salvation history, the intratriune life is not addressed in the apostolic witness; accordingly, it is not the subject of dogmatics. Theological inquiry based on personal encounter is preoccupied with God acting through the Holy Spirit in human history to reveal Christ as Lord and to realize his kingdom. The doctrine of the divine triunity, in contrast, focuses not on what has been disclosed in Christ but on what remains veiled. The "what" affirmed in the doctrine—God is Father, Son, and Spirit, and the Father and Son and Spirit are one God—is central to the kerygma, and to this extent Brunner recognizes its necessity as a legitimate doctrine. On the other hand, the complex history that led to the formulation of *una substantia—tres personae* can lead to dangerous and unproductive speculation that supersedes the limits of dogmatics altogether.

3

Case Studies in *Dogmatics*

"Genuine faith and critical reason cannot be opposed to each other, for they are created for each other."

—Brunner, *The Word and the World*, 34

In *Dogmatics I*, *II*, and *III* Brunner considers the main themes of systematic theology: the doctrines of God, creation, redemption, human beings, and the consummation of all things. The purpose of this chapter is to test the extent to which Brunner is reliable in his practice of that which he outlines in the *Prolegomena* as the nature and limits of the theological task. *Dogmatics* is a trustworthy introduction to his theology insofar as it is succinct in scope, pedagogical in tone, and representative of his overall thought. Each volume will be treated in parts 1 to 3 of this chapter, selecting key examples from Brunner's work that illustrate his approach. The study will conclude with part 4 in which two specific issues connected with Brunner's practice will be examined: *Entmythologisierung* and *Heilsgeschichte*.

Towards this end I list the motifs already identified that serve both to ground and guide Brunner's methodology. They first and foremost seek to be consistent with the apostolic witness to the risen Christ who reveals the fullness of the Godhead.

1. God is free and personal in his self-communication.

2. Human history is the context of divine revelation in Jesus Christ.
3. Human beings are responsible and free.
4. Truth is personal encounter with God as creator, Lord, redeemer, and reconciler.
5. Every encounter with God is personal encounter with Jesus Christ.

My first goal in the following exposition is to interpret Brunner according to his own model, which means beginning with his appreciation of the nature of theological inquiry as personal encounter and its limits as the authoritative witness to the historical event of Jesus Christ. Schrader suggests that, for Brunner, theology "is *realistic, dialectical,* and *existential.* The primary basis of all theological reflection is the encounter with God and, of course, the being both of God and the individual human subject."[1] Hauge also confirms these findings when he comments that Brunner's methodology appreciates God alone as the absolute subject of theology, and Jesus Christ as "the true dogmatic norm . . . since he is the truth. In the final analysis it is not the Bible but the Christ witnessed to in the Bible who is the norm of dogmatics."[2] Thus, our communication about God is worthy of consideration to the extent that it begins and ends with God's self-communication in Jesus Christ.

Brunner's conception of the work of dogmatics is accomplished practically by submitting the creedal confessions of Christian tradition to the critique of the apostolic witness. He does not clearly demarcate what the apostolic witness is in his *Prolegomena,* so we will be attentive to his description of it in these volumes. By it does Brunner mean only the personal eyewitnesses of Jesus? Is it comprised only of the synoptic gospels? Does it include the work of Paul?[3] What is the relationship of the apostolic witness to the law and the prophets? One thing is sure for Brunner, that we must come to the apostolic witness with ears to hear what it tells us, whether our intellect agrees with it or not. Indeed, the cross of Christ is foolishness to some, but it is none the less true for being so. The final critique of any doctrine must be: does it both follow from, and lead to, personal encounter with Jesus Christ? Does it foster a realization of Emmanuel, God with us, the kingdom of God in the here and now? If it does, the result will be a

---

1. Kegley, *Theology of Emil Brunner,* 12.
2. Ibid., 145.
3. Brunner clearly accepts Paul's apostolicity as genuine. The issue for him is that Paul was not an eye-witness of Christ in the same manner as the twelve.

positive response to his loving and holy lordship in worship and fellowship. Personal discipleship is the test of theological truth.

A statement about the difference between theology and ethics is timely, for as much as we are concerned with Brunner's theological methodology in *Dogmatics*, he is neither ignorant of nor irresponsible about the moral import of our doctrinal affirmations, as already discussed. Just as encounter is the beginning of revelation for the believer, personal transformation is proof of its authenticity. In this light ethics needs to be mentioned, though for the sake of my stated purposes it will not take a central role in this chapter but be mentioned only briefly in the final section pertaining to eschatology.

PART ONE: THE CHRISTIAN DOCTRINE OF GOD

The Christian Doctrine of God, Dogmatics I addresses the basis of God's self-revelation. The divine nature and will form this substratum which is crucial to Brunner's approach because it expresses a oneness of nature and will that reflects the unity of the triune being. "By refusing to separate person and work," observes Dowey, "[Brunner] avoids such trifling as the decision about when, how, and in 'which' nature Christ functioned thus."[4] This first part will consider Brunner's treatment of the divine nature by examining the name of God and the doctrine of the divine attributes. A shorter discussion of the divine will, focusing on the doctrine of predestination, will follow.

The Divine Nature

The category of mystery already suggested indicates, among other things, that God's self-communication is also his self-limitation. "We are here confronted by a remarkable dialectic," writes Brunner, "which will accompany us throughout the whole of our study of dogmatics. The better we know God, the more we know and feel that His Mystery is unfathomable. The doctrine which lays the most stress upon the Mystery of God will be nearest to the truth."[5] Brunner's admonition is that the dialectic of mystery and revelation be sustained.

---

4. Ibid., 200.
5. Brunner, *Dogmatics I*, 117.

Part I: Believing Thinking

The Personal Name of God

What is the name of God by which he discloses himself to human beings? Brunner insists that it is, above all, a personal name and a personal introduction. God is not a philosophical category such as that suggested by the Greek fathers, who insisted that the Old Testament name of YHWH, "I am that I am," amounted to an ontological statement of divine being. "The 'Name' of God, suggests further that God is Person: He is not an 'IT'; He is our primary 'Thou.'"[6] His is not a general name that can be deduced from an impersonal power or a timeless ideal. It is a proper name that God himself names and that he reveals to specific human beings in historical context. God names his name and in so doing makes himself known.

This movement of self-unveiling is "the act by which God steps out of the sphere of His own glory and self-sufficiency, in which the One who exists *for Himself alone* becomes the One who exists *for us*."[7] History testifies to this divine self-giving and to the communion it creates, visible first in God's covenant with Israel and second in the reconciliation achieved through Jesus Christ. God's name keeps at the forefront of our thinking the historical revelation of his condescension, for we can only ever know God through his name, never through abstract ideas, concepts, or theories. This point is central: God gives himself to his creatures to be known personally, something that no other deity in any religion does.

Christian theology, however, has not always respected God's nature as such. Brunner charges that "the penetration of the Neo-Platonic idea of the identification of the *summum esse* and the *summum bonum*," as seen in Augustine's thought, among others, wrenches theological reflection out of the soil of scriptural narrative and transplants it into the ground of metaphysics. Brunner further alleges that medieval scholasticism could not avoid speculation about the divine names because its foundation was *theologia naturalis* and not the apostolic witness.[8] Hence, regardless of its form, Brunner rejects all "natural, philosophical speculation about God... [that] begins with the sublime knowledge, with the hidden majesty, with God as He is 'in Himself,' because—as the God of speculation—He is not the God of revelation, the God who is 'for us.' Luther calls this speculative doctrine of God 'clambering up to the Divine Majesty.' In so doing, God becomes

---

6. Ibid., 121.
7. Ibid., 124.
8. Ibid., 129.

an '*objectum*, namely, the God who is not revealed.' There are only these two possibilities: either the natural knowledge (of God) with its '*objectum*,' the *Deus absconditus*, or the knowledge of God given in revelation."[9] Such an attestation confirms the boundary that revelation places on theological investigation: God, as he is known only unto himself, is not for us to scrutinize. We are invited to know God through revelation, but we possess no independent access to data about his inner being.

It becomes plain once again that the historical event of Jesus is the source of knowledge of the divine name. God breaks into history in Jesus Christ and subverts human self-sufficiency. Through personal encounter he addresses each human being as "Thou" so that each person must respond to him personally as "I." The gospels testify to varying reactions to encounter with Jesus; some respond by following him, others chase him away for fear. It is Brunner's contention that we also are unable to exist as indifferent automata when we encounter God. In his revelation, God in Christ condescends, naming each person and inviting each one to step out of self-determination into relationship. This is how divine encounter subverts our delusion of independence and reveals God as Lord.

Personal encounter reveals that Jesus Christ, the one who draws near to us as truly human, is truth and grace. When this happens, says Brunner, we recognize that the God who stands over against us is totally other as the Lord. This is how he communicates himself to Israel and to the church: "I am the Lord your God." Scripture shows him to be the one who willed creation of the cosmos and the one who sustains it. He is, moreover, the one who re-creates it according to the same choice to be known. Isaiah prophesied towards this end with his anticipation that one day "the earth shall be full of the knowledge of the Lord as the waters cover the sea" (Isa 11:9b). Brunner highlights that this creating, sustaining, and recreating is an expression of divine freedom and sovereignty, for there is no shadow of constraint in any of God's actions.

Creation is only the first expression of divine lordship, for God has shown himself also to be the Lord who forgives. Brunner makes his point with certainty when he writes, "the highest manifestation of the freedom of God takes place where He sets the sinner free, where He, the King, gives to the rebel soul the life which had been forfeited."[10] Again the cross and resurrection are understood as the culmination of God's word about

---

9. Ibid., 170–71.
10. Ibid., 148.

himself revealed in the law and the prophets. Brunner is keen to note that God's loving forgiveness realized in Jesus Christ in no way compromises his righteousness revealed to Israel, for in Christ God has fulfilled the law through the cross. He has pardoned us despite the law, the law that determined long ago that human beings could never know God because of our failure to reflect his image in love and holiness. In this way, argues Brunner, God's act of self-disclosure in Christ is a demonstration, not a concession, of his freedom and sovereignty.

The Doctrine of the Divine Attributes

What more does revelation communicate about this personal God who draws near in Christ? He is depicted as righteous, almighty, merciful, and eternal through his interaction with Israel and with the church. To the extent to which the biblical narrative speaks in these terms, we also can talk of God as such. It is Brunner's assertion, though, that early church thinkers went a step beyond this boundary. Brunner judges that they, being well trained in Greek thought, did not sufficiently differentiate between philosophical speculation and reflective consideration of Jesus Christ. "Thus, without realizing what they were doing, they allowed the speculative idea of the Absolute to become incorporated in the *corpus* of Christian theology."[11]

This speculative idea of God is, according to Brunner, irreconcilable with the biblical revelation. He reiterates the theologian's task: "dogmatics does not consist in constructing a system of Biblical statements, but it is reflection upon revelation, on the basis of the religious evidence of the Bible."[12] The distinguishing element of the written word is that it speaks about God in relation to his creation. Although this point has already been introduced, Brunner's reminder here is timely. The Bible invites us to contemplate who God shows himself to be in relationship to the world that he has made and that remains contingent upon his will. We do not know God in abstraction, as a being who remains isolated within himself from eternity. We worship him instead for what we know through his self-disclosure in flesh and blood. Consequently, the evidence of God's activity in human history is the only adequate basis for discussion of God's character.

The eternity of God will serve to illustrate Brunner's approach to the doctrine of the divine attributes. What does revelation tell us about the

---

11. Ibid., 243.
12. Ibid., 246.

triune being's relationship to time? Brunner posits that if we begin where classical Christian doctrine begins, with the concept of immutability, we immediately encounter the distorting infiltration of Greek philosophy, not the historical evidence of revelation. The Platonic concept of eternity as timelessness had influenced Christian ideology to the extent that the concept of the divine being was interpreted though the "timeless ideal" paradigm. The idea of eternity in classical theology consequently came to be represented as absolute timelessness, thus effacing any element of personal being.

According to Brunner, this transposition poses an unavoidable difficulty for dogmatics, because revelation affords no such permission to apply metaphysical concepts to an understanding of God. If this is true, where does that leave us with respect to divine eternality specifically, and to the doctrine of divine attributes more generally? Time as created (an affirmation that results from Brunner's treatment of the doctrine of creation) means it cannot be a divine quality because the creator pre-exists the creation. Time, therefore, is subject to God like the rest of the cosmos. What, then, is divine eternity? Eternity, contends Brunner, is not synonymous with timelessness but is God's "sovereign rule over Time and the temporal sphere, the freedom of Him who creates and gives us Time."[13] As supreme Lord, God is not subject to time, and because he is not subject to time he remains unrestricted by the movement of the temporal.

Brunner asserts that time is the positive sphere in which God ordains that which he has created to become most fully what he intends it to be. Time also possesses a specific character because God chooses to reveal himself in time and to involve himself in human history; as such it is not a universal truth. Brunner goes so far as to say that God "—in a certain sense—is not unchangeable . . . God, too, is 'affected' by what happens to His creatures."[14] Christian theology might speak of God as immutable, but this description is possible only when he is viewed as an idea. In such a case our understanding of the divine being takes on the unchanging character of a timeless concept at the cost of God's true character revealed in personal encounter. Following Brunner's line of thinking, it becomes evident that the traditional defense of divine immutability is at variance with divine revelation. The apostolic witness testifies to a personal being who engages

---

13. Ibid., 270.
14. Ibid., 268.

in relationship with his creation and consequently allows himself to be impacted by his creatures.

Are we to understand Brunner to say that God actually changes or is even unpredictable? His answer is offered in a discussion of divine holiness and love. Scripture unequivocally affirms that God is holy in his very nature, and in his very being he is love. These are not qualities that are manifested to differing degrees depending on the situation; rather, everything that God is and does expresses his loving and holy nature. He is not like human beings who possess a multiplicity of characteristics of which none is the sum of one's person. Some might say, for example, that one is loving when one attends to another in need, as did the so-called good Samaritan; or that one is growing in faith when one confesses God's goodness to all people, stunning Jesus with courage like the Canaanite woman. Nevertheless, such an individual is not the sum and substance of love or goodness since "no one is good except God alone" (Luke 18:19). We do not know God as good, loving, and holy because we recognize something of his nature in ourselves; it is the life, death, and resurrection of Jesus Christ that lead us to declare that God is love and that God is holy.

Brunner draws attention to the kind of love displayed in the incarnation and atonement as reflected in the New Testament word *agape*. It is by definition rooted solely in the decision of the lover and is freely bestowed upon the one who is loved. When Scripture identifies God as love, it refers to his condescension to humankind for our salvation. It is the action of revelation—in contrast with the impersonal concept of immutability—that reveals God as agape. This divine love is the self-communication of God in personal encounter, culminating in God's free act of mercy in redemption. Brunner helpfully extrapolates this intricate connection between love and revelation. Love condescends; it gives of one's self. In God's case, this is his self-communication, his self-unveiling. "The idea of self-communication gathers up into one the two elements love and revelation. The distinction between a 'formal principle' and a 'material principle,' between 'revelation' (Bible) and 'grace'(Justification) is a misunderstanding. Revelation is gracious love and grace is revelation."[15]

Two conclusions can be made here that are relevant to Brunner's treatment of revelation and the divine nature. The first was suggested in chapter 2, that the revealer and the revealed are one. The God who unveils himself in the incarnation and atonement is the same Father who loves

---

15. Ibid., 187.

the Son from eternity. The second point is concordant, that the personal being of the revealer is also the personal being of the one revealed. "The 'I' of God who speaks to us is the eternal 'I' of God," explains Brunner. "His Self-existence as an 'I' is not an historical manifestation, but it is his eternal nature."[16] Thus, encounter with God by faith in Christ through the Holy Spirit is encounter with the unique creator-Lord who is holy and who is love.

The boundary to theological inquiry established by the apostolic witness is illustrated here as the dialectic between mystery and revelation upon which Brunner insists. Scripture reveals God as person and personal in the very fact of his self-disclosure to specific human beings. Brunner is emphatic that God's nature and attributes are revealed only in this context. When this unity of being and will is disregarded by theology, reflection is diverted from the apostolic witness to objective speculation about an impersonal deity or a timeless ideal.

The Divine Will

The scriptural witness identifies God as creator-Lord, as the one who stands over against that which he has made. His personal self-communication by which he initiates fellowship with his creation is an expression of his love. It is this agape that Brunner identifies, not only in God's self-limiting act of creation, but as most dramatically manifested in Jesus Christ in whom the divine nature and will are unified. In the event of the cross, which is the center of the Christian faith and of human history, God reveals his unchanging will for our salvation. The theological articulation of the unity of nature and will, often referred to as the doctrine of eternal divine decree, asserts that from eternity God predestines some to salvation and, by implication, others to condemnation. Brunner holds that as a doctrine it is contentious at best.

Scripture speaks of a God who sees us from eternity past, and it is precisely because he sees us that life has eternal meaning. In fact, the gospel could be summed up as the eternal God calling temporal creation into eternal communion with himself. The scriptural premise on which the doctrine of predestination is based is similar: human life has meaning within the context of the divine life. There exists, however, a significant variant between the two foundations. Brunner points out that if the doctrine is

16. Ibid., 229.

based on an eternal idea of being, then personal existence in relation to it is "merged in the life of the All" and thereby loses its particularity.[17]

There ensues a dangerous implication if God sees each person from eternity past, even if it is for fellowship. If everything that happens in human history is eternally decided by the will of God, then human freedom becomes an illusion and human destiny is predetermined completely apart from human agency. What do we say of the gospel and of the import of faith if this is the case? Silence is the only answer, for even in personal encounter with God our response would be predetermined. Nothing could be more contradictory to the divine nature, though, if Brunner's understanding of revelation is accurate. The realm in which we have to live and on which we have to think is the historical one, not "the eternal Divine Decrees." There are mysteries which God himself knows and it is not for us, nor would it be possible for us, to know what these are. This is not theology's task nor is it faith's desire.[18]

From Brunner's perspective, Scripture offers us neither a message of double decree nor a message of universal salvation. Both concepts subvert divine freedom by declaring what God wills before God wills it, whether it is forgiveness or judgment. He contends that the dialectic between the love and the wrath of God cannot be resolved by any doctrine but only by God's self-expression through the Son through whom we encounter wrath and mercy, holiness, and love. For that reason, a concept of election can only be understood and articulated when divine love and holiness are dialectically maintained. The fullest picture of this tension is seen in Jesus Christ. "What God is in Himself is identical with that which He is for us—in Jesus Christ, in faith. But outside of Jesus Christ, outside of faith, God's Holiness is not the same as His Love, but there it is His wrath; there what God is 'in Himself' is not the same as that which He is 'for us,' there it is the unfathomable, impenetrable mystery of the *'nuda majestas.'*"[19]

Cairns's commentary on this point affirms what we have discerned. "It is not a 'knowledge that,' but a 'knowledge of.' We know God thus by being confronted by Him in His Son, the Word, in an act of revelation . . . But it is a personal knowledge of faith, created in us by the Holy Spirit bearing witness to God in Christ."[20] Our conclusion confirms that knowledge

17. Ibid., 305.
18. Ibid., 303.
19. Ibid., 337.
20. Kegley, *Theology of Emil Brunner*, 80.

for Brunner is not the theoretical knowledge of a universal truth, but it is grounded in the historical event of Jesus Christ, confirmed by the apostolic witness.

PART TWO: THE CHRISTIAN DOCTRINE OF CREATION AND REDEMPTION

Dogmatics I is primary in Brunner's methodology to the extent that it establishes the doctrine of God as the origin and content of revelation. That said, volume II, *The Christian Doctrine of Creation and Redemption*, rivals the first in priority in so far as it is concerned with the historic mediator of that revelation, apart from whom we would know nothing about the divine being or will. It also clarifies further the human context of revelation.

Creation

Genesis 1–3 is the *locus classicus* of the doctrine of creation. Nevertheless, Brunner asserts that to begin the investigation of the doctrine with the Old Testament story is to invite debates we are not yet prepared to address, for the simple reason that the Eden account was not intended to serve as a factual register of an historical event. He suggests another way to interpret the creation account, which determines "that in all theological statements about the divine revelation we must begin with Jesus Christ, as the Word of God Incarnate, and that we are not bound by any Biblical passages taken in isolation, and certainly not by isolated sections of the Old Testament."[21] He reiterates this approach in his sermons on the Apostles' Creed where he makes the connection between the creator in Genesis, who is revealed in the New Testament as none other than Jesus Christ.[22]

From this example we can extrapolate to explain the relationship that Brunner posits between the Lord of Israel and God's self-revelation in Christ. The biblical pattern begins with God's self-disclosure to Israel as YHWH, the Lord. It is only from his subsequent acts of revelation in salvation history, though, that they come to know him as creator and redeemer. This difference is noticeable if we compare, for example, Abram's knowledge of God at the moment of his call in Genesis 12 to follow a God

---

21. Brunner, *Dogmatics II*, 52.
22. Brunner, *I Believe*, 18.

he hardly knew to a land he had never seen, with David's worship in Psalm 51 that reflects an intimate, long-standing relationship. Brunner posits that God's self-unveiling in Jesus Christ follows the same form: Jesus is first revealed to his disciples as Lord through his acts of power, and it is only subsequently that their understanding grew to acknowledge him as creator, redeemer, and reconciler of all humankind. A comparative example illustrates his point. The experience of the twelve in response to the feeding of the five thousand shows their ignorance of just who this rabbi is, whereas the post-Pentecost preaching of the apostles is most noticeable for its confidence that Jesus is the Son of God.

It is imperative to keep straight this order of knowledge if we are to be faithful to the apostolic example even in our consideration of the doctrine of creation. Brunner's paradigm is difficult to ignore: we know God through the I-Thou relation of Christ, not through an impersonal story of origin. If the latter were the source of our knowledge of God, then God could remain a nameless universal, unknown in any personal measure. Yet Scripture communicates quite a different story; God is the one who draws near in human form and who initiates personal relationship. Furthermore, the necessity we sense to respond to God's lordship is not prompted by the doctrinal affirmation that God is creator of the cosmos; it is instead the reply to the revelation that God meets us in Christ and therefore we are "his property," no longer our own. Elsewhere Brunner highlights that how the Old Testament speaks of the creator indicates the relational context of this knowledge. He does not disclose himself "as the God who is to be known from nature, but, rather, as the God who reveals himself as the Lord of his people through historical deeds, through prophetic Word. Before Israel knew God the Creator of the world, God was known as Israel's Lord . . . Knowledge of the Creator belongs not to *theologia naturalis* but to *theologia revelata*."[23]

The connection between God's will in Christ and the doctrine of creation requires further explanation. Based on what has been stated about the divine being, we affirm that God is not bound to the world by any kind of need in himself. It is God's free decision to create. The doctrine of *creatio ex nihilo* appears on the surface to corroborate this thesis. Nevertheless, Brunner straightforwardly rejects the doctrine by arguing that it is founded on the concept of a pre-existent form of darkness and chaos which contradicts

---

23. Brunner, "The Significance of the Old Testament," 251.

the premise that God alone is pre-existent.[24] How could God create out of nothing? This is impossible to imagine, which is why the traditional exposition of *creatio ex nihilo* sometimes resorts to creation out of some disorderly, pre-existent material.

Brunner concedes that the idea of an original chaos is logical enough if we consider creation through the lens of the Genesis account only, but his view of scriptural revelation requires us to begin with the apostolic testimony. John's gospel introduction, "In the beginning was the Word" (John 1:1), sometimes has been rejected as an account of creation because it presses against the limits of our understanding and seems to counter Genesis 3 read as a more technical description. As apostolic witness, though, it clearly testifies that it was God alone and his word who achieved creation, and this must be taken into consideration.

Brunner's problem with *creatio ex nihilo* goes beyond a fascinating intellectual conundrum. If anything other than God existed before the creative moment, it follows that that *nothing* is really *something* co-existent with God from eternity. In such a case, God is neither Lord nor creator in the sense that revelation declares. Brunner perceives two options: "either human thought has power over God—and then God is no longer Lord, nor is He Creator; or God is Lord and Creator, and then human thought has no power over Him; then God can only communicate Himself and His Being as Creator by His own act, and man cannot reach this truth by his own thought, he can only accept it in faith."[25] He concludes that, by implication, to refuse that which we cannot imagine by reason—true creation out of nothing—is to refuse God's lordship.

The best meaning of *creatio ex nihilo* from Brunner's perspective is that God is dependent upon nothing and that he alone determines all that exists. The cosmos exists simply because God ordains it. "God's will is the *ratio sufficiens* of the Creation" and it is the expression of his power and love. "The love of God is the *causa finalis* of the Creation. In Jesus Christ this ideal reason for the Creation is revealed."[26] The *telos* of the divine plan is the realization of God's rule in unhindered relationship between the king and creation. Schrotenboer's summary is difficult to improve upon: "According to Brunner . . . creation is not causality for although God created by the Word, the Word is not only instrumental; the Word is also the

24. Brunner, *Dogmatics II*, 10.
25. Ibid., 12.
26. Ibid., 13.

Part I: Believing Thinking

plan, the goal, the meaning of creation. Creation expresses the notion of the contingency of reality . . . Creation, according to the Bible, signifies the irresolvable 'overagainstness' between the creator and the creature. It signifies unbridgeable distance. That God is the Creator means that he is *totaliter aliter*."[27]

Imago Dei: freedom and responsibility

The Christian faith holds that God ordered the cosmos in such a manner that human beings are its crown and are set apart by God's own image, possessing the same freedom for personal encounter that he himself possesses. While Scripture confirms this story time and again, the exact significance of the *imago Dei* as doctrine has been anything but obvious over the centuries. We will circumvent the historical debate and go straight to Brunner's definition. He describes the image of God as personal freedom, and because the human is free he is responsible.[28]

To know God as creator means to know oneself as creature, but what does creatureliness signify? This concept, if undeveloped, can lead to the confusion of self with the divine. If one is unaware of, or refuses to recognize, God as God, then there always remains the danger that the individual, the "I," becomes the center of existence. The individual assumes, however intentionally or unintentionally, the place of God. On the other hand, we have seen that a person becomes aware of his contingency when he encounters Christ as Lord. As a result, he also becomes aware of himself as a free agent.

In this light, we could anticipate that a discussion of the doctrine of *imago Dei* would begin with the subject of human freedom and responsibility. Brunner's approach requires a different point of departure, though,

---

27. Schrotenboer, *A New Apologetics*, 32.

28. Brunner's theological anthropology is a significant pillar of his work and it invariably receives mention in secondary sources. One expression of his felt urgency for a theological anthropology is captured by the following comment. "The most powerful of all spiritual forces is man's view of himself, the way in which he understands his nature and his destiny, indeed it is the one force which determines all the others which influence human life. For in the last resort, all that man thinks and wills springs out of what he thinks and wills about himself, human life, its meaning and its purpose." Brunner, *The Christian Understanding of Man*, 146. The whole of this chapter is a summary of Brunner's theological anthropology. Regarding secondary commentary, see, for example, Humphrey, *Emil Brunner*, 65–89 and most recently, McGrath, *Reappraisal*, 118–212.

which is Jesus Christ. "In Jesus Christ we know ourselves to be creatures of God," Brunner explains, "who, in contrast to His other creatures, have been created not only through the Word, but for the Word and in the Word of God . . . The true human quality which is due to this call of God is existence-in-love and is received in faith."[29] We can anticipate that he who is truly human is the one who defines for us what it means to be truly free, truly loved, truly responsible, and in unhindered partnership with God.

It might appear as if human responsibility is derivative of human freedom according to this definition of *imago Dei*. Brunner maintains that the two concepts emerge twinned in the broader study of what it means to be human, and they must be treated in tension. We receive life as a free, loving act of God, and we are given, in our very existence, the capacity to reflect divine freedom and love. Brunner contends that a human being realizes this purpose only when he responds to his creator-Lord in personal relationship. We must appreciate the centrality of this detail, which is ultimately no detail but the very crux of faith. "Responsibility is a relation; it is not a substance," declares Brunner.[30] In contrast to the view that equates *imago Dei* with the endowment of reason, regardless of one's relationship with the creator, Brunner claims that the divine image is visible because we always stand before God in I-Thou relation, whether in faith or in unbelief.

Sin and imago Dei

One significant issue arises from this that demands investigation but that cannot be addressed simply, which is the impact of sin on the *imago Dei*. As we begin it is constructive to attend to a few terms that are central to the issue of human personhood. John Baillie offers a worthwhile lexicon of Brunner's vocabulary on this subject:[31]

- *Ansprechbarkeit*—the human's "addressability"
- *Wortmächtigkeit*—the human's "verbi-competence"
- *wortempfängliches Wesen*—the human as a "word-receptive being"

---

29. Brunner, *Dogmatics II*, 73.
30. Ibid., 59.
31. Baillie, *Our Knowledge of God*, 29. McGrath translates *Wortmächtigkeit* as 'a capacity for words' and his treatment of the *imago Dei* within the context of natural theology offers relevant discussion. See McGrath, *Reappraisal*, 118–20.

Baillie aims to illustrate Brunner's conclusion that we do not exist apart from relation with God. To be a human is to receive the word addressed to us from the source of our existence. This is the positive response of faith to the divine–human encounter. It is as a *wortempfängliches Wesen* that each person is created, lives, and passes. This includes the human's capacity to respond to God. The effacement of this capacity because of sin means to be separated from the word of God addressed to us, which is nothing less than to die.

Baillie interprets Brunner as asserting that, while as fallen human beings we remain responsible subjects (we still retain the capacity for words, materially the *imago Dei*), human beings' ability to respond to divine address is lost because everything about us is distorted by sin.[32] The most important result of this treatment of the doctrine is the establishment of human beings as free and as responsible to respond to God, either in faith and obedience or in sin and self-sufficiency. Both Scripture and history declare a "guilty" verdict, however, for we have chosen to use our freedom in defiance of the lordship of Christ. "None is righteous, no, not one" (Ps 14:3; Rom 3:10). At the same time, it is because of the image of God in the human person that man, woman, and child alike can recognize in Jesus their trustworthy Lord. If the *imago Dei* is freedom and responsibility, and if that freedom and responsibility is in response to God's word addressed to each person in encounter, then it can be said, and indeed has been said of Brunner if not directly by him in *Dogmatics*, that there is some genre of natural knowledge of God present in every human person.

A caveat is needed at this point. As stated in the introduction, I will not be revisiting the Brunner-Barth debate about natural theology except to the extent that its concordant concept of *Anknüpfungspunkt* is relevant to our study. This is for four reasons. To begin with, the debate belongs more to an examination of apologetics than to dogmatics.[33] Next, this one element of Brunner's theology is just that—one element. The sands of time along with theologians' pens have inflated the significance of natural theology to being more important than it is in his actual thought. Also, the relational impact of the debate was likewise much more significant than Brunner himself would have wished or felt it merited. Finally, it would be hard to improve

---

32. Baillie, *Our Knowledge of God*, 30. See also McGrath, *Reappraisal*, 119.

33. See also Hart, *Barth vs. Brunner*, 214, and Johnson, "Soteriology as a Function of Epistemology," 168–69.

upon McGrath's treatment of the subject, which I recommend to those who are most interested in this point.[34]

That aside, we now must follow Brunner's argument in *Dogmatics I* if we are to understand him accurately. He begins by noting that the problem of *theologia naturalis* is a modern one. The debate is in essence the conflation of two questions: "the question of the revelation in Creation" and "the question of man's natural knowledge of God. While one side was mainly anxious to deny the validity of a '*theologia naturalis*,' the other side was chiefly concerned to affirm the reality of the revelation in Creation." He clarifies that his affirmation of revelation in creation does not equate to a doctrine of natural theology. "On the one hand, the reality of the revelation in Creation is to be admitted, but, on the other hand, the possibility of a correct and valid natural knowledge of God is to be contested."[35]

The question remains as to whether or not the person who has not received God's disclosure in Christ is able to respond to revelation in creation.[36] What is clear for Brunner is that there is no natural theology that leads to specific knowledge of God, but there is a kind of natural theology that is legitimate within the field of anthropology. This difference is due to how we intellectually conceive of the divine. Brunner suggests that Romans 1:19 is straightforward in its meaning: human beings think on the divine because what we experience in creation is made evident to something within us. It is this "point-of-contact" *(Anknüpfungspunkt)* in every human being that enables us to recognize the word of God.[37] Brunner defends the existence and validity of this original revelation according to the biblical witness to the knowledge of sin that is present in human beings even before they are addressed by the specific word of God in the law and the prophets. One's inherent sense of guilt is, for Brunner, evidence of knowledge of one's sin.

---

34. McGrath, *Reappraisal*, chapter 4.

35. Brunner, *Dogmatics I*, 132–33.

36. Smith comments, "Brunner had always taught that there is an objective revelation of God in the created world and in man created in God's image. But at the same time he has always denied that man can obtain a valid and genuine subjective knowledge of this objective revelation apart from the historical revelation in Christ." Smith, "Emil Brunner's Theology of Revelation," 8.

37. For a thorough treatment of the place of *Anknüpfungspunkt* in Brunner's thought see Heideman, "The Relation of Revelation and Reason," 35–49. McGrath's comments are also constructive in *Reappraisal*, 38–39, 68–70, 119–20.

Even though a point of contact remains in every person, we are unable to know God fully based on this information alone because sin distorts our vision. One response to this lack of true knowledge of God is a philosophical interpretation of seeds of truth gleaned from natural knowledge. The difficulty is that this attempt ultimately fails because it serves only to exaggerate the chasm between human thought about God and the full revelation of God in Jesus Christ. Baillie suggests that Brunner's differentiation is not between natural and revealed knowledge but between general and special revelation, both of which are revealed.[38] The fact and choice of one's sin, for which one is entirely responsible due to natural revelation, blinds one to this knowledge so that salvation is only possible through the special revelation of God in Christ, which is sourced in the Old and New Testaments.

This topic is too immense to treat in full here, but still we must ask what role it plays in *Dogmatics*. On the one hand, if the historical event of Jesus Christ is the definitive revelation of God, we could appropriately conclude that any deduction of the being and will of God on the basis of the fallen world cannot lead to an accurate reflection of the creator-Lord. Yet, surprisingly, Brunner is not as categorical as we might expect. It is true on an ontological level that there is no comparison; the intrinsic difference between creator and creation renders authentic parallel impossible. Brunner goes on to say that, in spite of this, we cannot avoid some measure of comparison if we hold to revelation's doctrine of creation which highlights two inescapable elements: word and person. In their capacity for speech and in their personhood human beings reflect something of the divine being. This positive claim is not an equation of natural theology to biblical theology, indicating that natural revelation discloses God to the same extent as special revelation. It is clear that our perceptions of both natural and special revelation have elements of truth and elements of error. Brunner's point is that we are not to disregard natural theology altogether, because it has something to contribute to anthropology and it preserves the vital point of contact for the word of God among human beings.

Redemption

The unity of the divine nature and will verifies that God the creator and Lord is also the reconciler and redeemer of humanity and of the entire

---

38. Baillie, *Our Knowledge of God*, 35.

created order.[39] He is one and the same God, and we know him through one and the same revelation, Jesus Christ. In his treatment of the doctrine of redemption, Brunner persists in the particular order of knowledge that must be respected in dogmatics. He writes, "If, from the point of view of *knowledge,* Jesus Christ comes first, and all that we can say about God is secondary, yet actually God, the Three in One, comes first, and the Incarnate Son, Jesus Christ, comes second. When this distinction between the *ratio cognoscendi* and the *ratio essendi* is misunderstood, it necessarily leads to speculation and fantasy."[40] Brunner's concern here is to remind us that Jesus Christ, though determined as the incarnate word from all eternity by God, only became the God-man at a certain point in history. As the full revelation of God, our knowledge of God starts with him, but it is the eternal, triune God and not the incarnate word who is the source of all existence.

Up to this point there might be little novelty in Brunner's assertion of the order of understanding. He goes one step further, however, and herein lies the crux of his insistence: "We know Jesus Christ through Jesus Christ; we believe that Jesus is the Christ, because He is the Christ. But if this statement is to be more than mere tautology, it must be placed at the end, and not at the beginning of our Christological inquiry."[41] At the heart of Christology, then, is the issue of how one becomes a Christian, how one comes to recognize Jesus as the Christ.

Jesus as the Christ: Historical Criticism and Believing Testimony

The synoptic accounts tell us of a man from Nazareth who spoke with authority, healed with power, and exhibited wisdom beyond his years. None of this means, of course, that everyone who met Jesus accepted him as divine. According to Brunner, the New Testament leads us to believe that it is only in light of the Easter encounters that the disciples fully acknowledge Jesus as the Son of God. It is on this point that Brunner's view of the apostolic witness hangs. The knowledge of Jesus as the promised one of God comes

---

39. Does Brunner imagine the redemption of all of creation, the non-human world included? *Dogmatics III* affirms that will of God is for the salvation of all, citing Col 1:20; Eph 1:10; 1 Tim 2:4, 6; but Brunner stops short of stating whether this includes non-human entities or not. Brunner, *Dogmatics III*, 415.

40. Brunner, *Dogmatics II*, 239.

41. Ibid., 240.

only after the faith encounters of Easter, and it is on the basis of such belief that they pen their testimonies. Consequently, we would not fully recognize Jesus as the Son of God apart from his post-resurrection appearances.

Brunner reminds his readers that no gospel record portrays Jesus overtly declaring himself as the Messiah. "The task which God had entrusted Him was not to proclaim the Christ, but to be the Christ."[42] Does this imply that Jesus himself was unaware of his identity? It does not, according to Brunner, who maintains that Jesus was cognizant of his unity with the Father during his earthly ministry and was eager for his disciples to recognize it. What it does suggest, though, is that Jesus never overtly proclaimed his deity but left it for his disciples to do so when they came to believe the mystery of Emmanuel, God with us.

It is Brunner's claim that the process of awareness that grew in the apostles offers a model for us to follow in dogmatics. This is one way he explains it:

> The way to the knowledge of Jesus leads from the human Jesus to the Son of God and to the Godhead . . . It is the miracle of the divine condescension towards us that He wills to meet us in a human being. If God has opened this way to Himself for us, we ought to follow it too; we have no right to try to reverse the process. That is why the Gospels, the records of the human life of Jesus, are placed first in the New Testament, in order that, meeting the Man Christ Jesus, we may, through this encounter, come to the knowledge of God. Only so can our Christian faith become our "own." We must see for ourselves—certainly not apart from the witness of the Apostles—who this Jesus really is.[43]

Of utmost importance for Brunner's methodology is its starting point. Knowledge begins with the man Jesus, and then proceeds to know him as the Son of God, in whom is revealed also the Father and the Spirit. This outline reiterates why Brunner rejects out of hand theological reflection that begins with the invisible divine being or that pursues its study apart from the apostolic witness to Christ. Hence, "who this Jesus really is" is the subject of the following sections.

---

42. Ibid., 249.
43. Ibid., 322.

Jesus as the Christ: The Doctrine of the Three-fold Office

Brunner's exposition of the so-called doctrine of the three-fold office of Jesus Christ is thorough and robust, worth digesting in detail, but we are interested in it mainly from the perspective of his claim that we know the person of Christ through his work. He finds the Reformation principle trustworthy: *Hoc est Christum cognoscere, beneficia ejus cognoscere.*[44] The New Testament titles of Prophet, Priest, and King point to the centrality of Jesus' work, and salvation history reiterates in its own manner this emphasis by focusing on God's self-communication in his activity. Brunner points out that statements of metaphysical or ontological substance are noticeably lacking in the biblical material, and early church titles for Christ are marked by their functional emphases.[45]

Christ's title of Prophet illustrates one of Brunner's preferred themes. Jesus is in every way greater than the prophets. He does not receive a calling from God as they did, because he is "the One in whom Word and Person, that which is revealed in the Revealer, are one."[46] Furthermore, the prophets spoke a word about the future work and word of the Lord, but the word of Christ is the work of God that not only declares but also creates the day of the Lord by his presence. Jesus is greater than the prophets because he is and he acts as the Messiah, the one anticipated by Jeremiah, Isaiah, and Daniel.

The title of Christ as Priest emphasizes his atoning work on the cross as the heart of God's revelation. The cross and its atonement are the heart of the New Testament because in it we see divine love and divine righteousness, as well as the dramatic reality of the human being for whom Christ died. Alongside this Brunner shows throughout *Dogmatics* that Jesus' whole life is his work of redemption as high priest for all nations. In contrast to the false division of Protestant orthodoxy between his *oboedientia activa* and *oboedientia passiva*, Jesus' whole life, including his death, effects atonement.

If priestly atonement is the work of the life and death of Jesus, what is the purpose of the work of Christ as King? Brunner contends that this title reveals the kingdom of heaven as present in him. The goal of history remains God's fellowship with his people as their sovereign ruler, and in

---

44. Ibid., 271; see also *Truth as Encounter*, 46–47.
45. Brunner, *Dogmatics II*, 273.
46. Ibid., 254.

Christ the kingdom of God is initiated here-and-now in a completely new manner to that of the law and the prophets. The kingdom inaugurated in Jesus creates communion between man and God. This is a gift, not a demand, realized in the cross where the self-sufficient 'I' of sinful humanity is transformed, realizing God's kingdom in the unity of divine and human will.

Jesus as the Christ: The Eternal Godhead of the Son

Christ's work reveals him as being greater than a prophet, as the Priest who offers himself in final atonement, and as the King in whose reign the rule of God is realized. Brunner identifies the Easter event as the confirmation of these offices. Along with the apostolic community after the resurrection, we also come to see Jesus as the Christ, and it is as the Christ that he reveals himself to us as the Son of God. What are the implications of this scriptural pattern for theological inquiry? It is worth reiterating Brunner's approach, again in his own words.

> This is the way of knowledge which lies before us plainly in the testimony of the New Testament. The earliest testimonies of primitive Christian faith do not yet say anything about the eternal preexistent Son of God. The early letters of Paul are confined to the confession of the Risen Lord, and their main theme is the work of the Redeemer. It is only the later Epistles which, with some clearness, show the background of this work of salvation, the fact that Jesus is the Eternal Son of God, but even they do so in such a way that the historic work of salvation is still in the foreground of interest. The eternal Sonship of Christ only becomes the main theme of the Christian message in the Gospel of John. This way of primitive knowledge is also the way of every individual Christian, and therefore too the way marked out for dogmatic Christology: from the historical foreground to the "super-historical" background. Only thus does living personal Christian faith arise.[47]

Two points are to be noted. First is the stress Brunner lays on the subject matter of the apostolic witness. The gospels center on what Christ disclosed of himself as the fullness of the Godhead in visible form. Even the affirmations of certain Johannine and Pauline passages that speak in terms of Christ's origins do so in a manner that keeps their readers' attention on

---

47. Ibid., 340–41.

Jesus' life; the word "was in the beginning with God" is the same word who "became flesh and dwelt among us" (John 1:2, 1:14). The kerygma of the early church was not based on esoteric, theoretical, or philosophical speculation but on the life of God with us in Christ. Brunner stresses that our proclamation and theological thinking should respect these same boundaries.

The second element is Brunner's recognition that the Easter event goes beyond straightforward history. In contrast to much of the apostles' testimony that communicates the sights, smells, and sounds of daily life, the resurrection transcends the general evidence of historical fact. The truth of the resurrection is not comprehensible in the same way as other aspects of the life of Jesus are accessible to believer and unbeliever alike; it is intelligible only to the response of faith. A comment from *The Mediator* elucidates. "It is the very essence of revelation and of faith that we should become Christians not through the historical picture of Jesus, but through the picture traced by the Gospels in the light of the Resurrection faith which has grown out of the testimony of the apostles, and has become the witness to Christ of the Christian Church."[48] In this way Easter is determinative for our perception of Jesus as the Christ, because it is the basis of the apostolic testimony that is given only in light of the resurrection, not before this event or apart from it.

PART THREE: THE CHRISTIAN DOCTRINE OF THE CHURCH, FAITH, AND THE CONSUMMATION

After considering the divine nature and will, as well as humankind and salvation in Christ, Brunner's *Dogmatics* culminates in *The Christian Doctrine of the Church, Faith, and the Consummation*. "The chief concern of this concluding volume," Brunner remarks, "is to vindicate the Biblical concept of faith in contrast to that supplied by the tradition of the creed."[49] A fresh appreciation of the church naturally follows, as does a refocused vision of Christian faith and hope.

---

48. Brunner, *Mediator*, 159.
49. Brunner, *Dogmatics III*, xi.

Part I: Believing Thinking

Ekklesia

The three different topics under consideration in this volume—church, faith, and eschatology—are presented as integrated, but it is not immediately clear what Brunner perceives the unifying feature to be. Is it the Holy Spirit, the presence of the risen Christ who is with us as Lord? Is it the life of the *ekklesia*, the community of believers who have responded by faith to Jesus Christ and live together in the presence and power of the Spirit? Is it the hope of a final consummation according to the loving and holy will of God, which animates the believing community in its present existence? We are left with two options for a main theme after initial investigation: the presence of the Holy Spirit or the life of the *ekklesia*. Brunner unsurprisingly launches his investigation from the apostolic witness, which displays a synergy of *ekklesia* and faith.

The Nature of Ekklesia

The New Testament portrays individuals in communion with one another as they share *koinonia pneumatos* and *koinonia Christou*. Brunner concludes from this evidence that "to be in Christ through faith and to be in this fellowship are one and the same thing. This fellowship is not an addition of secondary importance or even an *externum subsidium*. It is rather the conjoint fellowship which has its ground in Christ, fellowship with one another on the basis of fellowship with God."[50] He points out that this conception differs from the Reformed and Roman Catholic interpretations that perceive the church as an institution. Fellowship in these cases is often subordinated to the hierarchical structure that has become the primary identity of the church, an identity that is both rooted in and fostered by an extra-biblical conception of Christian communion.

As Brunner explains, however, nothing could be further from the reality shown us in Scripture, which demonstrates that "fellowship is nothing other than the existence with each other whose ground is God's existence with us, and conversely sin is nothing other than existence apart from Him and apart from each other."[51] Such a description preserves the personal nature of the divine–human encounter, as well as responsibility to respond to God in the obedience of faith. This draws our attention to Brunner's

---

50. Ibid., 21; cross-reference Rom 5:5; Gal 5:6, 22.
51. Ibid., 21.

critique that the *ekklesia* of agape fellowship differs radically from the historical understanding of the church. *"Ekklesia"* in Brunner's terms means the brotherhood of faith, and by "church" he understands the hierarchical institution called by that name.

We will not entertain here the historical discussion concerning the *ekklesia invisibilis* and the *ekklesia visibilis*, but it is important to note three aspects of Brunner's understanding of *ekklesia* that have traditionally been associated with the concept of the latter. They are the church as (a) *coetus electorum*, (b) *corpus Christi*, and (c) *communio sanctorum*.[52] Brunner maintains a key premise to which he has been faithful throughout *Dogmatics*, that the final test of an individual's understanding of truth is his response to God in worship and fellowship. In this way we see that creation's purpose becomes visible in salvation's *telos* through Jesus Christ: human beings are fully restored to communion with their creator. Brunner discerns this goal in the *coetus electorum* through which God is creating a new humanity. The image of the *corpus Christi* is also used in the New Testament to portray the fellowship of Jesus' followers in a believing, post-resurrection organism. Brunner helpfully emphasizes that the *ekklesia* was not something the first disciples had to believe in order to live; they simply became the body of Christ through the power of the Holy Spirit. Finally, the *communio sanctorum* represents the addition of post-apostle believers to Christian community, thus creating fellowship with Christ himself. Faith is simultaneously the ground and the fruit of fellowship.

What is Brunner's conclusion to this treatment of the church? He writes, "The Ekklesia is a thoroughly uncultic, unsacred, spiritual brotherhood, which lives in trusting obedience to its Lord Christ and in the love to the brethren which He bestows, and knows itself as the Body of Christ through the Holy Spirit which dwells in it."[53] It is this concept of the *ekklesia* that Brunner acclaims as the true meaning of church.

Ekklesia and the Christian

The Holy Spirit's role in the formation of the *ekklesia* reminds us of the necessity of faith in the individual's response to revelation, the result of which is the formation of a believing community that is both the seed and the fruit of faith. Brunner acknowledges that on one hand the *ekklesia* is the means

---

52. Ibid., 23–26.
53. Ibid., 33.

to the end of the advent of the kingdom of God, without being synonymous with the kingdom itself. On the other hand it is an end in itself in so far as it is the reality of the body of Christ, through which he is present by the Spirit. Faith, consequently, is described as "existence in fellowship."[54] It comes to individuals through the fellowship and proclamation of the *ekklesia*, and association with the institutional church is not prerequisite for its realization. The implication for Brunner is obvious: to be a Christian is to be part of the *ekklesia*. One is not a Christian outside of the *ekklesia*, nor is the *ekklesia* composed of persons other than those who in faith have responded to Jesus Christ and live under the lordship of the Holy Spirit. Life together is the consummate expression of self-giving love because divine agape is poured out in our hearts in abundance through the Spirit.

Regarding the relationship of faith, discipleship, and the *ekklesia*, Brunner explains that confession of *Kyrios Christos* is accompanied by an inner transformation. He who acknowledges another lord is no longer his own; he has surrendered his charade of autonomy for the obedience of faith. In this light, faith is no less an encounter for those disciples who heard the good news second-hand through the apostles even though they did not walk with Jesus in the flesh. Jesus Christ was made real in the proclamation of the gospel and those listeners encountered him as Lord. Brunner concludes that for the early church, as for the *ekklesia* of all ages, faith is the obedient response to God's invitation to become God's own and to belong to his people. The witness of the *communio sanctorum* is dual, including the proclamation of the word of God and the witness of its life together.

Faith

An edifying, but lengthy and intricate, exposition of the nature and workings of *pistis* introduces the final section of *Dogmatics III*, in which Brunner undertakes an historical survey of the understanding and the misunderstanding of faith in the Christian tradition. The nature of faith is of primary concern in light of the doctrine of justification. This subject is more than a detail and we shall see that on it much of Brunner's system hangs.

---

54. Ibid., 138.

Divine Address, Human Response, and Justification

In Brunner's opinion, Luther's expression of *Christus solus* brings us closer to the Pauline interpretation of faith than does any other formula. It preserves God as the sole author of salvation and keeps the focus on the kingdom of God instead of on human activism as the salvation of humankind as in liberal Protestantism. Simply stated, salvation is God's advent in the Son's self-giving love and forgiveness, both as historical event and as ongoing encounter. The human response to God's initiative must be by faith. It occurs when we understand that God calls us his children and when we receive that identity for ourselves. This apprehension of faith is true to the apostolic witness in its concern to make God's initiative in Christ the source and goal of theological articulation, including conversion, discipleship, and sanctification as the event of faith.

We have come full circle to confirm the tenet that started this chapter, that every encounter with God is encounter with Jesus Christ. Not only does it happen personally, it can *only* happen personally. The crux of faith is that God calls us his children even though nothing could be further from reality in light of the pervasive effect of sin in self and society. In Brunner's exposition, his emphasis is always on the sufficiency of the word of God and the act of personal address, which is why he affirms the principle that justification is effected by the word of God alone. Justification of the sinner occurs through God's pronouncement of "justified," followed by the response of faith "which 'hears' this Word 'from below' and repeats it obediently, the *hypakoē pisteōs* of the man who entrusts himself, who forsakes all security and takes shelter in the security of the God who opens His heart and communicates Himself in the Word, a pure venture of faith without any safeguards."[55] This was the way of salvation for the apostles and it is also ours.

There is no doubt that God initiates this event. Brunner has argued at length that human beings possess absolutely nothing to raise themselves to communion with God. Separation from God is not just the ramification of sin; it is the primary motivation of corrupt hearts to preserve a sense of authority by rejecting divine lordship. At the same time, however, Brunner acknowledges the apparent contradiction between divine willing and human responsibility in the process of reconciliation, illuminating the dialectical nature of personal encounter. Every human–human relationship is

---

55. Ibid., 201.

reciprocal in that personal interface requires the decision of both parties. Divine–human relationship is no less reciprocal, he suggests, but this is not due to the mutual and equal decision of human and divine wills. Rather, the defining feature in our relationship with God is that God initiated it definitively, once for all time in Jesus Christ. Our participation is the decision to accept or reject his gracious invitation.

Faith, Hope, and Eschatology

God's self-disclosure in the Son remains the substance of our theology to the very end of time. This is the hope with which Christians live in the world. Brunner's premise can be stated thus: eschatology is birthed in and sustained by hope, and Christian hope is the essence of faith. Christian hope believes that just as God has loved us from eternity past, he will love us for eternity to come, and that just as we have encountered God in Christ here, revelation continues in the power of the Spirit as we respond to him and to one another in love. The reign of God is thereby realized in the present while we simultaneously anticipate the promised culmination of God's full and unmediated presence with us.

Brunner insists that as Christians we are to conduct ourselves differently in the "now" because we live in the light of an eternal kingdom. Certain questions naturally follow, such as, What relationship is a hopeful Christian to have with the world in general and with the state in particular? Does the hope that animates the Christian's life become the rule according to which he lives and engages in relationship? Brunner's answer is positive in a first instance. We are free to behave according to the wisdom of the cross and no longer the wisdom of this world because we know ourselves to be perfectly loved. The result is freedom to love others, believers and nonbelievers alike, with the same self-sacrifice as Christ showed on Golgotha.

At the same time, human experience attests to another power that rules this present age. Because of this, Brunner gives a second and negative response by stating that we cannot live in the world and relate to earthly powers according to the same law that characterizes the life inside the *ekklesia*. He maintains that the Sermon on the Mount was given by Jesus, not as a general rule of society, but as the rule of agape that shapes Christian fellowship. The unity of believers is a force for transformation in the world, but "the improvement of the secular order can at the best be only a pointer to the coming Kingdom of God, never its realization."[56] The work of the Holy Spirit that powerfully effects change in and through the Christian community must be balanced with hope for the world. Supernatural power does indeed flow through the *ekklesia*, but Brunner cautions that this does not mean that the fullness of the kingdom is accomplished in the here-and-now.

How does the faith we exercise in the present relate to the promised yet delayed glorious return of the Lord? The fullness of revelation is what we anticipate in the Lord's second coming. "Just as the beginning of a speech has no meaning unless it comes to an end," reflects Brunner, "so faith has no meaning unless it comes to its goal in the fullness of revelation, in the unveiling (*apocalypsis*) which is called the Parousia, and in the Parousia which is called the *apocalypsis*."[57] The entire history of salvation is a history of waiting, but it is not a waiting in vain. The past advent of the Lord to save his people, to which the Old and New Testaments give evidence, assures of his future and final return. The Christian hope of the consummation and of eternal life is anything but mythical, as some imagine it to be. We already possess the evidence of the reality of the consummation because it is born of and maintained by the presence of Christ with us by the Spirit.

PART FOUR: FINAL CONSIDERATIONS

Brunner's paradigm throughout *Dogmatics* yields a positive evaluation of both material and methodological consistency in his work in at least three ways. First, the limits he places on theological inquiry in the *Prolegomena*, based on the apostolic witness as source and criterion, are respected. Second, he affirms the "what" of God's revelation in Christ while eschewing speculative subjects regarding the "how" of the divine being. Third, he maintains the reality of God's revelation as on-going and personal. Additionally, Brunner has shown that the believing witness of Scripture remains the rule of truth, whether in reference to the divine nature and will, the doctrines of creation and redemption, or the nature of faith and the *ekklesia*. He affirms *Kyrios Christos* as the unashamed proclamation of the entire early church by which Jesus' witnesses corroborate his own claims, that "whoever has seen me has seen the Father." "No one has ever seen God; the only God, who is at the Father's side, he has made him known" (John

---

56. Ibid., 313.
57. Ibid., 396.

14:9b; John 1:18). The divine–human encounter of faith proffers the same revelation today.

An area for further study relates to the connection between the historical facts of Jesus' life and its super-historical import. Responding to this area of ambiguity requires attention to the broader theological discussion of which Brunner is a part. This necessitates the next section in which we briefly examine Bultmann's *Entmythologisierung* project that received so much attention in the twentieth century and the interpretation of history as *Heilsgeschichte*.

Entmythologisierung

Rudolf Bultmann's demythologizing project figures periodically in *Dogmatics* and we survey it here in the briefest of forms in an effort to hear as best we can Brunner's dialogue with the theology of his day. Brunner had some measure of personal engagement with Bultmann in a small group of theologians who met during the 1920s, including also Barth, Eduard Thurneysen, Friedrich Gogarten, and Georg Merz. At least in the 1920s, both Bultmann and Brunner were proponents of dialectical theology alongside Barth and Gogarten, though their individual theological developments would lead them in different directions in the following years.

It was Bultmann's conviction that the kerygma must be freed from its temporal cultural, linguistic, and worldview elements in order for its existential import to be measured for the hearer. "What matters is that the incarnation should not be conceived of as a miracle that happened about 1950 years ago," Bartsch explains, "but as an eschatological happening, which, beginning with Jesus, is always present in the words of men proclaiming it to be a human experience."[58] The presupposition driving Bultmann's hermeneutic is that the New Testament message is less about an historical event and more about human self-understanding.

Brunner on Bultmann

Bultmann has two aims in this program according to Brunner: to interpret the New Testament faith with an eye to its existential significance, and to offer a "demythologization" of the New Testament that prunes all that is

---

58. Bartsch, ed., *Kerygma and Myth*, 191–92.

extraneous to such an interpretation. A principal impetus for this radical shift is the recognition of the pervasive influence of science on the modern worldview. In essence it aims to neutralize the "mythical" element of the biblical perspective so as to access the a-historical kerygma of the gospel, with an eye to communicating it in a relevant manner to contemporary listeners. Brunner describes it as working towards the "'de-kerygmatization,' that is, a fundamentally unhistorical interpretation of human existence," not the least of which is the rejection of any kind of actual revelation or salvation worked out in human history.[59]

The most important implication of this process for Bultmann follows on from this. Once the preacher has demythologized the text and distilled the kerygma, the issue of interpretation is at the door. Bultmann identifies the preacher as key because for him the pulpit is the primary realm in which the message of Scripture must be interpreted for its hearers. Barth asks in *Kerygma and Myth*, "Granted that these problematic elements in the New Testament do exist, how far are they capable of being interpreted? . . . Bultmann's answer is that the only honest exegesis, dogmatics and preaching is the existentialist interpretation."[60]

It is sufficiently apparent that Brunner's agenda is not precisely Bultmann's, for the very heart of Brunner's work is that Christ's advent stands alone as an objective fact: the incarnation is datable. Just the same, there is also evidence that what is of greatest consequence as far as the biblical testimony is concerned is not primarily the historicity of the incarnation or atonement, but that these historical events are attested to by faith. This is the central tension for Brunner, and for this reason he remains unsympathetic toward Bultmann regarding the unlimited nature of this demythologizing process. At the same time, he is willing to recognize a mythological element in Scripture in the sense that everything we say about God is somehow inadequate to communicate the fullness of his reality. Faith is required to embrace God's self-revelation in a historical moment. Theology must speak of God through signs such as "the symbolism of God's Personal Being (anthropomorphism) and by His intervention in history (miracle)."[61] References to God as a judge or shepherd or king, even as Father and Lord, reflect anthropomorphic imagery, not literal description, and the element

---

59. Brunner, *Dogmatics III*, 404.

60. Bartsch, ed., *Kerygma and Myth*, 111; see also Karl Barth, "Rudolf Bultmann—An Attempt to Understand Him."

61. Brunner, *Dogmatics III*, 405.

of the supernatural is captured in terms of God speaking, acting, or moving in the realm of space and time.

Although there are aspects of Bultmann's program that are problematic for traditional theology, are there other features that contribute to sound theological thinking? Brunner acknowledges the value of Bultmann's insistence on one's self-understanding through the lens of the gospel. As Lord, God is wholly other, and knowing him leads to a deeper understanding of who we are in Christ as the new humanity through whom God is reconciling the world to himself. Furthermore, demythologizing aids us in recognizing the limits of human speech, as well as the need to interpret that which the doctrine of verbal inspiration mistakenly takes at face value. "The mythical form of expression," explains Brunner, "is simply the necessary consequence of the incommensurability of the Creator and the creature, whose transcendence we can hope for only when that final revelation occurs which is the object of our faith. 'For we know in part . . . But when that which is perfect is come, then that which is in part shall be done away' (1 Cor 13:9, 10)."[62]

Despite these contributions, Brunner does not adopt the demythologizing project without critique, for although he acknowledges an element of clarity in Bultmann's distinctions between the biblical world and the modern, he rejects the extent to which Bultmann applies this principle. The difference is paramount for the true meaning of faith is uncertain in this debate. If Bultmann is right, Brunner's entire methodology, as well as the certainty of the incarnation and atonement, is unfounded. We effectively become God in our self-understanding and there is neither redemption nor eschatological hope of a new creation. While Brunner accepts that the kerygma of God's revelation in Christ is mythical, he rejects the conclusion that the gospel can be divorced from this form.

The concrete, historical event of the incarnation is unavoidably at the heart of this issue of history, myth, and revelation. This is the theme that has guided us thus far, without forgetting the role of the apostolic witness in establishing boundaries to that revelation. Brunner's methodology reliably brings us back to the response of faith, for in responding by faith to God's self-communication, we both receive eternal life and are transformed in our existence. In this encounter "we transcend . . . the one-sidedness

---

62. Ibid., 406–7.

of subjectivism, according to which faith is not concerned with the Jesus Christ of history, but only with the *kerygma* about Jesus Christ."[63]

Brunner's reiteration comes as no surprise: faith is not objective explication of doctrine but a personal response to personal address. That said, the difficulty is that Brunner has still not stated in unequivocal terms what apostolic witness is. Is it the New Testament as a whole or something contained within it? The issue at stake is that, while it is evident that Brunner disagrees with Bultmann's presupposition that Scripture is enshrouded in myth, it is less evident to what extent he thinks a mythical element characterizes some parts of testimony. The discussion of revelation as the word of God in *Dogmatics I* will both clarify the role of faith as well as illuminate Brunner's definition of divine revelation. To this we now turn.

Delimitations of Revelation as the Word of God

In *Dogmatics I* Brunner pointedly asks, "How can human doctrine spring from divine revelation?" Otherwise stated, how do our words reflect, in any meaningful measure, the reality of who God is? The written word records for us this revelation, which is God's speaking and acting in history. The prophets are singled out by Brunner as a unique expression of God's word: "here the Word of God is present in the form of revealed human words, not behind them." Such a statement rejects out of hand the premise on which demythologizing is founded because it insists that the prophetic word is not a cover under which the word of God can be found but is God's direct address to his people through a human messenger.[64]

The New Testament is similar to the Old in that it also conveys the very word of God, but there exists an essential difference between the two. The prophetic word about Jesus is different from the word that is Jesus. Jesus Christ is divine self-disclosure "beyond all intellectual concepts."[65] Brunner highlights a difference between the indirect revelation of the spoken word and Jesus himself who is unmediated revelation. Even when we consider a text paramount to Christology such as John's prologue, we must remember that the written word about Jesus is servant to the Lord himself whom we meet in personal encounter.

---

63. Ibid., 224.
64. Brunner, *Dogmatics I*, 22–23.
65. Ibid., 25.

Brunner suggests that faithfulness to the apostolic example will enable us to avoid the error that the Logos theologians made by over-emphasizing the role of intellectual inquiry in faith. The doctrine of verbal inspiration, an enduring point of contention for Brunner, is one result of this mistake. "This (aprioristic) Bible-faith is neither the *pistis* of which the Apostles speak nor the *emuna* of the prophets and psalmists," he asserts. "Rather it is a theorem about the Bible, which is not of Christian origin, but stems from the doctrine of the verbal inspiration of Scripture which was taken over from Judaism."[66] Here we see the value of his insistence on the apostolic witness as authoritative both for the nature of theological inquiry as dynamic and Spirit-led as much as for its content.

Brunner offers no indication that the apostles' testimony is in any way manufactured, imaginary, or self-protective as demythologizing could lead one to think. It is, on the contrary, a trustworthy, firsthand account of Emmanuel. The timeless witness of the Spirit directs our interaction with the written word in such a way that the Spirit always points to, and in this sense is not independent of, the revelation of Christ. "The witness to the Son constitutes the genuineness, and thus the validity of the witness of the Spirit. And the testimony of the Son constitutes its inexhaustible content." This is not just true for the first apostles, Brunner maintains; post-apostolic Christians have real knowledge of Jesus through the same Holy Spirit even though the way in which we receive it is different. He concludes, "their witness can never be the *basis and the object* of faith, but only the *means* of faith. We do not believe in Jesus Christ *because* we first of all believe in the story and the teaching of the Apostles, but *by means of* the testimony of their narrative and their teaching."[67] We come to know him through their testimony, making their historical record about Jesus the vehicle by which God's address continues to be heard.

We have come close to the heart of Brunner's methodology and to the very essence of what he believes can and should happen in proclamation and in theological thinking. One other detail requires attention before this chapter on *Dogmatics* is brought to a close: the issue of history and salvation history.

---

66. Brunner, *Dogmatics III*, 189.
67. Brunner, *Dogmatics I*, 31–33.

Heilsgeschichte

The subject of history and its relationship to revelation is a complex one and the associated issues are numerous: the nature of scientific knowledge versus faith, resurrection as historical fact or only as proclamation of faith, and the historic Jesus versus the Christ of faith are only a few. The overlap between this discussion of history and its suggested subdivision into sacred and profane is intertwined with the demythologizing debate. A certain amount of repetition is impossible to avoid, but my goal is to isolate the precise considerations that concern Brunner's methodology in the following manner. Firstly, we will overview the meaning and purpose of *Heilsgeschichte* within Brunner's approach to dogmatics. Secondly, we will consider the particular treatment of the incarnation and resurrection. Finally, we will suggest the correlation that this program has to his methodology, particularly as it concerns the definition of apostolic witness.

The Meaning and Purpose of Heilsgeschichte

Rudolf Bultmann's differentiation between *Historie* and *Geschichte* is sufficiently well-known that a full exposition of it is not required here. The significance for the present analysis is the preoccupation of *Historie* with the data of history—dates, geography, politics, wars, whereas *Geschichte* is concerned with the existential sphere of human life. Fergusson comments, "In Bultmann's theology, the paradigm example of this is the cross of Christ. As a datable event under the rule of Pontius Pilate it is a *historisch* event which is accessible to scientific study. Yet it is also a *geschichtlich* event by which existence before God is set on an entirely new basis. When taken up in faith the crucifixion becomes not only *Historie* but *Geschichte* also."[68]

To the extent to which Brunner observes such a distinction between *Historie* and *Geschichte*, what impact does it have on his work? What is the relationship between salvation history as Brunner describes it and his identification of the apostolic witness? How is an historical event the point of departure for theological thinking, as well as its goal and its criterion, when it is the believing witness of the apostles, not history, that leads us into knowledge of God's revelation? To the sceptic, this resembles a mind game more than serious theological thinking. For Brunner, the problem is decisive.

---

68. Fergusson, *Bultmann*, 56–57.

This question of history will serve as a test case for what Brunner is doing with various categories of thought and specific language in dogmatics. "History is not a Biblical concept," he explains in *Dogmatics III*. "The Bible does not speak of history. And yet it is the most historical of books. Christian faith, Biblical faith in general, is historical existence in the highest sense of the word."[69] History does not figure in Scripture as a stand-alone subject for it is not the purpose of either Israel's or the early church's story to record only facts of their respective epochs. At the same time, though, the very heart of what we believe as Christians is an historical event. Brunner identifies the event of redemption as *Heilsgeschichte*, as the historical revelation of God's salvation, which includes both the Old and New Testaments.

What, then, is salvation history? Brunner responds by proposing three elements derived from the scriptural story. The first implication is that humankind is portrayed as a single entity based on its relationship to the creator. The fact that humanity is depicted as beginning with the one man, Adam, is not the most significant point of the creation story; the foremost meaning according to Brunner is that we stand as one before God. We share biological commonality as *humanum*, but over and above that we possess the qualities of *humanitas* that unites us before God.

The second feature Brunner identifies is that humans are intended for a specific and active purpose, that is, for relationship with the rest of creation. Humankind was not created simply to exist for itself but to participate in the greater goal of community as well as in decision-making on behalf of the rest of creation. It is the good plan of the creator-Lord that we proactively participate in our temporal existence. This is part of what it means to be human.

The third implication follows on from the first. Scripture tells us that all human beings, regardless of nationality, are caught up in the trajectory toward the goal of God for humanity, which is salvation in Jesus Christ. This is the goal of history, the perfect rule of and communication with God in his kingdom, intended for the whole cosmos. Within this frame Brunner posits that the genesis of Israel is to be interpreted as a new beginning, not just for one nation but for all humankind.

It is not long before Brunner's particular interpretation of *Heilsgeschichte* focuses this general description. He refers, for example, to Old Testament salvation-history as "a later Priestly theological construction, which probably contains historical elements, but at the same time conceals

---

69. Brunner, *Dogmatics III*, 367.

as much as it reveals of the real course of events."[70] What exactly does he mean by this? To some ears this might render the authority of the Old Testament vague at best and downright spurious at worst. This would be a valid response if what we are looking for were a substantiation of the doctrine of verbal inspiration, which Brunner rejects. His point is that the priority of the Old Testament witness is less the temporal reality of God's appearance to Abraham or his conversations with Moses and more the spiritual reality to which it directs our attention—God redeeming the world.

This line of reflection leads to the concept of progressive revelation. "In His revelation God took into account the stage of development man had reached . . . What He gave to the primitive people of the time of the Judges is not the same as that which He gave through His prophets in the later years of the Monarchy."[71] There is no sense of change in the content of revelation itself, only the indication that the Old Testament plays a preparatory role, anticipating the full and complete revelation in the incarnation.

Implications for the Incarnation and Resurrection

Brunner locates the consistency between the law and the gospel in the dynamic nature of revelation. The crux of the matter is that in both testaments God reveals his person through mighty acts, not through a written book. "The Book is never the canonical form of His revelation," Brunner explains, "but the Living Word, expressed as His acts in History, as His intervention in the history of men."[72] The conclusion that God discloses himself within the confines of human history reiterates that the divine being is personal being, not a timeless, universal ideal. Furthermore, testimony to encounter with the personal Lord is not meant to be objective in the sense that it is written to report facts alone; no testimony is objective because every witness speaks subjectively about what he believes he experienced and saw.

If Brunner's approach to *Heilsgeschichte* is correct, what is the relationship between faith and historical event? To begin with, the death of Jesus Christ is the crossroads where we discover salvation history. The cross as atonement and redemption is God's self-unveiling and therefore cannot be restricted in terms of an historical event. This is what makes the

---

70. Brunner, *Dogmatics II*, 199.

71. Ibid., 199. Brunner goes on to reference Irenaeus for this view of progressive revelation with the idea of "economy of divine revelation."

72. Ibid., 201.

cross of Christ utterly unique, "something that by its very nature either has happened once and for all, for all times and for every man, or else has not happened."[73] Thus, the believer affirms that the crucifixion happened and as such it is not especially unique as an historical event, but the supra-historical import of the cross renders it absolutely unique as a faith event. The cross as atonement will not, cannot, and does not need to happen again; the resurrected Lord cannot die and the redemption achieved therein cannot be reversed or compromised. It is truly finished. Furthermore, "the meaning of world history does not lie in world history itself. This meaning comes from beyond history to history in Jesus Christ, the One who comes, the consummator and bringer of the Kingdom of God."[74] The whole of humankind is addressed by this event and in it is represented the spiritual reality of reconciliation.

In this commentary Brunner clarifies the limits of demythologizing, which otherwise rejects the idea of any kind of revelation or salvation being concretely worked out in the stories of nations and peoples. He distances himself at this point from Bultmann by insisting that truth is not found in existential self-reflection at the expense of historical reality but at the intersection where God encounters his creatures in space and time. This is the keystone of faith: God reveals himself exactly in this manner and such revelation cannot be attained or obtained by anything humans do but only by a gracious willing of God.

Conclusion

Having surveyed *Dogmatics*, three short questions and answers serve as a summary of the nature and limits of theological inquiry as we have seen Brunner practice them. (1) If the theologian's task is to critique the church's language about God, *what criterion is to be used as the measure of truth?* It is God's self-revelation in Jesus Christ. (2) *What is the source of that criterion?* It is the believing declaration of the apostles that the resurrected Christ is with us. (3) *What is the apostolic witness?* It is this very testimony concerning God's redemptive activity in human history, which gives access to the spiritual reality of his self-revelation in Jesus Christ.

What can these investigations contribute to an analysis of Brunner's methodology? Brunner reiterates time and again that the gospels are

73. Brunner, *Dogmatics III*, 369.
74. Ibid., 374.

not intended to be purely historical documents because they are written through the eyes of faith. They nevertheless can be trusted to be accurate testimony to the spiritual reality of the resurrected Christ with us and in this way serve as the means to personal encounter. This reorientation of dogmatics to the Bible as trustworthy testimony is one of Brunner's significant contributions to theology in his day and retains, I suggest, value for believing thinking in ours.

PART II

Bounded Theology

4

Beyond *Dogmatics*

"The first and most important fact that we can know about God is ever this: we know nothing of Him, except what He Himself has revealed to us. God's revelation of Himself always occurs in such a way as to manifest more deeply His inaccessibility to our thought and imagination . . . That God is mystery means that we cannot solve the enigma."

—BRUNNER, *OUR FAITH*, 20–21

GIVEN THE CENTRALITY OF revelation to Brunner's methodology, this chapter deals with topics related to the event of God's self-disclosure. It moves from the foundation of theology as believing thinking to the actual discipline in itself, which is circumscribed by the authoritative witness to its absolute subject. In part 1 of this chapter we will explore the movement of revelation in the apostolic witness; part 2, what revelation is not; part 3, what revelation is. Finally, part 4 will consider human–human encounter as one of revelation's implications that, though perhaps less well known, will contribute to our inquiry as appropriate. What we will find here is consistent with what has gone before, including the apostolic witness as the boundary to dogmatics, although in these volumes that go beyond *Dogmatics* Brunner deploys language that he has not used hitherto.[1] While

---

1. I reference titles as they arise in the study instead of giving an exhaustive list

the apostolic witness remains the criterion by which theology is evaluated, Brunner's interpretation of revelation goes beyond the vocabulary of the written word. Revelation is first and foremost event: the past event of Christ's revelation to the apostles, the present event of personal encounter, and future event of the final consummation. With this in mind, our understanding of Brunner's definition of revelation needs to be more specific. To this task we now turn.

PART ONE: THE MOVEMENT OF REVELATION IN APOSTOLIC WITNESS

Our discussion on demythologizing and *Heilsgeschichte* prompts a more precise description of the relationship between historical event and revelation. Brunner argues that if theological investigation begins with terminology that results *from* dogmatics, it risks controlling the gospel message according to philosophical constructs. "Revelation has always and everywhere the character of a sudden event," and whatever language is used must respect that character.[2] It is my goal, therefore, to show in greater detail the actual connections Brunner suggests from the event of the apostolic witness to doctrinal articulation. Four occasions are fundamental to his conception of revelation: the incarnation, the cry of *Kyrios Christos*, the cross and resurrection, and on-going revelation.

The Incarnation—Revelation as Super-Historical Event

The emphasis that Brunner lends to the incarnation requires further explanation if what it discloses is super-historical. Thus far Brunner has affirmed that (a) the heart of the Christian faith is the eternal Son of God become a temporally-bound man, (b) and that this is a movement from God to humankind, not humanity's reaching up to God, (c) which invites a response of faith. It is this very faith-response that is sought by God in the incarnation: *nostra assumit ut conferret nobis sua*. Brunner concludes that the origin and impact of God's self-movement in the incarnation is determined outside of the sphere of human origin. Redemption is not the result of human ingenuity or effort. It is neither an occurrence that takes place in

---

here, and they all come from Brunner's eristic-dogmatic period.

2. Brunner, *Revelation and Reason*, 30.

the natural order of things, nor can it be explained in human categories of thought or being. Although we know some of the facts of the life of Jesus, the fullness of his existence remains a divine mystery.

What exactly does Brunner intend to communicate when he speaks of the super-historical significance of the historical revelation? It is the unique factor about Christianity that faith hangs upon an historical fact; yet it is not the fact alone that determines Christianity but the reality of eternity entering time that takes place within it. He is keen to stress that the historical fact at the heart of faith is the event of Jesus Christ, and the "fact of the actuality of that upon which it depends" is the impossible paradox that eternity becomes bound by time.[3] For this reason Brunner insists that this tension be maintained between the historical and the super-historical if we are to fully understand what is being revealed. Christian theology does not content itself with identifying anonymous, if remarkable, events through time. This is the preoccupation of philosophical speculation and certain world religions. The Christian faith instead pursues its end in understanding the unique revelation that underlies its historical events. This pursuit is consistent with the eschatological goal of divine revelation of knowing God and Jesus Christ whom he has sent. Brunner states in *Eternal Hope*, "the basis of the Christian hope lies in the revelation of God given in Jesus Christ. Divine revelation is not a book, not a dogma, but a history, the history of Christ."[4]

Regarding the incarnation specifically, the apostolic witness leads us from the historical event of the Synoptic birth stories to their theological interpretation that explains what God was accomplishing in those episodes. A comparison between the Synoptics and the gospel of John suggests that, although the former focus more on historical narrative and the latter on an explanation of that narrative, they all share the same intention and the same testimony. In all the gospels it is the God-become-flesh that stands as the *sine qua non* of revelation and the focus of their witness. Nothing is more common in human history than the birth of a baby, yet the birth of Jesus is the most radical, incomprehensible, and powerful happening of human history, infused by its super-historical origin and goal.

---

3. Brunner, *Mediator*, 153.
4. Brunner, *Eternal Hope*, 26.

Part II: Bounded Theology

Kyrios Christos—Revelation in I–Thou Encounter

That said, the incarnation as defined by the historical event of Jesus' birth is not necessarily the full recognition of Jesus' divinity by those who experienced pre-resurrection encounters. Though Brunner does not do so, one could easily challenge this interpretation by reminding us that the gospels were written from the perspective of faith that Jesus is the Son of God. They were not written, the challenge proceeds, and presumably their witness was not passed down, in a progressive form as we have portrayed Brunner as stating: the progressive form of a partial recognition of Jesus' extraordinariness in a first encounter; further understanding though remaining incomplete during his ministry; then post-resurrection faith in him as the Son of God.

We might ask, though, is it entirely out of the question that the gospel writers attempt to show this growing faith as they write if it is consistent with the occasion of revelation? Although the Scriptures were written from the perspective of faith, we experience with the characters in the narratives the tension of not fully understanding as their knowledge of Jesus progresses. Despite their slowness, there is evidenced a greater comprehension of who Jesus is in various experiences of evolving faith-response, both before and after the resurrection. Luke 5:8, for example, tells us of Peter's reaction to the miraculous catch of fish that Jesus commanded on one occasion: "Depart from me, for I am a sinful man, O Lord." This answer is reflected in John 21:7, this time in John's words when he replies, "it is the Lord," to a similar miraculous catch after the resurrection. What is the point to be made? In the incarnation is hidden the super-historical event of God become man. Through the life and work of Christ, revelation of his deity becomes fuller, accompanied by an increasing recognition of his lordship. We have in the witness of the early church even greater certainty that Jesus is the Christ, such as in Acts 2:36–38. The disciples' testimony also is one of repentance in I–Thou encounter: "Let all the house of Israel therefore know for certain that God has made him both Lord and Christ, this Jesus whom you crucified . . . Repent and be baptized every one of you in the name of Jesus Christ for the forgiveness of your sins, and you will receive the gift of the Holy Spirit." Such accounts illustrate Brunner's point, that the faith-response *Kyrios Christos* symbolizes the believing reply to him as "Thou" and submission to his lordship.

The response of faith, however, is not the only possible reaction to personal encounter with the Lord. As we have already explored, the responsibility and freedom that characterize the human being leave one as free to reject God as one is to submit to him. "The freedom we have to say yes or no to God is the mystery of man,"[5] comments Brunner in *Our Faith*. He emphasizes this contradiction felt within the human heart as the conflict between that which we know we ought to do and that which we choose to do despite that knowledge. Though well aware of the extensive discussion in moral philosophy regarding the "ought" of human existence, he is mostly keen to highlight that revelation defines the same contradiction as the heart's rebellion against personal encounter with the Lord.[6]

This contradiction according to Brunner is a fundamental discontinuity between the human and the divine. It is the expression both of the personal rebellion of sin and the universal problem of evil. It is, in sum, the very heart of sin—the will to be independent, to exercise one's will, mind, and power free from relationship with and accountability to God. The garden interface between Adam, Eve, and God is reduplicated, theologically speaking, every time we say "no" to divine fellowship. As cases in point, the rich young ruler prefers his own life plan to that of Jesus (Luke 18:23), and nine of the ten lepers are too taken by their healing to respond in faith to the one who had mercy on them (Luke 17:17). These examples are not specific ones that Brunner offers, but they evidence the point he makes about the freedom we possess to respond to Christ either in faith or in self-sufficiency. *Kyrios Christos* is a cry that requires a faith response to revelation.

The Cross-Resurrection in Revelation

Roughly stated, the gospels trace the order of the historical events of revelation in this way: a first encounter with the man Jesus is followed by the disciples' confession of faith that he is the Christ (or the non-disciple's rejection of his lordship). This confession culminates in a faith-response to the cross and resurrection in which revelation finds its fulfilment, for it is only with the eyes of faith that one can recognize the wisdom of God in the scandal of the cross. Brunner concludes, "If human death—in contrast to death as a natural event—is the effect of sin and the divine wrath, that is, of man's perverted relation to God, then conversely, the consequence of the

---

5. Brunner, *Our Faith*, 40.

6. Brunner's discussion of the "ought," the moral imperative, is extensive in *The Divine Imperative*.

newly established communion with God in Christ is the re-establishment of 'existence-unto-eternal-life'" and this through Christ's death.[7]

The relation between the two categories of history and super-history remains complex but what matters for present purposes is that Brunner classifies the cross and resurrection alongside the incarnation as revelation. He points to the believing witnesses who attest to the risen Christ by faith, thus showing that the ultimate import of this twofold event cannot be seized by human logic alone but only in the context of Jesus' presence through the Spirit.[8] The cross firstly shows Jesus' descent to death as his enduring the consequence of sin to be borne by every human being. The signification of Christ's "descent into hell" is not obvious from the apostolic witness, observes Brunner; it is not given us to know exactly what happened or how it occurred. *That* he did die a human death is the key to grasping the import of God's revelation in this event. Brunner indicates the super-historical significance of the cross this way in *The Mediator*.

> Hence the Cross, conceived as the expiatory penal sacrifice of the Son of God, is the fulfilment of the scriptural revelation of God, in its most paradoxical incomprehensible guise. It is precisely in His revelation that the God of the Bible is incomprehensible, because in His nearness He reveals His distance, in His mercy His holiness, in His grace His judgment, in His personality His absoluteness ... It is thus that He is God, the One who comes to us in reality: who comes in the likeness of sinful flesh, the One who Himself pays the price, Himself bears the penalty, Himself overcomes all that separates us from Him—really overcomes it . . . This real event is His real coming, and therefore it is both the revelation of that which *we* are and of that which *He* is.[9]

The meaning of Christ's death lies secondly in the fact that from this lowest place of all Christ ascended to the right hand of the Father. Furthermore, for Brunner, "the resurrection is not the reason, but the result, of the Godhead of Jesus, and belief in the resurrection is not the basis, but the result, of faith in the Godhead of Jesus. No one believes that Jesus Christ rose from the dead who does not first of all believe that He is the Son of God."[10] The order of belief is determinative for the experience of I-Thou

---

7. Brunner, *Man in Revolt*, 475.

8. A helpful treatment of the resurrection through the lens of faith is found in Brunner, *Eternal Hope*, 142–54.

9. Brunner, *Mediator*, 473.

10. Brunner, *Revelation and Reason*, 305.

encounter and the subsequent expression in theological terms of that event. For people of every age it proceeds along these lines. A person first believes by faith that Jesus is who he says he is on the basis of the believing testimony of the apostles. Then, when he acknowledges by faith that Jesus is his Lord, he responds in submission and thereby personally experiences reconciliation and the forgiveness of sins. Through this lens of faith he then interprets Jesus' person and work as divine revelation. Brunner stresses the sequence as relevant. Revelation does not happen in the opposite sense, that is, a person encounters God through some means other than revelation and as a result of that experience comes to know Jesus Christ. God's self-communication happens in the personal encounter of the individual with the risen Christ as he surrenders to Christ's loving authority. It is only on this basis that the individual comes to believe in the super-historical significance of the resurrection.

Brunner writes with a confidence that perhaps deserves a measure of moderation. Must we say, as he does above, that "*no one* believes that Jesus Christ rose from the dead who does not first of all believe that He is the Son of God"? Even if this statement holds true for the apostles, does it hold true in the same way for every generation that does not experience encounter with the risen Lord as the twelve did? Brunner's answer was indicated in chapter 1: subsequent generations of believers have the same knowledge of Jesus as the apostles had, through the same Spirit who enlivens our hearts to faith, and the order of our faith is the same as theirs. His emphasis is not that one is prohibited from believing in the resurrection if one does not believe Jesus is God, but that it would be absurd to do so.

With this affirmation in mind we proceed with our investigation. The order suggested above could be emphasized in the following manner. (1) The *event* of the incarnation reveals the *theological category* of super-historical revelation. (2) The *event* of the disciples' faith proclamation reflects the *theological category* of contradiction—the contradiction between the logic of human reason and the mystery of divine revelation in Christ. (3) The *event* of the cross and resurrection reveals the *theological category* of divine love in response to that contradiction.

Of critical interest is the relationship of divine revelation to this movement both in history and in theological reflection. One way of stating the process is: God begins to disclose himself in the baby of Bethlehem; God further unveils himself in the work and words of Jesus of Nazareth; God reveals himself most fully in the crucified and risen Christ. It is not surprising that Brunner declares the event of the resurrection as being fundamental to all apostolic witness even though it is not the historical starting point of revelation. The apostles' testimony is differentiated from the word of the prophets and from our own, the former that looked forward to the victory of the resurrection and the latter that looks back in faith. The witness of the twelve to the risen Christ is one of first-hand, present-tense, and therefore historically-expressed recognition of God's revelation in Christ.

The Kingdom of God—On-going Revelation

What exactly is the relationship of the apostolic witness to the rest of the canon? Is it a case of Joseph and his brothers—all their father's sons but one apparently of greater worth? Brunner upholds the Reformation principle that all Scripture reveals Jesus Christ; we need both testaments to understand God's revelation. He thus confirms that the entire word of God remains the means through which the Spirit continues to reveal the living word. The believing testimony of the apostles to the living Christ is at the center of this word, but its significance and meaning depend on the entirety of Scripture.

The historical happening Brunner identifies is the continuing event of revelation that takes place by the Spirit through the written word in the Christian community. For Brunner, the connection between the work of the Holy Spirit and the living community of the church cannot be overemphasized. He does not establish this as an historical event in the same manner as the incarnation and resurrection. The incarnation and resurrection are *sui generis*, whereas God's on-going revelation is reproduced wherever and whenever the Spirit of God reveals the Father through the Son, as he did to the apostles and continues to do today.

While the incarnation and the cross-resurrection are "once-for-all" events, the faith response of the apostles is mirrored in the on-going revelation in the church. There results an argument for placing continuing revelation as a fourth historical event. The testimony of the early church certainly allows us to point to on-going revelation in at least Acts if not in the entire New Testament. Classing continuing revelation as historical event would also make sense in the broader vision of the kingdom of God inaugurated in the life of Christ as, from a theological perspective, "*now* is the day of salvation" (2 Cor 6:2) and every encounter with the risen Christ is unique.

PART TWO: WHAT REVELATION IS NOT

It is imperative to keep Brunner's concept of revelation in the forefront of our minds as we continue to explore his methodology. One of his aims is to show that the content of theology must be sourced in the self-unveiling of God in Jesus Christ as testified to in the witness of the apostles, the church, and the Holy Spirit. We have just shown how this is expressed, from the incarnation to on-going revelation. Brunner goes one step further, though, by discussing what revelation is not. He highlights in this analysis two things: revelation is not an infallible written word, and revelation is not the logos of reason.

In *Revelation and Reason* Brunner reminds his readers that all religious traditions claim special revelation of one kind or another. The Christian notion of revelation is no different in its premise, except that it asserts personal knowledge of someone, not of something. The interface of this personal being with human persons is the meeting "of the Unconditioned with the conditioned subject, the self-manifestation of the Absolute to the relative person."[11] This kind of knowing is distinct from all other knowing, be it natural or revealed, because it has for its goal the transformation of the knower instead of the anticipated intellectual acquisition of ideas. Brunner's distinction is critical for his understanding of revelation, personal encounter, the personal address of God's word, and ultimately theological inquiry.

An Infallible Written Word

Brunner is constant throughout his work in his emphasis on biblically patterned personal encounter, not only as a message of the gospel, but also as the lynchpin of his methodology. There is no doubt that he regards the written word as authoritative for Christian faith as we have seen. It is likewise clear that the Spirit leads us to encounter the risen Christ through scriptural testimony, but at the same time, Brunner argues, the Bible does not contain the sum total of God's self-disclosure. His difficulty with the doctrine of verbal inspiration in particular is its use as proof of the Bible's verbal inerrancy, thereby equating the written word with revelation. It is this comparison that he categorically dismisses for three reasons.

---

11. Brunner, *Revelation and Reason*, 27.

Part II: Bounded Theology

The first reason is the perennial nature of God's address to humankind that, in his view, has been active from the creation of the world. Four examples illustrate the point: in the event of creation, "And God *said* . . . and it was;" through the prophets, "the *word* of the Lord came to me, *saying* . . . ;" in the definitive word, Jesus Christ, "And the Word *became* flesh and dwelt among us;" and in the on-going work of the Holy Spirit, who "will *teach* you all things and bring to your remembrance all that I have *said* to you."[12] Brunner insists that God's address remains strictly God's prerogative and therefore cannot be limited to any human expression. Additionally, as a word it is constantly renewed as an expression of his love for humankind. To say that God's word is confined, defined, and delimited by the sum total of the Old and New Testaments in Brunner's view contravenes God's sovereignty over his self-expression and its living nature. He roundly declares, though a little harshly, "For orthodoxy, the Bible as a book is the divinely revealed truth. It is thus a revealed thing or object. For unperverted Christian faith, however, Scripture is only revelation when conjoined with God's Spirit in the present. The *testimonium spiritus sancti* and the clarity of God's word are one and the same thing . . . The real thing is Scripture to the extent that it is the witness to the revelation of God in Jesus Christ. 'Scripture is the cradle in which Christ lies' (Luther)."[13]

The second point is that the equation of the Bible with revelation is at odds with the Reformation principle *Christus dominus et rex scripturae*. The law, the prophets, and the New Testament together indicate Jesus Christ as the word given by God. There is no other word apart from him. Yet, when pushed to an extreme the doctrine of inerrancy turns this credo on its head. It ultimately concludes that the human words we possess *are* the revelation, almost implying that the living word, Jesus Christ, exists to prove the veracity of the written word. In contrast, Brunner maintains that the words of the Bible are human words and for this reason he contends that "the Bible is the human, and therefore not the infallible, witness to the divine revelation in the Old Covenant and in the history of the incarnate Son of God."[14] Underlying this assertion is the conviction that Jesus Christ alone is the perfect expression of God's being and will. The written word is a means to the end of knowing Christ, but as human expression it cannot be considered infallible and must not be equated with revelation in the

---

12. Genesis 1; Jer 1:4; John 1:14a; 14:26b.
13. Brunner, *The Philosophy of Religion*, 152.
14. Brunner, *Revelation and Reason*, 276.

same manner as Christ. Its trustworthiness is not dependent upon a human doctrine but on the fact that God remains its Lord.

The third reason Brunner offers, though possibly the weakest in its exposition, reflects his concern regarding the doctrine's conflict with science. The particular interpretation of the doctrine that he rejects renders as unquestionable everything that the Bible contains. Through the church's commitment to verbal inspiration, he explains, "everything in the Bible was canonized—the historical narratives, the cosmological, zoological, anthropological world-view of the old Semitic civilization and of antiquity in general."[15] Conflict with the scientific worldview was inevitable, and it was only a matter of time before Scripture would be considered by an unbelieving modernity as antiquated and anti-intellectual because of this mistaken hermeneutical commitment.

The issue with a strict type of inerrantist position is that it presents all of Scripture through a literalist lens, which has difficulty allowing for differentiation among genres of expression.[16] This dogmatism is not the work of the *testimonium spiritus sancti* according to Brunner, because it leads the believer to put his faith in a literal meaning of the written words without taking into consideration the contributions of biblical criticism that mediate between radically different historical contexts of the pre-modern, Near Eastern writer and the modern, Western reader.

Brunner has been taken to task at times for his positive regard towards modern biblical criticism, certain elements of which do not consider Scripture as a means of God's self-communication. Nevertheless, if we hold, as Brunner does, that the word of God in Scripture comes through human expression, then biblical criticism becomes necessary and constructive. He states, it "is nothing but the act by which we recognize that the crib is not Christ, that the ground is not the gold, that God's Word is only indirectly identical with the Bible word, although we have the one only through the other."[17] The heart of his concern is that we not confuse the biblical worldview and its very time-bound details with the message of revelation. This modified perspective creates more room for listening to the continual revelation that transcends the written text of Scripture and points to the triune

---

15. Brunner, *Word and World*, 97.

16. We must recognize that Brunner over-generalizes the inerrantist position, as some inerrantists do acknowledge the variety of scriptural genres. In a similar manner, some propositionalist theologians overstate Brunner's position; for example, Henry, *Christian Faith and Modern Theology*, chapter 4.

17. Brunner, *Word and World*, 102.

Part II: Bounded Theology

Lord whom the words were intended to communicate. Stated differently, the significance of the incarnation points above and beyond a Bethlehem stable; the reality of redemption is not limited to an empty first century tomb.

This said, the real problem for biblical faith in the modern era according to Brunner is not science but the view that the individual is his own authority. The drive to self-sufficiency is recognizable in both those who reject the Bible as authoritative for faith and in those who define the word of God according to the doctrine of verbal inspiration. Though different in their conclusion and consequence, it is at least plausible that these two approaches to Scripture share a similar root—the desire to control. Taken to their logical extremes they ignore God as the creator-Lord of the cosmos and the personal Lord of the one who seeks to know. Both miss the dynamic nature of divine revelation in Christ. Both ignore the personal character of truth as it comes to us in human form in the one who is the way, the truth, and the life.

As debatable as this point might be for some people, let us grant it to Brunner for the present time and see what relationship it has to the broader theme of theological method. We are exploring in this chapter the order of revelation as it unfolds in the biblical narratives: a person believes that Jesus is the Christ through the Holy Spirit's witness that the apostolic testimony is true. The ultimate goal is not that he would believe in the written words of the Bible as divine dictation, but that he would meet God in his holiness and love to which Scripture points. The doctrine of verbal inspiration prioritizes the former goal, thus disregarding personal encounter and transformation as the end of theology.[18] The argument is coherent even if one remains suspicious of its appearance. When the doctrine of inerrancy determines theology, the "'believer' is now no longer, as in the New Testament, a person who has been claimed and transformed by Jesus Christ, but a person who accepts what the Church offers him as divinely revealed doctrine, since he is aware that either the Bible or the doctrinal authority of the Church constitutes an authority to which he must submit without question."[19]

Has Brunner auctioned off the doctrine of verbal inspiration at too low a price? True it is that he refuses to credit the written word with revelatory significance in and of itself apart from personal encounter with Jesus

---

18. Brunner, *Revelation and Reason*, 174.
19. Ibid., 9.

Christ. This does not mean for Brunner, though, that the Old and New Testaments are not the constructive and even irreplaceable means to the end of God's self-communication. Brunner's dismissal of the doctrine is reflective of his commitment to revelation as God's coming to us in Christ in present-tense, personal address. He rejects the objectification of the Bible as *the* word of God because it short-circuits the dynamic nature of revelation and denies Christ as its Lord.

The Logos of Reason

Hence we see that, in Brunner's view, when God's self-expression is confined to words on a page, the element of personal encounter is minimized if not effaced entirely. The issue of how we know God takes center stage once again and brings us straight to the question of the relationship between revelation and reason. Brunner argues that the so-called contradiction between the knowledge of reason and the truth of revelation is not evident in the Bible and therefore is not theology's business. The issue in Scripture is rather the actual person in his very being before the self-revealing God. Personal encounter retains priority.

How did the problem of revelation versus reason become so important in modern theology?[20] From Brunner's perspective this occurred when the church attempted to establish proofs for the existence of God upon a rational explanation of the divine being instead of upon his revelation in Jesus Christ. One of the effects of this decision was that "the *theologia naturalis* and the *theologia revelata* appear in unquestioned agreement, mutually supporting and completing each other."[21] The response to this marriage has been pendular throughout history. My goal is not to resolve the issue in its breadth but to focus our investigation on the question of *logos* and its use in Brunner's writing.

The logos denotes in a first instance that which has "unity of thought of any kind," regardless of the source of that thought.[22] The emphasis lies

---

20. Though published before *Revelation and Reason*, Brunner traces the development of the relationship between revelation and philosophy in Protestantism in *Philosophy of Religion*.

21. Brunner, *Revelation and Reason*, 310. Heideman suggests that *theologia naturalis* in Brunner's thought means "that not only the Christian, but also the natural man can be understood only in his relation to God." Heideman, "The Relation of Revelation and Reason," 41.

22. Brunner, *Revelation and Reason*, 310.

Part II: Bounded Theology

in the internal consistency of a matter, in its logical uniformity. What is a logical problem becomes a theological problem when God is viewed as the source of what we know by human reason. Brunner comments on this connection between human reason and the divine being in the context of his anthropology. One of the characteristics of being human that is widely acknowledged is that we seek something greater than ourselves. Truth, beauty, goodness, justice, and the holy are some examples of this "greater than." Such a quest reflects within the human being a sense of the absolute, also referred to as the logos of reason.

According to Brunner this logos is not the logos of God, who is specifically the word, Jesus Christ. The distinction is a critical one. Brunner expounds:

> There are two statements which sound exactly the same, and yet lie as far apart from one another as the world of the Platonic theory of ideas and the world of Biblical revelation. They are these: God is (the same as) *the Truth*; and *God* is the Truth. In the former instance, that of Platonism, the concept of God is filled out with content: truth . . . In the second instance, that of the Biblical faith, we say that that which we call "truth" in abstract terms is in reality God, the God whom we know from revelation. Abstract truth is only a reflection of the Truth which is God, the Creator, the Revealer.[23]

One way of stating this difference is the logos of God differs from the logos of reason in that it is God who defines truth by his person, not truth that defines God. The point Brunner makes is fundamental for both doctrine and methodology: we know what love, freedom, and truth are because God is these things. We again follow the movement from the historical self-revelation of God testified to in Scripture to statements of his nature. Philosophical categories obtained from outside special revelation (such as truth, freedom, and love apart from Jesus Christ) do not determine our explanation of the divine being. Instead the opposite is true. Brown concludes, "perhaps all attempt upon truth of reality as it is in itself and for itself, apart from the human grasp upon it both of knowledge and action, is a mistaken adventure."[24] Faithfulness to the historical revelation is imperative if we are to avoid this error.

---

23. Ibid., 316.
24. Brown, *Subject and Object in Theology*, 127.

Can we further clarify how the divine logos is determinative for our understanding of Jesus Christ if the logos of reason has no such authority? Brunner declares Calvin's answer as concordant with the biblical witness. Calvin refers on the one hand to Jesus Christ as the incarnation in the context of the historical revelation; but when treating the word's pre-existence, he speaks specifically of the *sermo Dei*. Brunner surmises from this fact that "wherever anything true is perceived, the eternal Logos is at work; but Jesus Christ is at work where, upon the basis of His historical revelation, man believes in Him."[25] It follows that human reason only points to the divine logos, but encounter with the divine logos leads beyond reason to the revelation of faith. This is the revelation with which theology is concerned.

The debate between natural and special revelation rears its head at this point. Once again Brunner returns to the Reformers' claim that natural revelation and understanding borne of human reason are insufficient grounds for saving knowledge of God because of the fundamental perversion of sin. "Abstract speculative thinking by means of the *analogia entis* and the *veritas* idea does not lead to the true God but into the *merae tenebrae rationis* (Luther). The ascent of the soul to God is a false path, the *itinerarium mentis in Deum* does not end in the Living God, but in the *abstract ens realissium* of Neoplatonist speculation; the true God can be known only by His coming down to us, in the revelation of Christ which is disclosed to faith."[26] This expresses as lucidly as anything else thus far the limits on speculative theological inquiry. It becomes clearer that these boundaries are not a divine power play intended to stunt human knowledge as some may fear, but they are inherent within the divine design.

The strength of this argument for Brunner's schema is that it once again roots revelation in the event of Jesus Christ. Calvin writes along similar lines: "When the subject of faith is discussed in the Schools, by simply representing God as its object, they by empty speculation . . . hurry wretched souls away from the right mark instead of directing them to it. For seeing that God dwells in light inaccessible, Christ must intervene."[27] The Christ who appears to us in the accessible form of an historical figure is the ultimate ground of faith.

As we have seen, revelation always includes the role of faith, and faith is exhibited in obedience. Brunner deduces that theology is mistaken when

---

25. Brunner, *Revelation and Reason*, 320.
26. Ibid., 319.
27. Calvin, *Institutes*, 469.

this "necessity for decision is turned into a need for explanation,"[28] such as when theology tries to prove God's existence instead of acknowledging his reality by faith. If the written word is the source of God's revelation, as the doctrine of verbal inerrancy claims, then it is in the written word that we put our faith. It thereby takes priority over the incarnate word, and what the text tells us about Jesus defines Jesus. Yet this is not the order of revelation reflected in the New Testament. If Jesus is the logos of God, it is he who tells us who the Father is through the living witness of the Holy Spirit. The nature and role of faith has implications for theological inquiry, for if faith is personal relationship with him through the Holy Spirit, it cannot be faith in any written text about Jesus Christ but must be first person interface with a living person.

PART THREE: WHAT REVELATION IS

If theology is not the examination of Scripture as the infallible word of God, and if it is not appeal to the logos of reason, two queries follow. How are we to handle the written word *vis-à-vis* Jesus as revelation? What is the relationship between revelation and reason for the believer? In light of what revelation is not, the relationship of the Old and New Testaments to Jesus Christ requires elucidation. Furthermore, Brunner suggests that revelation is only revelation when it finds its mark in the human being, when the divine address is received by the human subject. This assertion also demands further study.

Through the Witness of the Old and New Testaments

There are four categories that Brunner uses in *Revelation and Reason* that will guide our discussion: original revelation, historical revelation, the revelation in the witness to revelation, and revelation as fulfilment.[29] Original revelation pertains to God's self-communication in creation and Brunner carefully differentiates between it and natural theology as we have seen, deeming the former as legitimate and important and the latter as suspect. The second grouping, historical revelation, indicates the Old and New Tes-

---

28. Brunner, *Mediator*, 344.

29. These categories are the subheadings for "Section II: The Fact of Revelation," in Brunner, *Revelation and Reason*, 58–202.

taments as they center on the historical event of Jesus Christ. The revelation in the witness to the revelation, the third category, refers to the continuing ministry of the Spirit through the written word and the church. As important as this element is, we will not treat it further in its own right but only in light of what happens in the human knower. Finally, revelation as fulfilment pertains to the future and complete unveiling, the promise and the end of that which we know in the present.

Brunner describes God's communication in the Old Testament as both revelation itself and a promise of fulfilled revelation in the coming of the Messianic suffering servant. Four elements comprise this actuality and anticipation: the word, act, name, and face of God.[30] Each component indicates "knowledge of God from beyond all human possibilities—truth which is given in the event which constitutes revelation, in the unique decisive occurrence of history, in the Word of God."[31] This remains the decisive factor of Christianity and of the issue of the word: truth comes to us from no other source than God's direct involvement in human history.

The first two elements, word and act, can be considered in tandem as the means by which God reveals himself in Israel's history. Brunner highlights the giving of the law, which could be considered the most systematic word Israel possessed, as making sense only within the context of the act of its divine giving and its human reception. The promises of God given to Abraham, Isaac, and Jacob similarly illustrate the binary nature of divine word and act in historical revelation. Brunner points out that "there is just as much narrative as teaching in the Old Testament, and both are recorded with equal emphasis and seriousness. For God reveals Himself through His acts in history as much as through the words which He places in the mouth of the Prophets."[32]

Indeed, it is the words of the Old Testament prophets that exhibit in greatest relief the character of special revelation. The prophetic word is a word from God, originating from outside the realm of human logic and not able to be known in any other way but via God's word. This divine word, expressed in act and prophetic speech, deepens, enhances, and develops that which is revealed in creation. At the same time, though, it is a revelation of promise by anticipating the fulfilment in Christ and the final revelation of the consummation.

---

30. Ibid., 109.
31. Brunner, *Word and World*, 16.
32. Brunner, *Revelation and Reason*, 85.

The Old Testament not only communicates the acts and the words of God, but it also records for us God's name and the revelation of his face. This name of God, when given to Israel—not deduced from reason—reveals God as a personal being. Israel's response to this disclosure is its willingness (albeit not entirely consistent throughout its history) to be the people of God "who are called by My name" (2 Chr 7:14). God unveils his name so that the intimacy of personal relationship can be realized. The revelation of God's face is recorded for us in Old Testament theophany. Brunner hastens to identify these events as the result of divine willing, not as the fruit of human feeling. "The fact that God unveils or hides His face is more than a general disposition; it is an act."[33]

The limited nature of revelation in the Old Testament theophanies is also a revelation of promise, anticipating God's personal presence in Christ. This is the relationship we are looking to identify between the historical revelation and the promise. Christ is divine word and act in a manner in which the Old Testament word and act never could be, but at the same time the fullness of divine unveiling in Christ does not side-line Old Testament revelation. Brunner recognizes in John's declaration that the word became flesh that "it is not denied but, on the contrary, affirmed that God has revealed himself and his Word before the coming of Jesus Christ."[34] The apostles eventually recognize the I AM in Christ because they knew the I AM of the old covenant.

Nevertheless, the sober warning against speculation beyond Old and New Testament historical revelation is still present. All that God communicates through his word, act, face, and name is not an invitation to speculate about that which remains hidden. This is just as true for all that Christ discloses. "The Johannine statements about the divine Being of Christ which are described as 'Trinitarian' or 'pre-existential' are not designed to give us information about the metaphysical and pre-temporal existence of the Logos," warns Brunner. "All they want to say is this: *whom* we encounter when we meet Christ; *who* deals with us, and *who* lays His claim upon us, where Christ acts and lays His claim upon us."[35] In this manner the boundaries for theological inquiry are respected.

Brunner concludes his discussion on historical revelation by returning to the goal of fellowship with Christ. This fellowship is the litmus test

---

33. Ibid., 91.
34. Brunner, *Faith, Hope, and Love*, 18.
35. Brunner, *Revelation and Reason*, 113.

of faith, not intellectual assent to doctrine. We are brought back to the subjects of the apostolic witness and the divine–human encounter that must be present if revelation is to achieve its purpose. In *The Philosophy of Religion* he reiterates that revelation is the occasion of personal address.[36] This impact of revelation and reason in the human knower is the next subject of our inquiry.

In Its Goal in Divine–Human Encounter

The divine word, act, face, and name are all expressions, according to Brunner, of the particular personal divine being, whose revelation is necessarily historical because it finds its end in the human soul. For this reason, we cannot "think" or deduce God from anything within our ken, but God has to address the person and disclose himself as love. This God alone, whose revelation is historical, is the Christian God because the God of love is the one who seeks personal encounter with his creatures. That said, this is not the only reason Brunner cites for the necessary historicity of revelation. Another reason is that the cross-resurrection event is in response to the fall; the solution to sin has to have the same form of event that the original sin took. Adam and Eve chose self-sufficiency, thus rendering intimacy with God impossible. Sin, as Schrotenboer explains, "is not due to sensuality or corporality, but to the misuse of freedom."[37] In spite of humanity's rejection of the creator, however, God's purpose does not change and fellowship endures as his goal.

The issue of how God relates to human beings post-breach is raised in the garden of Eden, though without an answer. In the fall, something of the divine design was obscured, broken. The problem for the human story immediately became how God would relate to rebellious human beings. As Brunner states, neither natural law nor timeless ideal would betray the divine decision to forgive or to condemn. Only an answer of the same order as the act of sin could reverse the predicament. He posits that the "religion of immediacy . . . be it mystical, speculative or moralistic," cannot answer the problem of guilt. It cannot tell us how forgiveness happens because it does not consider or treat the historicity of one's guilt and sin.[38] The answer

---

36. Brunner, *Philosophy of Religion*, 32.

37. Schrotenboer, *A New Apologetics*, 71. Schrotenboer captures accurately Brunner's concept of sin as well as his emphasis on relationality.

38. Brunner, *Scandal*, 17.

of the Christian story reveals God's will for reconciliation through the incarnation, cross, and resurrection.

Brunner is concerned to avoid the conflict between the historical and the timeless that has historically plagued such discussions of the cross. If God is an eternal idea he can never be expressed in the finite, for that which is finite belongs to the temporal realm and that which is universal cannot be reduced to the particular. If, however, God is the living God, then we can receive his intervention in human history as decisive and personal act that reflects his very character. For this reason the philosophical concept of God is inherently inconsistent with the personal being disclosed in the pages of Scripture. Brunner's indictment of contemporary theology on this offense is vehement. He writes in *The Word and the World*, "the evil lies here, that recent theology has been much more affected by modern than by Biblical thought, and that so-called Christian theology conceals under Christian phraseology an idealism, mysticism or moralism which stands to Christian thought proper in a mutually exclusive relation of Either-Or, and, so far as its bearing on reality is concerned, is a self-delusion on man's part."[39]

Revelation must be historical because it is only in this realm that divine–human encounter takes place and there is no evidence in Scripture for an a-temporal encounter between God and human beings. Brunner's critical rebuttal of modern theology's emphasis on immanence is evidenced in *The Theology of Crisis*. "Revelation accordingly means that God no longer speaks *out* of us, but *to* us; we do not know him as being *in* the world, and we do not know him *through* the world, but we know him as the One which comes *into* the world. For he himself is an other than the world, an other than the content of the soul. He is the *Other One*."[40] God requires revelation in order to be known because he is personal being and in his fullness cannot be deduced from the created order.

The role of faith is imperative if we are to know God for there is no other way to know him—neither through human effort or culture or reason. Knowledge of God only finds its goal in the trust of the one who responds to divine self-disclosure. This assertion targets a foundational tenet of Brunner's schema, that the God of the Christian faith cannot be proved. Proving is the human attempt to explain what is, by virtue of its own aptitude and power. This effort is foreign to faith because, in Brunner's words, anything that is provable has its origins in the realm of thought but divine

---

39. Brunner, *Word and World*, 8.
40. Brunner, *Theology of Crisis*, 32.

revelation, by its very definition, transcends human reason and is therefore not subject to proof.[41]

The relation between revelation and reason, particularly between the historicity of the former as superior to the universality of the latter, is intimately linked with the object-subject relation introduced in chapter 2. The issue of the relationship between these two elements is an unavoidable one. In *The Word and the World* Brunner writes of God as object and God as subject. What does he mean? As we have seen, the truth of reason presents itself as apparent and knowable apart from personal encounter with another. It "is implied in the fact of my own existence; it has only to be transferred from the state of potentiality to that of actuality."[42] As a result, the god who is known in this way is not the God who comes to the human being as wholly other but is the subjective god of human reason alone. This kind of god remains object, not subject. He is the immanent god of modern liberal theology and certain world religions, the god who is part of the self in such a way that one knows him as a projection of one's own being. Because there is no independence of being, personal encounter is impossible, as is revelation.

In dramatic opposition to this immanent deity stands the God of the Christian faith who is absolute subject. He addresses the knower as "Thou" in his revelation as creator-Lord. True knowing occurs only when, as the wholly other one, God tells the knower who he is. Statements about God express God only when God reveals himself as the intensely personal subject; he cannot be turned into an object of the intellect. The divine–human encounter requires a decision on the human's part in order for revelation to be complete. The response of faith accompanies the responsibility of the human being to reply to the divine revelation. When the person responds in faith and submission to the lordship of Christ, something happens that could not happen in any other way: the contradiction of sin is overcome. The divine word confronts the sham of human independence and, in its gracious address, issues the invitation to relationship.

The nature of this existential decision will be discussed in greater length in chapter 6 where we consider Kierkegaard's influence on Brunner's understanding of the gospel. For the time being, however, his warning is well-taken: human beings prefer the impersonal god of the philosophers because such a being does not impose any moral obligation, whereas the

---

41. Brunner, *Scandal*, 36.
42. Brunner, *Word and World*, 22.

God revealed in Jesus Christ requires an ethical response to his work of reconciliation. Brunner appreciates the stakes when he reflects, "The question how man, how you and I, may really live in this world, how you and I may become *real* in this life, is the same as the question how you and I may live *with* each other, how our *common* life, our agreements or agreements to disagree, may take shape. Man's reality is his life with others."[43] Thus the subject of ethics is our next and final topic.

PART FOUR: REVELATION'S IMPLICATION—HUMAN-HUMAN ENCOUNTER

Why is a treatment of ethics important to our overview of what revelation is and is not? In short, personal encounter with God leads to personal encounter with other human beings and theology has everything to do with community, and community has everything to do with ethics. The import of the witness of Scripture and of the church is faith and that faith creates moral obedience, which is at the heart of discipleship to Jesus Christ. Scripture declares that God alone is good and that God alone defines the good; that to do good is to love God and to love our neighbor; that we become more fully human the more we become like Christ in obedience to the Father's will. Brunner shows these claims as originating in the historical event of Jesus Christ. This connection leads to the question of the relation between the actual obedience of faith and the on-going nature of God's self-disclosure. So, we ask, how is revelation not only the source of ethics but also its goal?

The Divine Command

In order to ask the question, What is the good? Brunner begins his consideration of ethics in *The Divine Imperative* with the query, What is the problem? He wants to address ethics on a broad spectrum, in a similar fashion to his handling of the problem of evil in *The Mediator*. This is one of the strengths of Brunner's thought: he is remarkably consistent in his examination of the fundamental themes of Christian theology, the problem of evil being one of them.

---

43. Brunner, *Theology of Crisis*, xiii–xiv.

The introduction to *The Divine Imperative* culminates in the distinction between the categorical imperative as a universal sense of "ought," and the sense of contradiction in the human soul as the impact of the divine address.[44] He posits that the final result of the "phases of the immanent moral understanding of the self," being the moral idea, leads to the question of divine revelation.[45] The conclusion is that legalistic, rational morality cannot cause a person to do good, nor can it overcome evil of its own resources.

Brunner's judgment is justified throughout the rest of his discussion. He proceeds to show how philosophical ethics fails to adequately answer the question of the good because it retains its naturalistic and moralistic presuppositions, both of which rely on human experience. The person asking what it means to live according to the good is left to his own resources, which are saturated with the very problem he is trying to address—the irreconcilable gulf between what he does and what he senses he ought to do. Philosophical explanations ultimately fail to account for this disparity because they insist on finding resolution to the problem of evil from within human experience and reason, refusing the light of revelation.

Does religion offer a better definition of the good than philosophy? Certainly the common bond between religion and ethics is manifest especially where religious belief is determined by a strong sense of the holy. The problem according to Brunner is that it is impossible to determine "an 'original moral common sense'" that is universal to all religious systems. Yet ethics within the context of Christian theology has a different point of departure and arrives at a different end. "The answer of Faith to the ethical problem is the Word of Sin and Grace," avers Brunner.[46] Christian theology diverges from religion because it relies on revelation that addresses us from outside of our experience.

Even with this foundation, what the good is within the context of Christian theology remains uncertain. Brunner contends that legalism has failed to define the good because it is fundamentally misguided in its goal to enable us to stand in our own strength before God. He notes, "the legalistic understanding of God and of man is, it is true, the highest of which man is capable by his own efforts; but it is precisely upon this high level also the

---

44. See also Dyck, "Moral Requiredness," 141.

45. The "phases of the immanent moral understanding of the self" are as follows: immediacy, custom, intelligent purpose, sensible infinity, the aesthetic element as a form of life, the moral idea. Brunner, *Divine Imperative*, 22–25.

46. Ibid., 52.

decisive antithesis of the Gospel of grace."[47] Such an interpretation of the divine command directs away from personal encounter with God in which a person experiences both judgment and grace.

What does the Christian faith as revealed in Jesus Christ define as the good if divine revelation is its source and personal encounter is its goal? Brunner identifies it as the divine command, interpreted as "always doing what God wills at any particular moment."[48] The premier example of the life so lived is Jesus' obedience to the Father in every detail of his existence, illustrated by his affirmation to his followers, "My food is to do the will of him who sent me" (John 4:34). Jesus' definition of the good is specifically expressed in his response to the anxious lawyer: "You shall love the Lord your God with all your heart and with all your soul and with all your strength and with all your mind, and your neighbor as yourself" (Luke 10:27). Once again Brunner points to God's self-revelation in the God-man, where he recognizes that "only in the Mediator is the will of God, that is, the Good, known as Love."[49] It follows, then, that the divine command is identical in its expectation of us, that we love God with all our hearts, souls, minds, and strength and love our neighbor as ourselves. This is the good, to love God in every situation, in every moment, according to the standard of Christ's life.

If the good is obedience to the will of God and it results in conformity to Jesus Christ as Lord, what is its relation to dogmatics? The answer is patent for Brunner. He writes, "every theme of dogmatics is also inevitably a theme of ethics. Dogmatics does not exist independently, nor does ethics, but dogmatic knowledge as such always aims at existential, that is, ethical, thought, and ethical knowledge is rooted in the knowledge of dogmatics."[50] This intimate relationship between belief and praxis compels him to return to the issue of ethics throughout his writing.

The Practice of Ethics

To the extent that God has shown us what is good in Jesus Christ, we know how to live rightly and are without excuse. The logic might be straightforward, but the reality of righteousness is not because the contradiction

---

47. Brunner, *Revelation and Reason*, 334.
48. Brunner, *Divine Imperative*, 83.
49. Brunner, *Mediator*, 603.
50. Brunner, *Divine Imperative*, 86.

of sin means that as human beings we cannot achieve the good by our own efforts. Our rejection of God leads to the handicap of our capacity for the good. Once again we are confronted with our dependence upon God, whether on his mercy if we respond in faith or on his judgment if we rebel.

Dogmatics introduced responsibility as the significance of the *imago Dei* but Brunner extends that condensed definition as we read on. The effect of the divine–human encounter catapults the believer out of theoretical responsibility into the concreteness of relationship. In the "Thou" of personal encounter with God we also encounter fellow human beings as "Thou." We again see why, in *Encounter*, Brunner is concerned not only with the nature of truth but also with the relationship between truth and the knower. Both divine–human and human–human relationships disarm the masquerade of self-sufficiency and show us that we only become fully personal in I–Thou relationship. "God has so organized human life that no man can live for himself," observes Brunner. "He cannot live without the other . . . Human life is so ordered by God because God has created man for love."[51] This love is the power and purpose of community.

In *Man in Revolt* Brunner expands on the necessity of community for the full expression of what it means to be human, going so far as to state that one does not and cannot exist alone. From birth to death, human beings exist in relation to others, to the other. This being the case, it is imperative that theology address how we ought to live in community. Brunner suggests that the will of God is a social will; there is no service to God that is not at the same time service to other human beings. The role of faith is, indeed, critical for encounter, for knowledge of truth, and for personal transformation. "The *sola gratia, sola fide, soli deo gloria* of the Christian faith . . . ," contends Brunner, "is the only solid foundation for ethics; and faith in redemption through Christ is the only real source of that ethical renewal and energy to which Paul refers when he speaks about the new creation in Christ."[52] This is an outcome of his insistence that the goal of theology is simultaneously the goal of faith and that personal encounter exhibits itself in discipleship.

A return to the roots of dogmatics illuminates the connection between theological thinking and right living. In chapter 2 we observed the necessity of theology for exegesis, catechesis, and polemics for the greater goal of Christian discipleship. The arena for personal encounter with God

---

51. Brunner, *Our Faith*, 53.
52. Brunner, *Theology of Crisis*, 68–69.

in faith is in the flow of the human story. It is unsurprising, then, that Brunner expresses concern throughout his writing about how Christians live their faith in the world. To say that he is primarily an ethicist is to go too far if we regard ethics in the narrow sense of the study of morality. On the other hand, if we describe ethics as the response to such questions as, How can I best love God and my neighbor in this context? or, What is the proper use of my time and resources in this situation?, then we can say that Brunner is committed to doing theology in a manner consistent with redemptive, kingdom transformation. The goal of his short work *Justice and the Social Order* illustrates this connection.[53] For Brunner, the kind of faith that answers God's personal address is, simply stated, "obedience—nothing else—literally nothing else at all."[54] Encounter with the risen Christ is the beginning and the end of faith, and service to others is its proof.

Conclusion

By this point in our study we can state with a measure of confidence that the volumes considered in this chapter are consistent with what we discovered in *Dogmatics I, II*, and *III*. The insistence with which Brunner returns to the apostolic witness is also reliable and in this sense it can be said that he is faithful to his own methodology. The center of his schema holds: in his theological thinking he remains faithful to the historical event of Jesus Christ in the incarnation, cross, and resurrection, and the testimony offered in the apostolic witness provides the model for dogmatics. With this as its pattern, theology's foundation continues to be the historical events and the super-historical themes to which those events point. The heart of Brunner's argument, as well as its contours, is faithful to the historical event of Jesus Christ and to his on-going revelation in personal encounter.

We asked previously whether Brunner rejects all use of language and categories of thought that are not rooted in the actual vocabulary or at least in the events of the apostolic witness. Could it be for Brunner that certain subjects can be *theologically consistent* with the apostolic witness even if they use language not sourced directly in it? The issue for Brunner seems to be the *source* of categories used in dogmatics. Is X question or statement prompted by what God has revealed of himself in salvation history, or does it originate in what remains veiled? The former can remain faithful to the

---

53. Brunner, *Justice and the Social Order*, 8.
54. Brunner, *Mediator*, 592.

apostolic witness even if the vocabulary is fresh, while the latter follows the line of speculation that Brunner deems so dangerous. In other words, for Brunner the imperative starting and ending points for all dogmatic thinking is the full self-revelation of God in Christ. That said, in the work of understanding in faith who God reveals himself to be we are obliged to use expressions that go beyond the first- and second-hand language of the Synoptics. This is unavoidable as we strive to fathom a mystery and a scandal by faith but it is also unavoidable in our limited, fallen, and temporary human existence.

Is the role that Brunner affords reason a compromise to bemoan, something that unnecessarily limits or dangerously compromises the theological task? Or can we retain some confidence that God speaks to us through our faith reflection, that theology can approximate a measure of the divine reality we seek to know and to express? The use of human reason, and language that reflects that reason, is useful for the purpose of communicating the meaning of divine revelation in the apostolic witness. This is a different role than allowing philosophical categories to determine theological inquiry as a point of departure. For Brunner, the place of reason is self-evident in theology: it is believing *thinking*, and the first-hand witness of the gospel narratives remains the raw material to which that thinking always returns. His passionate concern is that one's whole person is encountered by the risen Christ, including one's intellect. Discipleship is as much about loving God with one's mind as it with one's heart and in one's service.

This leads to one point that requires further attention—the point at which Brunner's emphasis on personal encounter invites and involves existential concerns. Such a potential mélange of biblical and philosophical material could be discarded out of hand; after all, is not existentialism a court of appeal that arrives from the extra-apostolic domain that Brunner so carefully seeks to avoid? Adjudication on this point will be explored in chapter 6.

5

Beside Brunner—Karl Barth

"God's Word is God Himself in His revelation. For God reveals Himself as the Lord and according to Scripture this signifies for the concept of revelation that God Himself in unimpaired unity yet also in unimpaired distinction is Revealer, Revelation, and Revealedness."

—KARL BARTH, *CHURCH DOGMATICS* I/1, 295

HAVING EXAMINED KEY THEMES in Brunner's thought we now turn to consider, in whatever measure incommensurate with the man's stature, a theologian who worked beside Brunner, Karl Barth. My purpose in this chapter is to consider by way of comparison how one of Brunner's contemporaries presents the nature and the limits of theological inquiry. Barth is a logical choice because their similarities transcend history and geography to include, in broad outline, kind of theology. The two men are most often considered in light of their differences, or at least the differences that some perceive as being significant in their work.[1] The present study does not adopt the same approach but has for its focus the narrow field of the "do-

---

1. A concise example of the kind of differences in their thinking is illustrated in Brunner's article "The New Barth," which appeared in 1951 in response to *CD* III/2. This piece offers a feel for what is communicated as a latent ambiguity in the so-called distinctions between them.

ing" of theology in which we will concentrate on the doctrine of the Trinity and its relevant themes as a means to the end of analyzing Barth's approach.

Part 1 of this chapter explores the nature and limits of theological inquiry within the work of Karl Barth based on a close reading of his *Prolegomena* comprised in *Church Dogmatics* I/1 and I/2, but also drawing where appropriate from other volumes of *Church Dogmatics* as well as *Dogmatics in Outline*. Two issues relevant to the doctrine of the Trinity will be assessed in part 2, being the doctrine of the virgin birth and the miracle of Easter; at this juncture we will begin to highlight points of comparison between Barth's method and Brunner's. Finally, part 3 will remind us of Brunner's treatment of the Trinity in order to facilitate a summary of the salient points of contrast in their respective practices.

It is necessary as we begin to attend to one of Barth's primary motives discernible in his *Prolegomena*, which affects his entire approach to dogmatics. It is his unalloyed rejection of the role of *analogia entis* in theological thought.[2] His introduction to *CD* I/1 is characteristically candid. "I can see no third alternative between that exploitation of the *analogia entis* which is legitimate only on the basis of Roman Catholicism, between the greatness and misery of a so-called natural knowledge of God in the sense of the *Vaticanum*, and a Protestant theology which draws from its own source, which stands on its own feet, and which is finally liberated from this secular misery. Hence I have no option but to say No [to the *analogia entis*] at this point."[3] This reference sets the stage for our study in that it reminds us of the contest in the theological arena at the turn of the twentieth century. From a Reformed perspective, modern theology had sold out to a doctrine of immanence and rejected both God as the absolute subject of faith and Scripture as revelation. Barth summarizes this loss as a tragedy and asserts that with the loss of theology's object also came the loss of faith. Religion had replaced faith as the theological *plat du jour* and unbelief was the resultant poisoning.

Barth's rejection of the *analogia entis* also reminds us of his debate with Brunner over natural theology, which I have already acknowledged in passing.[4] I note here simply that the disagreement was a significant turning

---

2. Lovin offers an introductory study of Barth's rejection of the *analogia entis* in *Christian Faith and Public Choices*, 34–39. A more recent treatment of the issue, which helpfully explores the theological context for Barth's response to the *analogia entis*, is Johnson, *Karl Barth and the Analogia Entis*.

3. Barth, *CD* I/2, xii.

4. Furthermore, I share Lovin's appraisal of the dispute: "we must be careful not

point in their relationship and that their respective views on the possibility of natural theology impacts on their dogmatic method and doctrine. The doctrine of the Trinity is central to Barth's work so that we now turn.

PART ONE: BARTH'S DOCTRINE OF THE TRINITY

The Task of Dogmatics

Foremost in Barth's treatment of dogmatics is its relation to the church and to revelation. Succinctly stated, though in reverse order of its occurrence as task, his schema is summarized thusly: (1) dogmatics is a function of theology, (2) theology is a function of the church, (3) and the being of the church, as Jesus Christ, has for its primary purpose the proclamation of the word of God. "As a theological discipline," Barth writes, "dogmatics is the scientific self-examination of the Christian Church with respect to the content of its distinctive talk about God."[5] It seeks to answer the query, How does the language we use to communicate who God is and what he has done correspond to the actual content of his divine being and work?

A correct relation between proclamation and dogmatics is fundamental for the fulfilment of the church's commission on earth. Barth identifies proclamation of the word of God as the church's primary responsibility in the world. Because it is human proclamation, though, we acknowledge its potential to err. Dogmatics thus becomes necessary as the secondary task, though it always remains the ancillary endeavor and is also liable to err. It is critical to keep Barth's structure in mind: the datum of proclamation is revelation and faith; the datum of dogmatics is proclamation.[6]

---

to overstate the differences between them. Although much depends on this issue [of natural theology], the point of contention is small indeed." Lovin, *Christian Faith and Public Choices*, 63. For one view of the topic, see O'Donovan, "Man in the Image of God." Lest we forget their own expression of the disagreement, see Brunner and Barth, *Natural Theology*. As has already been mentioned, one insightful resource to the Brunner-Barth relationship, though only obliquely related to the natural theology debate, is Hart, *Barth vs Brunner*.

5. Barth, *CD* I/1, 3.
6. Ibid., 82.

The Purpose of Dogmatics

It can be said, therefore, that Barth views the theological task as offering "guidelines, insights and limits" to our language about God.[7] Dogmatics delimits our communication about God's self-revelation and, although the words we use may change throughout the centuries, the content of that revelation does not. This content is reflected in Christian dogma, which brings us to two critical presuppositions of Barth's understanding of the science of dogmatics.

Firstly, Barth propounds that the true content of Christian talk about God, sourced in the self-revealing address of God to men and women, can be known. This seems obvious enough in the Reformed tradition, so what is the unique consequence of this premise for Barth's methodology? It is the role of faith. Barth explains that while dogmatics is human thinking and for that reason is fallible, it none the less can be sure of the truth it seeks to know because its ultimate subject is God. "It is this intractable faith and its intractable object which make possible the certain divine knowledge which is at issue in dogmatics."[8] We know God through his self-communication that we receive by faith, and we know even while we are seeking to comprehend it further.

Barth adds to this first supposition a second, that the true content of our Christian-speak about God must be known. We recognize that Christ who is revealed in the word remains the measure of the content of our speech about God, even though our language is sometimes ambiguous. The word of God, therefore, is the sole criterion of theological inquiry, for apart from the word we cannot rightly assess our own conversation. As God grants the grace of understanding through his word, he is in his very being with us as Emmanuel, for "it must be said that here in God's revelation God's Word is identical with God Himself."[9] In this light, God's revelation is not to be separated from his act of speaking or from his being.

Further explanation is needed here. How is our language meant to accurately reflect the content that we encounter in God's self-revelation? In Barth's view inquiry is the only proper nature of dogmatics. We are never one hundred per cent sure of our theological conclusions because our insight is unable fully to represent the content of the divine reality, so

---

7. Ibid., 86.
8. Ibid., 13.
9. Ibid., 304.

our investigation is always in need of evaluation and correction, and it is ever an act of faith. This is not sufficient reason, though, to refuse the work of theology. Not only is talk about God's self-revelation necessary, Barth declares it possible by means of the constant self-critique by the church of its language about God. He concludes that it is impossible to undertake theological inquiry outside of the church and apart from faith because it is effective only as God gives real hearing and real obedience.[10] Theological inquiry is dependent upon the event of God's grace and his self-revelation in the person of Jesus Christ.

The Nature of Revelation

Barth insists that "God with us" is the content of the word, the word is the content of church proclamation, and church proclamation is the content of dogmatics. It is therefore the function of dogmatic theology to ensure that Christian language of proclamation is consistent with the self-revelation of God in his word because the word of God is the source of God's self-revelation. His three-fold form of the "what" of the word of God is well-known: the written word, the preached word, and revelation.[11]

The first designation of the written word Barth describes as the recollection of God's self-unveiling to men and women in the past. The Old and New Testaments are "the word of the prophets and apostles to whom it was originally and once and for all spoken by God's revelation."[12] As the expression of those who experienced Jesus personally, the written word establishes boundaries for our own talk about God. The words of Scripture do not constitute revelation itself, but through the event of God's grace they testify to God's presence with our forebears.

Scripture also promises God's presence with us in the future through the preached word, Barth's second designation. The one who believes the testimony of Christ's eyewitnesses is the one who "so hears their word that he grasps and accepts its promise . . . : Immanuel with us sinners, in the word of the prophets and apostles, this is the faith of the Church. In this faith it recollects the past revelation of God and in this faith it expects the

---

10. Ibid., 18.
11. Ibid., chapter 1, sec. 4.
12. Ibid., 88.

future revelation that has yet to come."[13] The decisive substance of church proclamation remains "Lo, I am with you always" (Matt 28:20).

How then does the word become the event of revelation, Barth's third specification? It is the unveiling of the veiled; by contrast, that which is not revealed remains veiled, hidden, unknown. Thus the event of God's grace determines when the written and the preached word become revelation, while also establishing their veracity. This last form of the word underlies the first two, for "it is the very one that never meets us in abstract form"[14] but only through the proclamation of future promise and the recollection of past revelation. It is the divine act of God's personal address, the event of God's grace.

This is how Barth establishes revelation as the content of the word of God. Likewise, the word, which is not the divine act of grace itself but recollection and promise of it, is the content of church proclamation. In one sense we are talking about the differing natures of revelation, word, and dogmatics. Revelation is divine act, and the word and proclamation are recollection and promise of the divine act. Theological inquiry is the critique of proclamation to evaluate to what extent it represents the word, even though neither the word nor proclamation nor dogmatics can be revelation. Proclamation cannot exist without the word, but the word-become-revelation remains the freedom of God's grace alone.

Can we then say that God self-reveals apart from proclamation of the word if revelation remains the prerogative of divine grace and not the effect of human activity? "*Nein!*" Barth declares in vigorous tone—at least not if this indicates any kind of knowledge of God apart from special revelation. He rejects "every (positive or negative) *formulation of a system* which claims to be theological, i.e. to interpret divine revelation, whose *subject*, however, differs fundamentally from the revelation in Jesus Christ and whose method therefore differs equally from the exposition of Holy Scripture."[15]

It is fitting to make one more comment regarding the word as Scripture. Barth's view of the Bible includes "its nature as sign, its relation to the thing which it signifies."[16] Two details are worthy of note here. One, Barth's reorientation of theology, dogmatics, and faith towards the Bible as divine revelation is a contribution to twentieth century Christianity for

---

13. Ibid., 108.
14. Ibid., 121.
15. Brunner and Barth, *Natural Theology*, 74–75.
16. Barth, *CD* I/2, 458.

which he is rightly credited. Two, the connection between a sign and the thing signified is a distinct topic to which we will return in part 3 when we discuss methodological implications.

Barth states that the Bible is "the basis and boundary, the presupposition and proviso" of preaching.[17] Scripture declares no other message than the good news that God is with us, that God has been with us, and that God will be with us forever. It is through this message that God shows himself as the Lord and comes to us personally. In this event of revelation, the divine "he" of the written page becomes the "thou" of personal engagement. The triune God is not only revelation but is simultaneously the one who reveals and the one revealed; and as such he is Lord.[18] Barth explains that "in the event which the Bible describes as revelation God deals with man as the Lord . . . as the authority which in distinction from all others is absolutely superior to man, but which, even in this absolute superiority, also concerns and claims man with the same absoluteness."[19] As Father, Son, and Spirit, God is thrice our Lord for he is also creator, reconciler, and redeemer. We will examine this in more detail in the next section.

This order of word, proclamation, and revelation is not only the core of Barth's theology but it is also the outline for his approach to the primary task of proclamation and the secondary endeavor of dogmatics. In Barth's view, divine freedom is paramount to all that God is and does. Revelation consequently remains God's prerogative, and human proclamation becomes divine self-unveiling only in the event of God's grace. This is the key to truth, the promise of the word, and the goal of theological inquiry. The word of God is the same, whether in proclamation, Scripture, or the event of revelation, but revelation—the "*illic et tunc visum Deo*"—is the primary form underlying the first two.[20] Emmanuel, God with us, is the recollection and the promise of the word of God.

What transpires in the event of revelation is that the mystery of God becomes disclosed. In Christ God meets us, speaks with us, reconciles us to himself as Father, and reveals himself to us. Creature meets creator; sinfulness encounters holiness. Faith is the event that makes possible the knowledge of God's word despite its inconceivability. Barth remarks, "If it is

---

17. Barth, *CD* I/1, 117.

18. See *CD* I/1, chap. 2, sec. 8 for exposition of "God Himself in unimpaired unity yet also in unimpaired distinction is Revealer, Revelation, and Revealedness."

19. Barth, *CD* I/1, 384.

20. Ibid., 118.

true that man really believes 1. that the object of faith is present to him and 2. that he himself is assimilated to the object, then we are led in conclusion to the third point that man exists as a believer wholly and utterly by this object."[21] Revelation is purely a divine act, and the content of the person's knowledge is true when it corresponds to the reality of the word of God itself.

The relationship between revelation and the word of God does not end there, though. "God's Word is God Himself in His revelation," Barth suggests. "For God reveals Himself as the Lord and according to Scripture this signifies for the concept of revelation that God Himself in unimpaired unity yet also in unimpaired distinction is Revealer, Revelation, and Revealedness."[22] This association between revelation and the triune divine being is a distinctive feature of Barth's schema and requires care in being understood.

The Doctrine of the Trinity

Here is where the doctrine of the Trinity takes on its full breadth in Barth's outline. The foundation for the doctrine of the Trinity is revelation. This connection cannot be overemphasized, either in *CD* I/1 or in a discussion of Barth's methodology. "The threefold yet single Lordship of God as Father, Son and Spirit, is the root of the doctrine of the Trinity. In other words the biblical concept of revelation is itself the root of the doctrine of the Trinity. The doctrine of the Trinity is simply a development of the knowledge that Jesus is the Christ or the Lord."[23]

Barth's concept of revelation is intertwined with his explication of the triunity of God as revealer, revelation, and revealedness and on the whole proceeds along these lines. It starts with the self-disclosure of God in the Son, significant because of the Son's relation to the one he reveals: Jesus is the Son because he is begotten of the Father. To speak of God as revealer is to consider the form of God's self-disclosure in the historic person of Christ, but to speak of God as revealed is to refer to God in his essence. For Barth, God as Lord means God is free both to reveal himself and to remain veiled.

21. Ibid., 244–45.
22. Ibid., 295.
23. Ibid., 334.

In the Son as revealer we encounter God as supreme over all life, the creator, the one from whom we receive our existence. Barth suggests that the Son shows us the Father in the historical event of the cross and resurrection, where he is revealed as Lord over death. To know God as Lord of life is subsequent to knowing him as Father, however, for he is Father eternally. He clarifies in this way: "Jesus did not proclaim the familiar Creator God and interpret Him by the unfamiliar name of Father. He revealed the unknown Father, His Father, and in so doing, and only in so doing, He told us for the first time that the Creator is what He is and that He is as such our Father."[24] Though Scripture does not offer objective statements about the eternal essence of God as Father, the biblical witness affirms that the Son is God's self-revelation and as such the Son reveals him as the Father.

Barth continues his explanation of the relationship between the revealer and the one revealed. "God's trinitarian name of Father, God's eternal fatherhood, denotes the mode of being of God in which He is the Author of His other modes of being."[25] Does this imply that God is the source of the Son and the Holy Spirit in such a way that they are secondary to him in their essence, derivative and therefore lesser? Barth explains that the sense of subordination in the Trinity is not a question of greater or lesser degrees of being because the works of the Trinity together testify to the being of the Trinity as undivided. Rather, the question of the intra-triune relations refers to their modes of being and how they are expressed in space and time. He concludes that "because God is the eternal Father as the Father of the Son, and with Him the origin of the Spirit, therefore the God who acts in reconciliation and redemption, and who reveals Himself as the Reconciler and Redeemer, cannot be a second and third God or a second and third part of God; He is and remains God *unus et individuus* in His work as in His essence."[26] *Opera trinitatis ad extra sunt indivisa.*

The oneness of the divine being and work is central to Barth's elucidation of the doctrine of the Trinity, which brings us to the third person, the Holy Spirit. The Spirit, also antecedently in himself, is simultaneously related to and distinct from the Father and the Son. One way in which Barth explains this relation is in terms of subjective revelation. "It is God's reality in that God Himself becomes present to man not just externally, not just from above, but also from within, from below, subjectively . . . God's

24. Ibid., 391.
25. Ibid., 393.
26. Ibid., 395.

freedom to be present in this way to man, and therefore to bring about this encounter, is the Spirit of God, the Holy Spirit in God's revelation."[27] Faith is essential for this revelation to become personal, as we have already attested. When we encounter God through the Spirit by faith, we confirm the promise of proclamation and we experience the testimony of Scripture that God is with us. Emmanuel is the grace of God imparted to us in the Spirit.[28]

Consideration of the Holy Spirit would be incomplete without reference to the vexed issue of procession. What is Barth's take on the debate? Firstly, the dogma establishes that the Spirit is not a temporal creature but shares the eternal nature of the Father with the Son. The distinction between the Son as begotten and the Spirit as proceeding is impossible to fully define because both refer to "the eternal genesis of an eternal mode of being of God."[29] Perhaps it is just as helpful to recall what the doctrine does not say, not only about the Spirit but also about the Father and the Son. "We cannot establish the How of the divine processions and therefore of the divine modes of being . . . The *ignoramus* which we must confess in relation to the distinction that we have to maintain between begetting and breathing is thus the *ignoramus* which we must confess in relation to the whole doctrine of the Trinity, i.e., in relation to the mystery of revelation, in relation to the mystery of God in general . . . Therefore for the sake of what the doctrine of the Trinity must state, namely, that the Father, the Son, and the Spirit are God, no more must be said at this point and no definition must result here."[30]

Is this Barth's attempt at evading a theological blind alley? Is he only illustrating the inefficacy of theological language to lead us into greater understanding of God's self-revelation? No; instead we have here a reminder that however positively one might regard the possibility of theological inquiry, it is God himself who defines the boundaries of our contemplation. He remains Lord of revelation.

---

27. Barth, *CD* I/1, 451.

28. "Therefore the Holy Spirit is the subjective reality of revelation," Barth, *CD* I/2, 242. Also, the Holy Spirit is both the reality and the possibility of revelation; Barth, *CD* I/2, 280.

29. Barth, *CD* I/1, 475.

30. Ibid., 476–77.

Part II: Bounded Theology

Implications

The correspondence that Barth draws between revelation and the divine modes of being critically shapes not only his expression of the doctrine of the Trinity and revelation but the whole of theology. We have summarized the significance of this reading of the doctrine for our interpretation of the Son as the revealer, the Father as the revealed, and the Holy Spirit as God's self-impartation. Barth's exposition reiterates at least three points: that there is a differentiation among the modes of being but no subordination of essence; that each person exists antecedently in himself; and that the work and being of God are one and the same.[31] The conclusion is consequential: God's self-communication cannot be separated from his person. He is his revelation.

Barth is unequivocal that the dogma of the triunity of God is the fruit of theology, the result of creaturely contemplation of God's revelation. The dogma is not biblical in the sense of being found, as dogma, in Scripture. It is interpreted from Scripture and through it we perceive how Jesus' deity creates revelation and reconciliation.[32] By this Barth does not intend a relegation of doctrine to second-rate status because expressions which are not directly identified in the biblical text cannot be regarded as truth. His perspective is quite the opposite; the value of theological language in general and doctrine in particular is that they can foster our understanding of God when they retain God as their absolute subject.

Barth asserts the usefulness of dogmatic theology by arguing that when it is done rightly, our rational grappling with divine revelation will affirm instead of dispel the divine *mysterium*. One element of modern theology most offensive to Barth is, in his words, "the constantly increasing confusion, tedium and irrelevance of modern Protestantism, which, probably along with the Trinity and the Virgin Birth, has lost an entire third dimension—the dimension of what for once, though not confusing it with religious and moral earnestness, we may describe as mystery."[33] Dogmatics can serve revelation by providing tools to understand it without pretending to master the divine subject in any way. God remains free to veil or to unveil himself as he pleases.

---

31. Ibid., 371.
32. Ibid., 415.
33. Ibid., xiv.

We are challenged by a paradox at this point. Theology has the possibility of leading us into some measure of knowledge, while at the same time it is impotent to master its subject. Let us investigate this further by considering the significance of the term "begotten" as it pertains to the Son and to the Father. As we have it in Scripture, the reality to which this term refers can rightly be described as divine. It comments on the fatherhood and the sonship of God as a unique relation, in contradistinction to the rest of the cosmos that is created by God and thereby not begotten. Though this relation is identified in the word, we recognize that we are limited in both our comprehension and communication of this aspect of the intra-triune relations. Because the word does not afford greater revelation than this, we comfortably use the term "begotten" in order to convey something of the Son's relation to the Father without suggesting that we fathom the dynamics of this bond.

Barth readily recognizes certain limitations of both the traditional approach to the doctrine of the Trinity and of his own treatment of it, of which the Son's begotten nature is one aspect. He comments, "the inadequacy of all concepts not only implies the menacing proximity of a philosophical criticism based on the immanent possibilities of meaning of these concepts . . . What it also implies is the menacing proximity of theological error."[34] Despite this danger, the work of theology remains valid. It is interpreting and explaining the mystery who is God; not that the goal or result is the dissipation of mystery but rather it is the rational understanding of what simultaneously remains not entirely comprehended.

At the same time that Barth acknowledges this possibility of dogmatics, he also identifies two limits to theological inquiry. First is the limit of divine mystery, as noted. When we refer to the Son as begotten, we are not speaking of truth in the logical and comprehensible sense, but rather truth as "untruth." We affirm in belief God as Father and Son and Holy Spirit even though this is hidden and unknowable.[35] Thus, although theology is capable of referring to the Son as begotten, it is simultaneously restricted by the impenetrable nature of this reality. The conclusion is that concepts such as begetting and begotten are unavoidable when we speak of the Trinity, even if such terms are only representative of the mystery and not exact.

A second and corollary boundary is the inadequacy of human speech to fully communicate theology's absolute subject. Dogmatics is never

34. Ibid., 367.
35. Ibid., 432–33.

identical to the mystery that it seeks to communicate and it remains unable to convey truth apart from revelation and faith. It is crucial to recall that our understanding of who God is "may always be pure illusion, and our thought within it and speech about it may always be pure ideology, if they are not grounded in God Himself and continually confirmed by God Himself. Because and to the extent that what the dogma states is true, that God's Word is the Word of God, for that reason and to that extent the correlation is also true."[36]

With this in mind, Barth exhorts us to remember constantly our own limits in considering the divine self-unveiling, lest we become carried away by thinking that we can in any measure possess God. Although the goal of our theological efforts is to be able to explain the word of God, this is something we are not able to do adequately because it is the one thing that the boundaries of God's mystery and human limitation rule out. Therefore, we can never assert that we possess as an object our knowledge of him. It is through the I-Thou encounter of God with us that we know God. As a result, the language used to express this event is not and can never become the encounter itself.

Barth offers a helpful point about the limitations of our language, especially as it pertains to the distinction between, and the unity of, the modes of the divine being. Commenting specifically on the creedal affirmation "We believe in Jesus Christ as light of light, very God of very God, begotten, not made," he writes, "we have good reason to recall that knowledge of God's Word can only be knowledge in faith . . . What we think and say will never be commensurate with it; it will always be incommensurate (inadequate)."[37] Even if our doctrine is a verbatim repetition of Scripture itself, we cannot—except by the grace of God—think that what we proclaim is the same as the reality itself. Our expression is ultimately unequal to its subject.

Synthesis and Critique

We now ask to what extent Barth's is work consistent with itself within *CD* I/1 and I/2. I begin with three strengths that his methodology possesses, including the centrality of the word of God, the potential of dogmatics to facilitate believing thinking, and the integrity of his treatment of the

36. Ibid., 422.
37. Ibid., 428.

doctrine of the Trinity. These comments will be followed by two perceptible weaknesses, specifically, Barth's structural decision to start the *Prolegomena* with revelation, and the confusion of the problem of the Trinity with the doctrine of the Trinity. Towards this end I will incorporate elements of Brunner's work that will facilitate the investigation.

Strengths

Even in the heat of their most publicized debate, Brunner credits his colleague with possessing the "greater mental impetus" required to "[give] back to Protestant theology its proper theme and subject-matter" of Scripture, thus altering the face of modern theology.[38] I affirm with Brunner that Barth's commitment to both the preached and the written word as the root of revelation and the criterion of dogmatics is a foundation to which he remains faithful throughout his work. The consistency between his theory and his practice in maintaining the centrality of Scripture for the theological task is indisputable.[39] Furthermore, his dismissal of any other source of revelation as authoritative was not only a decisive corrective to the post-Enlightenment enthrallment with a variety of distractions, it also addresses several decades later the confused winds of postmodern relativism.

Such praise, however, immediately begs the question of *how*. How does Barth use Scripture and to what norm is he consistent? We considered in the previous section his view on the limited capacity of theological language to fully reflect the divine reality, while simultaneously acknowledging that this is the primary means we have to engage God's self-revelation. Such is the line Barth tries to walk, confidently employing human speech for believing thinking while humbly acknowledging the veil that separates us from full knowledge of God. On the whole he does this in his *Prolegomena* without falling into philosophical speculation divorced from Jesus Christ and also without a paralyzing preoccupation with the actual vocabulary of Scripture. It is in setting such a pattern that he is able to treat in *Church Dogmatics* the breadth of theological topics in the constructive, reflective, and exhaustive manner that he does.

---

38. Brunner and Barth, *Natural Theology*, 17.

39. Take, for example, Thompson's appraisal: "Very few systematic theologians have devoted as much space in their theological work to extended interactions with the biblical text." *Engaging with Barth*, 171.

PART II: BOUNDED THEOLOGY

With this tension in mind, how does Barth execute the relationship between proclamation and dogmatics? He suggests in *CD* I/2 that proclamation, which is the church's vocation and mission in the world, is a human impossibility because of the preacher-theologian's fallibility.[40] Proclamation at the same time is possible when God himself renders Jesus Christ present as an event of grace. He remarks on an important connection. "The human frailty of the Church's proclamation must be constantly borne in mind to the precise extent that we have to be clear that both those who speak and those who hear in this matter necessarily rely on the free grace of God and therefore on prayer . . . But if they are dependent on prayer, undoubtedly they are also dependent on serious and honest work."[41] Consequently we know that God has given human beings the work of proclamation, even though we also know that human words never equal or capture God's word. God remains Lord over revelation; human speech has no control over it or even power to effect it.

Thus, the disciplines of preaching and dogmatics must be pursued side by side. The logic is straightforward for Barth: "bad dogmatics—bad theology—bad preaching. And conversely: good dogmatics—good theology—good preaching."[42] Dogmatics must ever anew call the teaching church to listen to God's revelation, and it must lead by example, specifically by offering "a thinking and speaking about God which is disquietened, delimited and confined by the norm of the Word of God."[43]

The strength of Barth's approach is evidenced in his treatment of the doctrine of the Trinity, which respects to a large extent the mystery of the *how* of the Father, Son, and Holy Spirit while seeking to understand what we can about God from Scripture as three persons in unimpaired unity and in unimpaired distinction. He affirms the capacity of the doctrine to "lead us . . . into revelation and faith, to their correct understanding."[44] Barth's exposition of the Trinity is effective for facilitating understanding of God as three in one and is consistent with the revelation of God as Father, Son, and Spirit in Scripture.

This brings us to an additional matter pertaining to the Trinity. If dogma is the work of human reflection, can we say anything more about

---

40. Barth, *CD* I/2, 750 and following.
41. Ibid., 755.
42. Ibid., 767.
43. Ibid., 813.
44. Ibid., 396.

divine triunity than has been said in the creeds, given their authority in the church for sixteen hundred years? The Nicene-Constantinopolitan Creed states the *that* of the divinity of Christ and God the Father and the Holy Spirit. According to Barth, this is the substance of what we can assert about God as triune. In his exposition, though, does not Barth go beyond the *that* of divine triunity? To what extent does he bear out in practice what he outlines as the responsibility of theological inquiry, to ensure the correspondence of church proclamation with God's self-revelation in the word? We will examine these queries in further detail in part 2 when we consider the doctrine of the virgin birth and Easter.

Because of Barth's view of revelation as fundamental to the scriptural witness, he does not perceive any unfaithfulness to the word by going beyond the terminology of Scripture when discussing the Trinity. He addresses such issues as generation of the Son and procession of the Spirit, as well as descriptions of the intra-triune relations, in so far as they concern the correlation of the revealer to the revealed and to the revelation. He can do this without infidelity to the word because he sees the bond between revelation and the Trinity as organic and indissoluble.

As a result, to extrapolate the doctrine of the Trinity from the nature of revelation as Barth has done is internally consistent even though at this point he is engaging the dogma and no longer the scriptural narrative. In Barth's schema the one follows from the other. Because God reveals himself to us in Christ we can regard both Scripture and proclamation of Scripture as God's word. The Bible and preaching "become" God's word based on revelation and in this way they confirm and affirm revelation as they become God's word.[45] This is his three-fold form of the word of God. We can say, therefore, that Barth is consistent with his method as he establishes it in his concept of revelation.

Weaknesses

We come now to two areas of difficulty in Barth's work overviewed here. The first pertains to what seems to be the questionable certainty of the divine act of God's self-unveiling, which results from beginning *CD* with the concept of revelation instead of a discussion of the nature of the one revealed. While on the one hand the on-going event of God's revelation is central to, though not identical with, his self-unveiling in the incarnation, cross, and

---

45. Barth, *CD* I/1, 118.

resurrection, there lingers a certain ambiguity regarding the certitude of the *hic et nunc* of revelation at any given point in time. Even if we trust that God does show himself to be Emmanuel today as he was Emmanuel in first century Palestine, is there any assurance that he will do so?

One anticipates the response to this question to be found in the divine character, that God's inexhaustible love assures us that he will never cease to come to us by his Spirit in the gracious act of disclosure. However, Barth's *Prolegomena* incites no such confidence, either before or alongside his exposition of the Trinity. Why is this potentially problematic? On the one hand we ought not to expect a treatment of the divine nature here when Barth has stated explicitly his approach to revelation and his purpose of reorienting dogmatics toward the word as its source. This is his first concern; and to the extent that he has stated his approach, has excellent reason for it, and indicates his intention in the title *The Doctrine of the Word of God*, he misleads no one. On the other hand, his choice can lead a reader to feel that his doctrine of revelation, for all its strengths, is founded on an insufficient understanding of God at this point in *Church Dogmatics*. We are pointing to an imbalance between concept and content: Barth's exposition of his conception of revelation could be understood to displace the substance of revelation.[46]

It is true that God's love is mentioned in various places throughout *CD* I/1 and I/2.[47] In his description of the simultaneous act of reconciliation and revelation that take place through the Son, for example, Barth identifies God's love and mercy as expressed in creation and revelation.[48] Furthermore, although the *Prolegomena* refers to God as creator, reconciler, and redeemer and thereby implies God's holiness and mercy, the specific references are few.[49] Barth never suggests that his treatment of the doctrine of the Trinity takes the place of the nature of God. Instead, the issue raised here is that because his discussion of the doctrine of the Trinity comes before an articulation of the divine nature, his argument, at least methodologically, is weakened. Brunner reflects this suspicion when he writes, "the

---

46. This disproportion points to what Stephen Williams indicates as something of an epistemological overdose in Barth; see Williams, *Revelation and Reconciliation*, 56, 79.

47. See Barth, *CD* I/1, 139, 409, 433, 470, 480, 483, 487. Also Barth, *CD* I/2, 248, 371–80.

48. See Barth, *CD* I/1, sec. 11, on God the Son.

49. In *CD* I/1, God's holiness is mentioned explicitly only once, on 322, and it is not stated at all in *CD* I/2. The attributes we are here concerned with are more implicitly indicated rather than explicitly treated.

doctrine of the Trinity only becomes really intelligible when first of all, and indeed in harmony with revelation, we speak of God's Holiness and Love."[50]

It looks at first glance as if Barth runs the risk of committing the self-same error that he has constrained himself to avoid—rooting dogmatics in something other than the word of God. Barth, however, would assert that this is the very thing he is sidestepping in his attempt to reorient, not just the doctrine of the Trinity, but all of dogmatics toward revelation. His primary concern is to begin with the person of Jesus Christ, the revealer, who makes known the Father as the one revealed, and consequently imparts to human hearts his own Spirit as revelation itself. As a result of this approach, one could say that God's activity as Father, Son, and Spirit is one with his person, and the *illic et tunc* of his revelation testifies in such a way that his mercy and love are revealed.

If this much is clear, where is the problem? Are we merely concerned with a "structural anomaly," as Brunner puts it, a misplacement of the doctrine of the Trinity in Barth's *Prolegomena*, which is a minor detail in the larger picture of Barth's program?[51] Barth himself emphasizes the importance of his choice in rejecting the traditional structure of dogmatics. He sees the triune being of God as the root of revelation and the basis for theological knowledge. There is no other sufficient starting point from his perspective. Does consideration of this intention in placing the doctrine of the Trinity in his *Prolegomena* spare Barth our critique? It does only partially because the issue with which we started this assessment—the certainty or uncertainty of the divine act of God's self-unveiling—remains unresolved.

This leads to a second weakness, brought into focus by Brunner's appraisal in *Dogmatics I*. "Barth does not distinguish between the *problem* of the Trinity which is set us by the message of the Bible, and the *doctrine* of the Trinity. He does not see that the doctrine of the Trinity is the product of reflection and not a *kerygma*. The *kerygma* is the God revealed in Christ, Christ, the genuine revelation of God. The doctrine of the Trinity itself, however, is not a Biblical doctrine, and this indeed not by accident but of necessity. It is the product of theological reflection upon the problem, which is raised, necessarily, by the Christian *kerygma*."[52] It is fair to say that Barth is guilty of no inconsistency with his own approach, so as with the first concern, this judgment is the result of our own methodological

---

50. Brunner, *Dogmatics I*, 237.
51. Ibid., 236.
52. Ibid.

priorities as well as Brunner's. Still, it needs to be addressed because if this conflation is true, then Barth has failed, at least in part, in his attempt to remain true to the content of God's self-revelation.

How does the argument proceed? Barth's preoccupation is to secure theological thinking and discussion in divine revelation, which has its center in the historical event of Jesus Christ as God's decisive self-disclosure. If dogmatics is to be consistent with anything, it must be consistent with Emmanuel. Does the life and work of Christ as we have it recorded in the Scriptures outline for us the Trinity as a doctrine? It clearly does not. Eventually evident to the apostles is the truth that Jesus Christ is God and that he acts in one will and action with the Father and the Spirit. This, however, is not a doctrine; it is the revelation of the reality of who God is through the action of Jesus' story. The advantage of the gospel narrative, as with most narratives, is that it has the capacity to sit with unresolved tension. The cross and resurrection accounts are only one example of such uncertainty, as the disciples experience something that they do not understand at the time. In contrast, the nature of doctrine, and we could almost say its purpose, is to answer questions and to define paradox, not in such a way as to efface it, but in such a way as to make it understandable.

That being so, why does the doctrine of the Trinity, with its accompanying explanations, explications, and qualifications, take center stage in Barth's *Prolegomena*, working hand in glove with his concept of revelation? He is no longer dealing with the narrative of the triune life of God as it is communicated in gospel stories. The result is, at least from Brunner's perspective, that priority is given to the doctrine of the Trinity which is not found in Scripture.[53] If this is indeed true, then we must admit that Barth does not entirely succeed in respecting his own methodology as concerns the Trinity.

PART TWO: FURTHER CONSIDERATIONS

We broaden our scope at this point to the doctrine of the virgin birth and the miracle of Easter to discern if there are other aspects related to doctrine or methodology that will facilitate our analysis. I choose these subjects for a couple of reasons. Firstly, there is an intimate connection among these creedal affirmations and the doctrine of the Trinity, namely Jesus Christ.

---

53. Ibid., 236–37.

Secondly, we have mentioned Brunner's take on these subjects in previous chapters and the juxtaposition of Barth's view with his is fitting.

The Doctrine of the Virgin Birth

Both Scripture and Christian tradition affirm the "prime mystery" of revelation as the incarnation. God-become-man is a belief that not only determines our Christology but also how we understand the Trinity. The Creed identifies this event as the *conceptus de Spiritu sancto, natus ex Maria virgine*. For Barth, the strength of this statement is that it declares the mystery without trying to explain it. In this way we are given terms by which to begin to affirm that God became a man, but the reality of the miracle of Christmas remains inconceivable. Barth pointedly asks in *Dogmatics in Outline*, "*Must* we believe this? . . . Perhaps even here we may joyfully say Yes."[54]

Barth refers to the miracle of Christmas as dogma established by the church but which is not entirely self-evident in the words of Scripture. He clarifies that the question of the virgin birth is not the same question as that of the two natures of Christ. It is the phrase "born of the virgin Mary" that marks the humanity and historicity of Jesus in his natural birth of a fully human mother.[55] At the same time, however, the church recognizes the supernatural, miraculous element of this birth: Jesus was conceived by the power of the Holy Spirit in an act of divine sovereignty, obedience, and condescension.

In this miracle of Christmas, as in the whole history of the Son, we witness the acts of the unified willing of the three divine persons. In the incarnation we see "the astounding conclusion of a divine obedience. Therefore we have to draw the no less astounding deduction that in equal Godhead the one God is, in fact, the One and also Another, that He is indeed a First and a Second, One who rules and commands in majesty and One who obeys in humility." Not only that, but this Godhead who is "One" and also "Another" is also a "Third;" the three sharing perfect fellowship and equality. We, too, are drawn into this fellowship via the divine obedience to which the virgin birth testifies.[56]

---

54. Barth, *Outline*, 95.
55. Barth, *CD* I/2, 187.
56. Barth, *CD* III/4, 202–3.

It is the role in Jesus' conception by the Holy Spirit as God that eliminates *a priori* any other explanation of Jesus' birth as entirely natural. Barth takes pains to highlight that it is only through the Spirit that God is present to man, that man participates in revelation and reconciliation, that the church is animated, and that we are made his children. He concludes that the essential presence of God by the Spirit is in the incarnation event and through this event the word of God and the Spirit of God, together in human nature, are God's revelation to humankind.[57]

A point of clarification is needed pertaining to what Barth perceives to be the sign of the virgin birth as that which signifies the reality of the Son's condescension. "Noetically, i.e., for us to whom this sign is given, who have to recognize it in and by this sign, the fact that Jesus Christ is the Son of God come in the flesh stands or falls with the truth of the *conceptio de Spiritu sancto*. But it could not be said that ontically, in itself, the mystery of Christmas stands or falls with this dogma."[58] In other words, Barth acknowledges the necessity of the sign of the miraculous conception to be critical to our recognition of, and faith in, Jesus as the Son of God. If he were not conceived by the Holy Spirit, and if we did not affirm this as an element of our faith, we could not affirm that Jesus is Lord. At the same time, this intellectual necessity must not be extrapolated to imply actual necessity. The order is that "the mystery does not rest upon the miracle. The miracle rests upon the mystery. The miracle bears witness to the mystery, and the mystery is attested by the miracle."[59] The fact that the Son is fully God means that he could so condescend to us in this way.

Brunner's concern about the legitimacy of *natus ex Maria virgine* as dogma brings us to a point of difficulty that Barth himself recognizes. He confesses that the breadth and precise form of the doctrine is not found in Scripture as clearly as it is stated in the creeds.[60] How one interprets the arguments for or against the scriptural data determines how one will classify the doctrine. It is precisely for this reason that Brunner considers it inappropriate and disproportionate with the scriptural emphasis to hold to the virgin birth as Christian dogma. In *The Mediator* he comments that his goal is not to attack the doctrine or rid the Christian faith of it altogether, but rather to assert that attempt to prove anything based on such inconclu-

---

57. Barth, *CD* I/2, 199.
58. Ibid., 202.
59. Ibid.
60. Ibid., 174.

sive evidence is, in the case of the doctrine of the virgin birth, "especially unfortunate."[61]

Another reason for Brunner's rejection of the virgin birth as dogma is that the apostles do not speak of the virgin birth in their affirmation of Jesus as the Christ. Only two of them, Matthew and Luke, mention the story, and it is quite possible that Paul and John teach and write about Jesus as the Christ apart from knowledge of these gospel accounts. Brunner is blunt in his analysis. "Apostles never mention this," he writes; "still less does it form part of the content of the original Christian *kerygma*." Therefore "the Apostolic doctrine of Jesus expounds the Nature of Him who rose from the dead, but not of Him who was born of the Virgin Mary."[62] The virgin birth simply did not figure in their witness to Jesus as Lord. As such Brunner deems it distracting as a dogma and non-essential to the church's proclamation of Jesus as Lord.

Barth, in contrast, argues that the very fact that the event is noted in the gospels means it demands attention by the church.[63] He acknowledges along with Brunner that there are questions regarding historical-critical details of the texts. To Barth's way of thinking, however, these uncertainties are not sufficient reason to reject it as dogma. "The final and proper decision is whether in accordance with the demands of Church dogma this testimony is to be heard, and heard as the emphatic statement of the New Testament message, or whether in defiance of Church dogma it is not to be heard, i.e., only to be heard as a sub-statement of the New Testament message which is not binding."[64]

A few variances between Brunner and Barth come into focus. Their conflicting estimation of the doctrine of the virgin birth illuminates their divergent starting points: Barth wants to maintain the doctrine despite uncertainties in the scriptural account, whereas Brunner does not acknowledge the event as dogma because it is not foundational to the apostles' proclamation. Brunner maintains that the kerygma "Jesus is Lord" forms

---

61. Brunner, *Mediator*, 324.

62. Brunner, *Dogmatics II*, 329.

63. We know of this event by Luke's account of Gabriel's appearance and word to Mary that the Holy Spirit would come upon her and she would conceive and give birth to a son. Matthew, however, only mentions the conception in passing (Matt 1:18, 20), and Mark is silent on the *conceptus de Spiritu sancto, natus ex Maria virgine*. Both interpretations are plausible: its mere presence in the gospels supports Barth's position, while Brunner's interpretation is also understandable when the minimal detail is emphasized.

64. Barth, *CD* I/2, 176.

the heart of the eyewitness testimony to Christ, and this testimony alone serves as the model for and the test of our theological thinking. A note of precision is required here. Brunner is not denying *that* Jesus was conceived by the Holy Spirit or born of the virgin Mary; rather he is emphasizing that these elements were not fundamental factors in the apostles' faith.

Barth's boundaries in contrast appear to incorporate a broader spectrum of teaching from the New Testament, to include the church's historical traditions that range beyond the first-hand account of the apostles. The determinative question for Barth regarding the doctrine of the virgin birth is whether the "rightness and importance" of the doctrine, both at the delimitation of the canon as well as the writing of the creeds, holds authority for us today. If so, we too must acknowledge the virgin birth as central to the gospel narratives and thereby to divine revelation, even though this knowledge is *a posteriori*. In answering his own question Barth posits that the dogma of virgin birth is based on a different level of testimony than the doctrine of the two natures. The former is not meant to be a reiteration of the latter but is something of a confession of that which we otherwise cannot explain.[65]

It is clearly not my intention either in this case or in this chapter to offer adjudication on disparities between Brunner and Barth. What interests me are the implications of this doctrine for their respective methodologies. Barth sums up the stakes:

> When two theologians with apparently the same conviction confess the mystery of Christmas, do they mean the same thing by that mystery, if one [Barth] acknowledges and confesses the Virgin birth to be the sign and the mystery while the other [Brunner] denies it as a mere externality or is ready to leave it an open question? Does the second man really acknowledge and confess that in His revelation to us and in our reconciliation to Him, to our measureless astonishment and in our measureless hiddenness the initiative is wholly with God? Or does he not by his denial or declared indifference towards the sign of the Virgin birth at the same time betray the fact that with regard to the thing signified by this sign he means something quite different? May it not be the case that the only one who hears the witness of the thing is the one who keeps to the sign by which the witness has actually signified it?[66]

---

65. Ibid., 176–77.
66. Ibid., 179–80.

Though one may wonder if Barth is not overcome by a disproportionate sense of disgruntlement here, his questions are germane to our study. Before we answer them, though, we take a look at a second element related to this issue, which is the miracle of Easter.

The Miracle of Easter

To Barth's mind the miracle of virgin birth and miracle of empty tomb are correlates that serve as signposts. They distinguish the life of Jesus Christ from all other human life as the historical existence identical with God himself. God is the ultimate subject of this life and no other. The virgin birth opens the sign while the empty tomb closes it. Barth is careful to say that it is not our interpretation of these events that these two signs demarcate but the reality of God's revelation.

How do the signs correspond to the things signified in these two events, and what do they have to do with revelation? Barth highlights several elements. First, the virgin birth signifies that it is God himself who chooses and acts to reveal himself in this mystery of incarnation. No human imagination or religiosity is at its source, but the triune persons are at the center of revelation. Second, Easter is only possible because of the veiledness of the incarnation. If God had not been born of the virgin Mary, if the divine had not hidden himself in human form in Jesus of Nazareth, there would be nothing to unveil at the resurrection. Thus Barth writes, "the mystery at the beginning is the basis of the mystery at the end; and by the mystery of the end the mystery of the beginning becomes active and knowable. And since this is so, the same objective content is signified in the one case by the miracle of the Virgin birth, in the other by the miracle of the empty tomb."[67] It is precisely the empty tomb that discloses what had been hidden in mystery.

Barth's view has much to promote itself. It is consistent with the divine mystery and disclosure of God as Father, Son, and Spirit; it is founded on a long ecclesial tradition; and it is certainly poetic to view the miracle of Christmas in the virgin birth and the miracle of Easter in the empty tomb as book ends to the life of the God-man. Yet a curious question is washed up in its wake, prompted by Brunner's critique. To what extent do the apostles uphold these doctrines as foundational to their witness to Jesus as Lord?

---

67. Ibid., 183.

In *Dogmatics II* Brunner regards the event of Easter as going beyond straightforward historical fact. We recall that he claims that the empty tomb "is not part of the historical *continuum*, but at this point the Beyond 'breaks into' history."[68] Easter is not accessible to the understanding in the same way the historical aspects of Jesus' life are accessible apart from faith. What makes Easter determinative is that it is the foundation for the apostles' believing testimony, thus forming the gospel basis for the Christian faith. It is in light of the resurrected Christ that they proclaim Jesus is Lord, not before this event or apart from it.

Brunner's approach requires further qualification. He asserts that it is not primarily or essentially because of the apostolic witness that we believe in the resurrection, but because it is the testimony of all of Scripture that Jesus is Lord. "Jesus Christ is Victor over death and the grave, not only because He is the Risen Lord, but because He is the Christ, the God-Man, which, as such, could not remain subject to death."[69] While it is to this Jesus that the apostles testify, the reality of this Jesus as Lord surpasses their testimony in scope and in effect. We are reminded of a key to Brunner's methodology, that the order of theological inquiry is established by the first Christian community. It is reflective of their own process of discovery—from the man Jesus, to be understood as the Christ and as Lord in light of Easter, and finally to be declared as the eternal Son of God.

PART THREE: THEOLOGICAL METHODOLOGY

There is one more element that requires acknowledgement, which recurs throughout Barth's *Dogmatics* and which is highly relevant to the subjects already addressed. It is the distinction he makes between a sign and the thing signified. This will be the first element examined in section 1 regarding implications for methodology. The second section will include final reflections on the differences between Brunner's and Barth's dogmatic *modus operandi*.

---

68. Brunner, *Dogmatics II*, 328.
69. Ibid., 372.

Sign and Thing Signified

Access into this subject is easily gained through *Dogmatics in Outline*, where Barth refers to the miracle of Christmas. There he says, "The truth of the conception of Jesus Christ by the Holy Spirit and of His birth of the Virgin Mary points to the true Incarnation of the true God achieved in His historical manifestation."[70] Barth comments that by declaring that Jesus was conceived of the Holy Spirit we affirm the mystery of the incarnation for which the virgin birth exists only as a sign. Certainly the incarnation stands alone apart from the sign that accompanied it, but it is the sign that is given to disclose it as a miracle.

What is the proper relationship between the form and content of the miracle then? Barth indicates that "the two should not be confused . . . [I]t would be wrong to conclude from that, that therefore 'only' a sign is involved, which therefore might even be deducted from the mystery. Let me warn you against this. It is rare in life to be able to separate form and content."[71] Just the same, the form of the divine revelation, which is the sign that points to its mystery, is necessary for the understanding of faith.

The issue of form being separable from content is a theme that Barth deals with in his *Prolegomena*. In *CD* I/1, in the context of a paragraph on the word of God and faith, Barth discusses the possibility of knowing God's word. This possibility of knowledge is a "pointer" to the word of God who gives the ability to know. God is the object of knowledge, not any of the markers pointing to him along the way. We never possess the form without the content, while at the same time our comprehension of the content is made possible by its form, apart from which we would not recognize the thing signified as from God.[72]

Barth extrapolates in *CD* I/2. "Sign and thing signified," he writes, "the outward and the inward, are, as a rule, strictly distinguished in the Bible, and certainly in other connections we cannot lay sufficient stress upon the distinction. But they are never separated in such a ('liberal') way that according to preference the one may be easily retained without the other."[73] How are we to apply this distinction, for example, to the miracle of the virgin birth and the mystery of the God-become-man? Barth contends in this

---

70. Barth, *Outline*, 95.
71. Ibid., 96.
72. Barth, *CD* I/1, 237.
73. Barth, *CD* I/2, 179.

case that affirmation of faith is put alongside the reality. The event which the Christian faith affirms as Jesus Christ being conceived by the Holy Spirit and born of the virgin Mary serves as the language symbol indicating the invisible event of the divine condescension.

It remains to be asked what could be the connection between the thing signified and dogma about that reality. From Barth's perspective the doctrine of the virgin birth is necessary because it serves to point to the otherwise invisible mystery of the incarnation. For him, everything depends on divine mystery being made known in the sign. This is his justification for retaining the doctrine of the virgin birth as dogma.

A potentially discomfiting choice between two conclusions ensues. If on the one hand Barth means that God's revelation in the incarnation depends on its occurrence in the virgin birth, we can accept its indication of the logical and biological constraints of human origin, for God could not be fully man unless conceived and born. Is it not the case, however, that we can affirm the physical process of the incarnation without elevating the virgin birth to the status of dogma? This latter interpretation, though, is not an acceptable one to Barth's mind, even though it appears to be Brunner's understanding, for which Barth takes him to task.[74]

On the other hand, if Barth insists that it is necessary to view the virgin birth as doctrine in order to recognize the mystery of the incarnation, does this not render divine self-communication dependent upon human establishment of dogma? He seems to argue that we only perceive the incarnation because it is revealed through the sign of the miracle of Christmas. Unfortunately, our second option is not any more comfortable than the first because the question remains: is not the incarnation identifiable as mystery and as real event apart from the virgin birth being established as doctrine?

---

74. Barth's critique is scathing, but perhaps it reiterates in turn the consistency with which Brunner maintains his methodology. There is, in my opinion, something to be said for both perspectives. "Brunner develops the queer objection that the doctrine of the Virgin birth means a 'biological interpretation of the miracle' (meaning the miracle of the incarnation), and is in fact an expression of 'biological inquisitiveness.' The divine miracle, he contends, is supposed to be explained here in its How, whereas we should be content in faith with the That. The Virgin birth is an event in space and time, a fact of observation, of the reality of which we may be aware without having faith in it. For that reason we ought to declare our indifference toward it. In reply to this we must first of all make an exegetical statement . . . : neither in the New Testament nor in the creed is the doctrine of the Virgin birth a 'biological' explanation. There is not a single word in which it takes anything to do with the biological happening as such—even on the analogy of the Easter story." Barth, *CD* I/2, 183.

Furthermore, is not the virgin birth part and parcel of God's word, not human story or interpretation? Barth anticipates this line of inquiry and offers clarification. "The true Godhead and the true humanity of Jesus Christ in their unity do not depend on the fact that Christ was conceived by the Holy Spirit and born of the Virgin Mary. All that we can say is that it pleased God to let the mystery be real and become manifest in this shape and form."[75]

The role of signs for human understanding of divine revelation receives further attention in *CD* I/2. Barth explains the process as beginning with the objective revelation from God to the human being. In this event the person's heart is opened up and identifies the truth of revelation, thus rendering it subjective truth. To Barth's way of thinking, what was objective revelation becomes subjective faith without suffering alteration. The revelation that is Jesus Christ remains, but the person understands this as more than a statement of fact; he comes to see that Jesus himself is in Christ. Therefore, Barth posits, that revelation exists for us and we for it. The process could be summarized in this way: *objective revelation + signs + the Holy Spirit in the human person = subjective revelation*. "In its subjective reality God's revelation consists of definite signs of its objective reality which are given by God."[76] These signs, these "instruments of the Word of God," do not possess within themselves anything that makes them signs, but it is God who makes them signs of his revelation out of his own free will. They are definite and concrete signs of the word of God; they are divine acts. This subjective revelation is the work of the Spirit of Christ speaking the word of God to the human heart.

What impact does this have on theological method, particularly on the limitations that Barth establishes for dogmatics? Furthermore, what does this mean for what we can state about the triune being? Barth discusses in *CD* II/1 the issue of limitations. He begins by stating that the limitation of our knowledge of God is that it is secondary objectivity. It is not identical with the knowledge that God has of himself because it is creaturely knowledge. The necessity of signs becomes clearer in its grounding in the paradox of the divine veiling and unveiling. "It is the case everywhere that when . . . He reveals Himself His hiddenness is confirmed."[77] If this is true, is it not possible for the human knower to mistake the sign for content and thus disregard the substance of God's self-communication?

---

75. Barth, *Outline*, 100.
76. Barth, *CD* I/2, 223.
77. Barth, *CD* II/1, 55.

This is a risk that Barth recognizes and, he suggests, one that God also recognizes and is willing to take: that human beings will receive the sign without receiving God himself as revelation. We must be aware of this danger in the work of theological thinking. "The reality of the fulfilment of the true knowledge of God, as the act in which God gives Himself to be known and is known, must always be distinguished from the necessary limitation in which it happens."[78] In other words, what we know of God in the context of our human understanding must be distinguished from the means and signs that God uses to communicate himself. While the means facilitate revelation that otherwise would not be possible, they also hide the divine subject because they are never commensurate with this reality. Consequently, the theologian must be ever mindful that God's word is God's and cannot be sealed to or by any human expression or explication.

Brunner–Barth Comparison

As I bring this chapter to a close, I summarize the key points of contrast between Brunner's and Barth's treatment of the Trinity and potential ramifications of their respective approaches for the dogmatic task. To begin with, we briefly recall their similitude. Firstly, both men regard the science of dogmatics as an ecclesial discipline. While dogmatics is critical to the well-being of the church and to its theological task of polemics, catechesis, and exegesis, it can never replace the church's primary function of proclamation of the word of God. Secondly, the word, both written and preached, not only records the past event of Emmanuel and announces the promise of God's full and future coming, it is also the means of God's presence with us in the here and now as the Spirit renders it revelation. This leads to a third parallel, that both concur that it is in the event of God's grace that the Spirit speaks to our spirits by which we know him in I-Thou encounter. Finally, there exists for each theologian a comparable emphasis on the role of the event of Jesus Christ and the event of God's self-unveiling. Both regard Jesus as the definitive revelation of God to humankind; on this there is no compromise.

---

78. Ibid., 56.

Brunner on the Doctrine of the Trinity

Let me give a thumbnail review of Brunner's view on the Trinity before we proceed with a critical comparison. Here we see the clear implications of his commitment to the written word as the source of all theological inquiry. He maintains that Scripture reflects the divine triunity in God's activity in human history: in the Old Testament testimony to the promised Messiah; in the Synoptic narratives about Jesus Christ; and through the New Testament apostolic witness to the Son of God. The word testifies to the Lord as one God, Father and Son and Spirit.

Brunner nevertheless tempers his position by affirming that discussion about how the Father, Son, and Spirit relate in their inner life is limited. Thus, because both the source of divine revelation in Christ and the criterion of our speech in the apostolic witness are restricted in their commentary on this point, so must our theological discussion on trinitarian existence be restrained. This illustrates Brunner's view on the limits of theological inquiry. Only those doctrines that are sourced in the substance of the biblical witness in both content and form ought to be considered dogma. This is why Brunner has such reservations about the doctrine of the virgin birth, as we have discussed. It is not that he wants to cast doubt on the gospel account of Gabriel's message to Mary. Rather, since this event was not part of the apostolic message of "Jesus is Lord," neither is it central to the preaching of the church.

If this is the nature and these are the limits of God's self-communication, it should also be the nature and, these, the limits of the content of our inquiry about the divine subject. When it comes to the Trinity, both Brunner and Barth agree that the doctrine is not formally part of the early church's kerygma and is therefore not the primary matter of church proclamation. It is, just the same, the defining doctrine and the decisive defense of the Christian faith since the Church Fathers. In the context of theological reflection, the doctrine of the Trinity is central even though it is not revealed via biblical narrative in the same form as we affirm it in the creeds.

This being the case, what, in Brunner's opinion, can dogmatics say about the intra-triune relations? Theology can declare only what is revealed through the apostolic witness to the self-revelation of God in Jesus Christ. It is through the historical work of Jesus Christ that he reveals the Father. Brunner acknowledges that there are expressions regarding divine transcendence in the writings of Paul, for example, that appear to surpass this measure, but he contends that even these citations eventually return to Jesus Christ as revelation's historical center. He also points out a similar dynamic in John, where the apostle writes about the eternality of Jesus as the word; but John too returns to the historic event of his life, death, and resurrection. Brunner concludes that the various New Testament writers all affirm, based on the historical revelation, the reality that Jesus shares fully in the divine being. He is the one through whom God communicates himself to humankind.

Critical Differences

It can be said that the boundaries to theological inquiry that Brunner establishes are valuable, not primarily for the speculation they prohibit but also for the coherent theological thinking they facilitate. They accommodate the narrative nature of Scripture, especially the apostolic witness to the personal word of God. Scripture establishes for us the limits to our investigation, both in its content of God's work of revelation and reconciliation and in its form of narrative. Brunner thereby identifies the appropriate subjects of theological dogma as only the themes of the biblical testimony. Because the shape of that testimony is non-propositional and is grounded in historical context, so also the expression of our theological thinking ought to be sensitive to the same conditions. This does not mean that the only appropriate genre for dogmatics is story, but rather that the starting point and criterion of dogmatics is the biblical account.

Brunner's approach refuses any other foundation for dogmatics than the apostolic witness. The reserve we sense in Brunner's affirmation of certain theological categories is perhaps reflective, not of his reticence to speak in theological terms, for he obviously does, but of his awareness of the primary witness and sole root of doctrine as the biblical narrative. This conviction is coupled with the commitment that our language will reflect the limitation of our knowledge. It is his contention that we cannot improve upon the categories of Scripture as the "stuff" of theological reflection. As a result we conclude that the apostolic witness for Brunner offers the substance of Christian dogma.

Although Barth similarly affirms the priority of the written word as authoritative testimony to God's self-communication, his conception of revelation is a different starting point for the doctrine Trinity. Even as Barth begins to talk about the triune nature of God, he uses theological terminology that is one step removed from the biblical witness. Instead of referring strictly to God the Father as the one revealed by the person of Jesus Christ, and to the Spirit as the one sent by Jesus, he follows a theological construal of the biblical narrative: the Father as veiling, the Son as unveiling, and the Spirit as impartation. We could say that the apostolic witness for Barth is the basis of dogmatics but not its entire substance.

This variance raises a critical question. If the word of God is the authoritative testimony to divine self-revelation, can there be any other legitimate foundation for the doctrine of divine triunity? In other words, does Barth's formula of revealer—revelation—revealedness do justice to the biblical testimony to God as Father, Son, and Spirit without importing suppositions that are not found in the apostolic witness? Is Barth employing an extra-biblical theological construct in order to investigate and affirm the divine triunity? If so, what might this imply about a source for the doctrine of the Trinity, or any other doctrine for that matter, that is other than the biblical narrative? Ovey warns, "If Barth follows his own program, then errors or obscurities in his own trinitarian theology, designed to stand at the head of his dogmatics, may have far-reaching implications."[79]

From Brunner's perspective a commitment to divine revelation allows us to endorse the use of theological terminology in our affirmation of God as triune, while simultaneously compelling us to reject any other source but the apostolic witness as the content of our faith. Brunner's aim is that the doctrine of the Trinity articulates in other language only that to which the biblical narrative testifies; Scripture alone must remain the root of the doctrine. Barth, in contrast, turns to a doctrine of revelation as the basis for explaining the Trinity and unabashedly so, for he regards the concept of revelation as the only legitimate root for the doctrine. Barth's approach is problematic on one fundamental point: he runs the risk of mistaking the concept of revelation for its content, thereby interpreting the historical manifestation of God's self-communication according to an extra-biblical construct.[80]

---

79. Gibson and Strange, *Engaging*, 200.

80. I am not alone in my concern, as Ovey reflects: "This term 'concept' provokes precisely the question whether Barth's revelation basis is really an analysis of a concept

We can conclude that while both theologians uphold the centrality of the written word for dogmatics, it is in different ways. Brunner insists on the biblical narrative as the origin of the doctrine of the Trinity, while Barth begins with what we might call a theological interpretation of Scripture. It would appear that Barth works from the doctrine of revelation that is borne from a different foundation than Brunner's treatment of the New Testament's witness to the Son, the Father, and the Spirit.

Is this merely a question of dissimilar starting points, with Brunner focusing on the *opus Dei ad extra* while Barth considers the *opus Dei ad intra*? This is perhaps a facile categorization, for Barth's emphasis in his *Prolegomena* suggests that his goal is precisely the contrary. "Who is God in his revelation?" he asks. By means of an answer we are to ask two other questions: "What is He doing? and: What does He effect?"[81] Later in *CD* I/1 Barth proceeds to identify the unity of the triune persons with the unity of their works. "The work of God is the essence of God as the essence of Him who ... is revealer, revelation and being revealed, or Creator, Reconciler and Redeemer. In this work of His, God is revealed to us."[82] The fact that Barth moves on to write for hundreds of pages about how the Father, Son, and Spirit are related as three in one may be consistent with their work revealed in Scripture but certainly surpasses the Scriptures' *ad intra* statements.

In contrast, Brunner's discussion of the Trinity is limited to what the person of Jesus Christ reveals about himself, about the Father, and about the Spirit. His commentary is restricted particularly to the emphasis of revelation in the immanent work of Christ. Jesus is the starting point who, as the revelation of the Father, firmly roots divine revelation in the created sphere. What can we learn from this event, if anything, about the origin of the Son or about the transcendent relations of the Father, Son, and Holy Spirit? The classical formula of the three persons expressed side by side might lead one to believe that we can know something about how they relate based on the life and death of Jesus. After all, the movement of the Son from transcendent presence with the Father to reveal himself in history and then to return to the Father gives us some clues, does it not?

Brunner argues that speaking of the Father, Son, and Holy Spirit in a certain sequence does not reflect an ontological succession but instead the order in which God has revealed himself to humankind in salvation history.

---

rather than of content, that is, of the revelation that actually occurred." *Engaging*, 215.

81. Barth, *CD* I/1, 297.

82. See ibid., 371 and context.

What are the implications of such a viewpoint? For one, he contends, we must abandon the fascination with a doctrine of the intra-triune persons where the Father, Son, and Spirit are examined independent of their revelation in time and space. In this light Brunner rejects the possibility of speaking in such terms as *tres personae* and *una substantia* as an "intellectual aberration which substitutes speculative and impersonal thinking for the line of thought controlled by revelation."[83] It is not the divine mystery they reflect but rather human fascination with a realm of knowledge that has not been made known to us in Christ.

Even though there is apostolic reference to his transcendent origin, the historical center of the life of Jesus always qualifies this connection. Because the biblical narrative forms the boundaries to his dogmatics, Brunner's treatment of the Trinity is likewise confined in its content and its language. This can be considered a strength to the extent that it fosters consistency with the written word. The prominent difference with Barth is that, while Brunner does not deny the reality of an intra-triune life, he refuses to discuss at length how this might look. The *ad extra*, in other words, forms the substance of dogmatic discussion, and the *ad intra* remains firmly lodged in the realm of mystery.

What is the real mystery of the Trinity according to either theologian if this is the case? It is that mystery which revelation accentuates, not which human speculation dispels. Both Brunner and Barth generally agree on this point, that inscrutability is inherent in the divine being and forms one of the boundaries to God's self-revelation. What Brunner rejects is the "pseudo-mystery" that presents us with an intellectual conundrum about the divine being as three-in-one and then asks us to respect this as the mystery of God. He contends that there is nothing in the apostolic witness that alludes to such a *mysterium logicum*; rather, the mystery of revelation is the mystery of the incarnation and the cross. Here we encounter the divergence between doctrine and kerygma. The doctrine of the Trinity belongs to the theological teaching of the church and not to the gospel teaching of Jesus and the disciples, whereas the work of revelation and reconciliation of God in salvation history is the sole preoccupation of church proclamation.

---

83. Brunner, *Dogmatics I*, 227.

Part II: Bounded Theology

Conclusion

This overview of Barth's handling of the doctrine of the Trinity has served as a comparative measure for what we have examined in Brunner's work. By way of conclusion one final question remains: where do our sympathies lie? How is this analysis of Brunner's methodology amplified and/or altered with these two approaches to the Trinity in mind? I firstly affirm that Brunner's treatment above all seeks to be faithful to the New Testament witness to Jesus Christ as the revelation of God. He begins and ends with the apostolic writings and considers the doctrine as the fruit of theological reflection on the triune being, not as its genesis. On this count Brunner seems to avoid the pitfalls of inverting dogma and revelation and confusing dogmatics with proclamation. Secondly, his approach leads to a valuation of the biblical narrative that is congruent with revelation as personal encounter and that affirms that God will meet us in our own historical context. It is not through ancient dogmas that we experience Emmanuel but through the Spirit's work as he speaks to us in Jesus Christ. This is the heart of revelation, past, present, and future.

In my view we can go as far as to suggest that Brunner's emphasis on divine revelation as personal encounter and his valuation of Scripture as the foundation for theological thinking provide a helpful response, not only to the aftermath of twentieth century liberal theology but also to some twenty-first century challenges. The particular relation between the strength of Brunner's approach and the struggle of theology today is the former's emphasis on God's revelation, particularly in the narrative character of Scripture, and the latter's quest to know an experience of God in personal story. Brunner gently yet unapologetically leads us back to the word as the exclusive record of God's self-revelation where we can encounter God through the story of Jesus Christ. Does Barth's methodology provide a similar corrective? No, it does not seem to do so in the same way. While Barth unequivocally values the word of God as the witness to divine self-revelation, and perhaps in a manner that few other modern theologians have done, he does not offer the same appreciation of narrative that Brunner does, and thus runs the risk of relying on dogmatics as source of theology instead of regarding it only as faith's fruit.

PART III

Transformed Being

6

Behind Brunner—Søren Kierkegaard

"The issue is not about the truth of Christianity but about the individual's relation to Christianity, consequently not about the indifferent individual's systematic eagerness to arrange the truths of Christianity in paragraphs but rather about the concern of the infinitely interested individual with regard to his own relation to such a doctrine."

—KIERKEGAARD, *CONCLUDING UNSCIENTIFIC POSTSCRIPT*, 15

THUS FAR WE HAVE outlined Brunner's methodology and critiqued its application throughout his published corpus. I have argued that his work is commendably consistent with both the believing witness of the apostles and his own schema. A brief comparison with Barth has served as a case study of sorts by which to further highlight what I see as the distinctive elements of Brunner's reflective process. We have not yet reached, however, what Brunner deems the ultimate effect of theology.

Certainly Brunner has had his critics through the decades on a variety of counts. Some scholars have argued that Brunner is no better off than the liberal theologians against whom he reacts, in part because the broad structure of his thought has deep philosophical roots, thus rendering his theology "hostile to the historic Christian faith."[1] This allegation is a

---

1. Van Til, *The New Modernism*, xiii.

serious one of which Brunner himself is aware. My goal in this chapter is not to engage a full examination of these claims and Brunner's response to them, which is an undertaking for another project altogether. Instead, my objective remains expository: to consider one philosophical voice that we hear clearly in Brunner's thought, that of Søren Kierkegaard. As we will see, there are several themes in Kierkegaard's existentialist reading of the Christian faith that are central to Brunner's theology: sin, the paradox of the incarnation, the contemporaneity of faith, and the role of faith in knowing, to name a few. A further parallel that will become evident is the corresponding conclusion that Christianity is utterly and entirely irreconcilable with philosophical idealism. In all of this I hope to show the third thread of this book that Brunner's believing thinking, which is done within boundaries given us in Scripture, in its fullest sense will lead to the transformed being of the Christian.

There are two goals towards the end of identifying Kierkegaard's influence on Brunner's work. The first is to hear Kierkegaard in his own voice by attending to three primary sources: *The Sickness unto Death*, *Philosophical Fragments*, and *Concluding Unscientific Postscript*. This will be done in part 1. I focus on these volumes in particular because they are the most frequently referenced of Kierkegaard's works in Brunner's writing. The emphasis on the doctrine of human being that we have seen in Brunner's thought directs us to *SD* for its impact on his anthropology. The choice of *PF* is guided by the very critique being addressed: the possibility of treating the Christian faith in non-theological terms. The final selection of *CUP* is made for its standing as Kierkegaard's *magnum opus*, as well as for its comprehensive assessment of the role of faith in knowledge.

The second goal of this chapter, treated in part 2, is to suggest specific ramifications for Brunner's methodology that result from Kierkegaard's influence. Questions will be addressed such as, What Kierkegaardian themes, if any, are reflected in the limits that Brunner places on theological methodology? Is there a correlative relationship between Kierkegaard's defense of "truth as subjectivity" and Brunner's definition of "truth as encounter"? If so, how can this connection illuminate our understanding of Brunner's epistemology? How does Kierkegaard regard Scripture, and does his treatment concur or conflict with Brunner's?

In part 1 the majority of space will be devoted to analysis of the primary sources under consideration. As a final element in each section on *SD*, *PF*, and *CUP*, select references to Brunner's work that either correlate or clash with Kierkegaard's motifs will be integrated, in an attempt to highlight important points for our overall investigation. Part 2 will consist of a "discussion" between the two men around the implications of Kierkegaard's influence for Brunner's methodology. There is no attempt here to give priority to one or the other perspective; the goal is to see where the two minds meet and where they part company, so commentary on each will be simultaneous.

PART ONE: KIERKEGAARD'S VOICE, BRUNNER'S ECHO

With Brunner's question from *The Divine–Human Encounter* in mind—How is knowing related to being?, it is constructive to evaluate subjective considerations that play a role in our knowledge of the truth of Christianity. *The Sickness Unto Death*, regarded as Kierkegaard's anthropology, is our slipway into that investigation. In response to this volume, Brunner comments that anthropology is the critical element that differentiates the Christian faith from humanism. It comes as no surprise, then, that there are some forty-five references to Kierkegaardian material in *Man in Revolt*, Brunner's own anthropological work. The reasons for Brunner's capitalization on Kierkegaard's thought soon will become evident.

The Sickness unto Death

The issue of the self before God and the issue of despair form our first focus, followed by a treatment of the Christian themes of sin, paradox, and offense. What we have already discovered of Brunner's anthropology must be kept in mind. His appreciation of Kierkegaard's contribution is emphatic, no doubt for, among other things, its faithfulness to revelation. He writes, "It was no mere whim of Kierkegaard, when he undertook to try to represent the whole of human life—in so far as it is not in 'faith'—as despairing, and its phenomena as countless variations on the one theme of despair; and the book in which he does so has become one of the finest of his writings," that is, *The Sickness unto Death*.[2]

---

2. Brunner, *Man in Revolt*, 201.

Part III: Transformed Being

The Self before God and Despair

We start with Kierkegaard's definition of the human being. Kierkegaard precisely describes the self as the synthesis between one's eternal soul and temporal being. Human existence is rooted in the dialectical tension of the finite with the infinite: we desire to know the eternal because our spirits are eternal, yet, being confined by the temporal, there is nothing we can do of ourselves to access the infinite. Without this awareness of the synthesis that distinguishes humanity from the rest of the created order, we cannot begin to know what it means to be a self. The fully human self thus is defined as the positive relation between the finite and the infinite.

That said, the dialectical synthesis does not stand in relation only to itself. In Kierkegaard's view, such an I-I relation is the result of speculative imagination dissociated from the reality of human existence. The distinctive element of the self is that it is in positive relation to "the power that established it."[3] Though Kierkegaard does not immediately identify this "power," we know it to be "the god" based on subsequent commentary.[4] We recognize, then, that the human being in relation to the god is a foundational presupposition of Kierkegaard's schema. To be fully human requires one to understand oneself as a spiritual as well as a physical being. Kierkegaard states that a person's life is virtually wasted if he "went on living so deceived by life's joys or its sorrows that he never became decisively and eternally conscious as spirit, as self."[5] Thus it is only before God that we exist, and it is only in the context of this spatio-temporal relation to the eternal that anything can be known.

Alongside this positive description of what it means to be human is the claim that there is a sickness that characterizes every person called despair. Despair, like selfhood, is understood in relational terms, though more accurately as relation's distortion. It is the misrelation of the self to the self and

---

3. Kierkegaard, *SD*, 14.

4. He discusses this power in part II as the love of God. His use of "the god" in place of the anticipated capitalized "God" is consistent with his project of defending the Christian faith in non-theological terms, which characterizes his enterprise in *SD*. Although Kierkegaard's conception of God is occasionally critiqued for being more Aristotelian than Christian, Law offers a reasoned defense of it as thoroughly Christian; see Law, "How Christian is Kierkegaard's God?" For the purposes of this chapter I will use "the god" when referring to Kierkegaard's material and "God" in most other contexts, recognizing that both designations refer to the triune God of the Christian faith.

5. Ibid., 26.

thus the misrelation of the self to the power that established it.[6] Despair is the determination not to be oneself, fuelled by the willful disruption of the synthesis within the human person. It is the result of the disorder between finitude and infinitude, the temporal and the eternal, freedom and necessity.[7] The impact of this misrelation is also the disruption of the self's relation to the power that established it. Kierkegaard continues his appraisal of the wasted life by saying that the person who never "became aware and in the deepest sense never gained the impression that there is a God and that 'he,' he himself, his self, exists before this God" is lost to himself and lost to his life.[8] Becoming fully human and knowing what is true is in this case an unattainable goal, and human existence is tragic.

It is clear in *SD* that Kierkegaard unreservedly pursues a Christian interpretation of humanness consistent with Scripture. Being one's self is to have one's particular shape, despite the fear of being unique. When a person does not assume his unique shape, he "forgets himself, forgets his name divinely understood, does not dare to believe in himself, finds it too hazardous to be himself and far easier and safer to be like the others, to become a copy, a number, a mass man."[9] The resultant despair takes two particular forms. The first form is despair in weakness—not to will to be oneself. Kierkegaard identifies this expression as the self's dependence on the sensate experience of the immediate without any attention to the eternal. Whenever something threatens this experience of the immediate despair sets in. There is neither self nor desire to be one's self in such a case; instead, the attempt not to be one's self or to be someone else takes center stage. The second form of despair is to will to be one's self in defiance of the power that established the self. In contrast to the first form, here the self possesses a measured awareness of the eternal but refuses to live in light of that self-consciousness. Such despair is equally as pervasive as the first form and the result equally alienating.

Kierkegaard aims to show how, lest something changes in one's existence, this despair is "the sickness unto death" for every human being.

6. Brunner comments, "This separation between the 'I' and the 'Self' is the central division of personality which characterizes the sinful man; it is that despair which Kierkegaard, in his *Sickness unto Death*, describes as the state of fallen man in theological ontology and psychology, as the decay of the original unity of the original elements of human existence." Brunner, *Man in Revolt*, 229.

7. Kierkegaard, *SD*, 15.

8. Ibid., 26–27.

9. Ibid., 33–34.

Despair presses one even further than death, for despair is also the inability to die when this is precisely what one desires in order to escape one's existence. He diagnoses despair's effect as inescapable, while at the same time acknowledges its impotence to "consume the eternal, the Self at the root of despair."[10] Its universal presence means that every person experiences this misrelation, whether it is in unawareness of one's eternal self, or in despair not willing to be one's self before God, or in defiance willing to be one's self apart from God. This is the condition of human existence in the disruption of the self's relation to the power that established it, which is the starting point of Kierkegaard's anthropology.

Sin, Paradox, and Offense

Having treated the self and despair in part 1 of *SD*, Kierkegaard expands his definition of human existence in part 2 to include sin, the paradox, and the offense of the Christian faith. Despair, although characteristic of human nature, remains ultimately the individual's choice to refuse to be himself before God. The first and most central point of this extrapolation, then, is the affirmation of despair as sin. Kierkegaard takes pains to contrast this definition with the Socratic view that sin is ignorance. Without reference to God, the latter definition focuses on sin as "a negation," as something that is fundamentally lacking in human existence, an inborn obfuscation of knowledge. This ignorance is, in the Socratic view, something for which humanity cannot be held responsible, thus concluding that sin does not exist. Because there is no inherent knowledge of the wrong, there is also no requirement to act in a certain (right) manner.[11]

In sharp contrast, Kierkegaard defends the Christian concept of sin as that which "most decisively differentiates Christianity qualitatively from paganism."[12] He takes up the orthodox view that sin is not a negation but a position, and that we do not know what sin is apart from divine revelation. The reality of sin is greater than a simple definition of position, however; that one continues to sin is a significant aspect of the misrelation of the self to God. It is not only that we are positionally misrelated to God, but also that we persevere in our enmity by choice. The state of sin in which one

---

10. Ibid., 18.
11. Ibid., 87–88.
12. Ibid., 89.

lives goes beyond the particular sins which one commits. It is the consistency of sin that characterizes human despair.

Kierkegaard goes on to describe sin as a paradox. The paradox is rooted in the absurdity of the fact that the individual exists "before God," and this "being before God" is the very position that illuminates one's willful refusal to be oneself. From this point the Christian paradox segues readily into the category of offense. Because the individual's position of sin has as its qualification "before God," it is a "qualification that in turn has Christianity's crucial criterion: *the absurd, the paradox, the possibility of offense*."[13] The message of the gospel is that human beings are intended for something other than despair. Sin is never a necessity of human existence because, to the extent that one is responsible, one is always free to respond to God's love in trust and surrender. Trespass nevertheless remains a possibility: we are free to reject divine forgiveness in disbelief, and this includes every small vice as well as the sin of dismissing Christianity altogether. Hence, the critical point for Kierkegaard is that sin is never an obligation.

The good news of the incarnation is that the eternal one has entered time in order that we might be lifted out of our despair. It is the paradox of the god-man that makes it possible to relate rightly to oneself and to the god. Kierkegaard exclaims, "Truly, if there is anything to lose one's mind over, this is it! Everyone lacking the humble courage to dare to believe this is offended. But why is he offended? Because it is too high for him, because his mind cannot grasp it, because he cannot attain bold confidence in the face of it and therefore must get rid of it, pass it off as a bagatelle, nonsense, and folly, for it seems as if it would choke him."[14] The qualification of offense is inherent in the Christian message and must not be disregarded; yet, insists Kierkegaard, it is the offense of good news. Because we cannot possess it by our intellect, it threatens to shake us out of our despairing status quo. The only option for those who do not respond to it by faith is to turn more deeply into sin.

Brunner's Echo

Although *The Sickness Unto Death* is the most cited of Kierkegaard's volumes in Brunner's works, we are also concerned with connections that go beyond direct references yet clearly exhibit a Kierkegaardian foundation.

13. Ibid., 83.
14. Ibid., 85–86.

PART III: TRANSFORMED BEING

For example, the actuality of the relation of the self to the eternal in the human soul and its subsequent misrelation is referred to in *Man in Revolt* in these terms: "Man is not merely what he is; his peculiar being is characterized by that inward and higher 'something' which confronts him either with a challenge or at least with pressure from without."[15] It is entirely consistent with Brunner's anthropology to say that this "something" challenging human existence in its relation to itself and in its relation to the source of its being is what Kierkegaard identifies as the eternal, the god.

Brunner is speaking along the same lines as Kierkegaard in the latter's treatment of the self's misrelation with itself. He states, "The real enigma of man is the conflict within his own nature, not the fact that he is composed of body and soul; the real problem does not lie in the fact that man is part of the world and is yet more than the world; the real problem is that the unity of all these elements—given by the Creation—has been lost, and that instead of complementing and aiding one another, they are in conflict with one another."[16] The misrelation with God is the rejection of our existence as "being in the love of God," leading to "existence-unto-death."[17] This disruption between the individual and God, of which the individual is acutely aware, is the very state from which the individual tries to free himself. This is the struggle of despair and the conflict of rebellion.

Fear's ubiquitous presence, which Brunner perceives in human experience, is another Kierkegaardian theme, also reminiscent of despair. It is a fundamental and pervasive fear of not finding one's place, a home, a space of belonging; a fear that affects everyone regardless of era or culture or age.[18] As for the reality of sin, there is also concordance between Brunner's and Kierkegaard's understandings. In terms similar to those of his predecessor, Brunner rejects the concept defined as a lack in the human being. He insists that sin is ultimately inexplicable in a-personal terms because it is a willed rebellion against the personal God that ultimately affects the sinner's being. Brunner points to Scripture's description of sin as turning away from God. Such self-sufficiency makes the human being "a sinner," thus affecting his entire existence. Here Brunner maintains the same contours of

---

15. Brunner, *Man in Revolt*, 19.
16. Ibid., 168.
17. Ibid., 164.
18. Ibid., 195.

sin as Kierkegaard does: despite its universal presence, sin never becomes a quality but remains a decision for which each individual is responsible.[19]

Notwithstanding these points of agreement, Brunner seems to diverge on the place of the communal in the treatment of anthropological concerns. Briefly stated, what seems to remain individual in Kierkegaard is treated as individual *and* social in Brunner. Though there is occasional reference in Brunner suggesting that their perceptions cohere,[20] he also indicates that "in the thought of Kierkegaard the idea of 'community' does not get a fair deal, but in principle it is included in his category of 'the individual.'"[21] It is Brunner's insistence on creation by the word of God, both as individuals and as a people, that establishes this distinction.

> In the Creation we are an individualized, articulated unity, one body with many members . . . [W]e are bound together in quite a unique way, in that way which is called mutual responsibility, which is, however, to be understood not as a task but as a gift, as a God-given life, not as an aim to be realized by us in the future, but as our Creation and Beginning in God. God has created us in this whole—so that only and precisely in this being-in-the-whole, in this personal existence which is based upon our relation from and to one another can each become that for which he is destined, a responsible person, a human [being].[22]

This reference raises the question, If we exist only in relation to the other, human as well as divine, what impact does sin have on social existence? How does the misrelation of the self to the self, and of the self to God, affect the relation of the self to an other human self? Brunner's attention to ethics comes to mind again; however, the central issue of the divine–human relationship, not just the human–human, is close at hand. What impact does the disruption of the I–Thou relation have on one's understanding of God and of the self? The following pages will yield some clarification.

---

19. Brunner, *Man in Revolt*, 148. Kierkegaard has much to say on this theme in *CUP*, particularly regarding the ethical as one becoming a subjective individual. See for example Kierkegaard, *CUP*, 133 and context.

20. For example see Brunner, *Man in Revolt*, 140.

21. Ibid., 285–86; see also references to Kierkegaard on 23–24.

22. Ibid., 140–41.

Part III: Transformed Being

Philosophical Fragments

As we have seen, *SD* illustrates well Kierkegaard's fundamental conviction that the authentication of Christian knowledge is found in the integrity of one's existence before God. Though *PF* is a prequel to *SD* in the temporal sequence of Kierkegaard's published works,[23] I have chosen to treat it after *SD* because it is constructive to establish the context of human being and knowing before addressing, as *PF* does, the content of and condition for obtaining knowledge of the truth. The thought-project undertaken by Kierkegaard in *PF* is closely related, if not identical, to Brunner's: to show the utter irreconcilability of Christianity with philosophical idealism. *Fragments'* guiding query is, "Can the truth be learned?"[24] Thulstrup even suggests that *The Mediator* "can be read as a modern edition of *Philosophical Fragments.*"[25]

The unique manner by which Kierkegaard undertakes this project begins with the Socratic, to show that Christianity is interpreted through a Platonic frame of reference.[26] *PF* is a defense of the Christian faith in non-theological language, which highlights the historical event of the incarnation as determinative for human existence. Study of this text will begin with a brief overview of the question, the problem, and the thought-project that *PF* addresses. I will then suggest several points of commonality between Brunner and Kierkegaard on which the latter offers clarification, including the themes of the paradox of the gospel, and the moment and the condition of knowledge.

The Question, Problem, and Thought-project

A key issue around which Kierkegaard's project in *PF* revolves is the problem of "the moment." He has in mind a Christian response to idealism's elevation of eternal truths of reason over truths of temporal existence. He explains idealism's view that truth is eternally present in the individual learner and needs only to be recollected. Truth is not something that the learner receives from outside himself, either from experience or a teacher.

---

23. *PF* was published in 1844 and *SD* in 1849.

24. Kierkegaard, *PF*, 9.

25. Ibid., xcv. Brunner makes this connection as well in his autobiography; see Kegley and Bretall, *Theology of Brunner*, 11.

26. Kierkegaard, *PF*, lxix.

Because the learner possesses access to the eternal truth within himself, there is no temporal moment in which he learns the truth. The significance of the historical for knowledge is rejected as a result. Not only does the gulf remain between truths of reason and truths of experience in the Socratic view, the chasm does not even need to be traversed.

One implication of this system is, that if the truth needs only to be recollected within the learner, the teacher is accidental. It is not the teacher who gives the truth or even who leads the learner to the truth; the teacher merely shows the learner how to recollect that which is already present. The particularity of the teacher in this case is incidental to the learning process, whether they are a parent, a postal worker, or the honorable professor. They are merely the occasion for the learner to recollect and any other teacher could stand in their stead. The moment of recollection is likewise immaterial, for "viewed Socratically, any point of departure in time is *eo ipso* something accidental, a vanishing point, an occasion."[27] The truth is supreme and eternal; the teacher and the moment are accidental and soon forgotten.

While this is clear enough, Kierkegaard is not satisfied with the theory because it cannot account for the learner's misrelation to the eternal that is evidenced by sin. He asserts that the very nature of learning requires one to come to know truth at a particular point in one's own existence. Kierkegaard posits that if truth is eternal and remains outside of time one does not know it, whereas if one knows the truth at some point in time then the truth itself, which is eternal, must come into historical expression at a particular moment. This is why identification of "the moment" is so crucial.

At this point Kierkegaard identifies two weaknesses in idealism's representation of timeless truth. One, if a person already possesses the truth, they cannot say that they come to know it. Because it is always with them there is not only no moment of learning, there is no learning at all, for learning is a movement from not knowing to knowing. Two, if a person does not possess the truth then they cannot seek it because they do not know what it is that they ought to seek. In this case, we are no further ahead in answering our question than we were when we first asked, how does one learn the truth?

Kierkegaard, recognizing this difficulty, suggests another approach based on the historical moment that avoids the weakness of idealism. He maintains that the misrelation of the self to the eternal is evidence that truth does not exist eternally within the human person. The actual condition of

27. Ibid., 11.

the learner is that he is "outside the truth (not coming toward it like a proselyte, but going away from it) or as untruth. He is, then, untruth."²⁸ This is the "preceding state" of the human being in approaching the question of whether or not the truth can be learned, which is the state of sin for which every human being is responsible. Kierkegaard is clear that this untruth is not simply an unhappy state of affairs, but that it is a situation for which the learner is at fault.

A further complication to the learning process is created by this actuality. Not only is the person not in the truth because he is responsible for being in untruth, he does not even possess the condition to learn the truth when he encounters it. The learner cannot set himself free nor teach himself the truth because he has already decided to employ his freedom in the service of unfreedom and therefore can no longer use it in pursuit of the truth. It becomes clear that revelation is required for knowledge of the truth to be possible. A radically new relationship must take place between the eternal and the temporal, completely outside the sinful human condition.

This alternative understanding of the learner demands clarification of the teacher's role. If the learner is in untruth as Kierkegaard contends, the only way he can come to know the truth is if the teacher creates the condition necessary for him to learn. It is not sufficient to give the truth; rather, the teacher must also instill the capacity to learn it, which implies removing sin and guilt. The resultant problem is plain: no human being possesses this capacity, because to create the right condition for the learner to learn requires fundamental transformation of his existence. Reformation of sinful habits is not enough; a transformation of personal being is required. Kierkegaard warns, "[If this] is to take place, it must be done by the god himself."²⁹ God alone is able to transform the human person in such a way that he can exist as himself, free from sin.

Kierkegaard goes on to demonstrate that there is no other way to know the truth apart from divine revelation. "Just as the person who by Socratic midwifery gave birth to himself and in so doing forgot everything else in the world and in a more profound sense owes no human being anything, so also the one who is born again owes no human being anything, but owes the divine teacher everything."³⁰ The moment in time in which this new

---

28. Ibid., 13.
29. Ibid., 14–15.
30. Ibid., 19.

birth takes place is the focus of Kierkegaard's thought-project and is the subject of the remainder of *PF*.

The Paradox and the Moment

It soon becomes clear why Kierkegaard squarely focusses his reflections on "the moment." Behind this subject lies the philosophical discussion of the relationship between revelation and history as expressed in Lessing, or between revelation and reason as treated in Hegel.[31] It is undeniable that a portion of the history of philosophy is playing out in Kierkegaard's mind as he writes. Though space does not permit a textual analysis of *PF*, the following themes are pertinent to Kierkegaard's influence on Brunner.

We begin with what Kierkegaard identifies as the "passion of thought" which is also "the ultimate paradox of thought: to want to discover something that thought itself cannot think." This is the unknown against which human understanding wounds itself and "against which the understanding in its paradoxical passion collides and which even disturbs man and his self-knowledge." What is this unattainable magnet of human longing? It can only be called the god.[32]

The god is foreign to human understanding for two reasons. Firstly, says Kierkegaard, he is "the absolutely different in which there is no distinguishing mark." The category of "the absolutely different" indicates that the knower cannot even imagine that which the god is, for if he could imagine the god, the god would not be utterly unknown. Instead it is the case that the learner cannot even think the absolutely different because the understanding can only think in relation to itself. Kierkegaard explains that, among all the different objects of human understanding including "the prodigious, the ridiculous, etc.," the one thing the mind cannot think is the absolutely different. It is to this category that the god belongs.[33]

The quality of absolute difference pertains not only to the god as distinguished from the human being but the human being as also absolutely

---

31. Thulstrup's introduction notes this background and, though painfully dense in parts, serves as an invaluable guide to the historical dialogue in which Kierkegaard is engaged; see "Commentator's Introduction, by Niels Thulstrup," *PF*, xlv–xcvii. For a more exhaustive consideration of related issues between Hegel and Kierkegaard, see Crites, *In the Twilight of Christendom*.

32. Kierkegaard, *PF*, 37–39.

33. Ibid., 44–45.

different from the god. This second absolute disparity, "caused by the individual himself," is what we already identified as the sin that human beings universally ignore.[34] This threatening and absolute difference between the god and human beings sets the scene and the dramatic color of the human predicament fills our eyes. There appears only one way out if a person is to learn the truth at all: the god must determine within himself to become the teacher, to give the condition and the truth. It is the love of the god who, despite no need within himself, desires to be known by human beings and, thus, to create them as equals to himself.

Critical in Kierkegaard's discourse is this precise moment at which the learner becomes aware of his sin. "Through the moment, the learner becomes untruth; the person who knew himself becomes confused about himself and instead of self-knowledge he acquires the consciousness of sin etc., for just as soon as we assume the moment, everything goes by itself."[35] It is also the moment of offense, though Kierkegaard insists that taking affront in no way proves any understanding of the paradox. On the contrary, it is our inability to grasp with the mind the paradox of the god's coming in the form of a human servant that wounds the pride. It could be said that it is at the very point of being offended by the paradox that the individual has the occasion to know the truth but only if the god has given the condition to do so.

Brunner's Echo

Connections are multiple between Kierkegaard's treatment of the paradox and Brunner's outline of the incarnation. Firstly, Brunner unequivocally identifies the historical event of Jesus Christ as the paradoxical element of the eternal entering time that is so clearly distinguished in Kierkegaard. "That revelation," he reminds us, "the divine manifestation—that is, eternal truth and everlasting salvation—has to be connected with a fact which took place once for all, or—it amounts to the same thing—that we can never approach God directly but only through the Mediator."[36] In Brunner's terms, the mediator is the divine means for human beings to know God.

Secondly, both Kierkegaard and Brunner maintain that the mystery of God-become-flesh offers both the condition and the truth necessary to

---

34. Ibid., 47.
35. Ibid., 51.
36. Brunner, *Mediator*, 42.

know God and one's self. The offense of the gospel is that we cannot reach the eternal of our own efforts. It is not only that reason cannot comprehend this; the bigger problem is "the humiliation of moral and religious self-sufficiency [which] is much greater, because it is far more personal."[37] Both men acknowledge the paradox as an offense to the intellect *and* the spirit (the moral), and that it is only the power of the paradox that can successfully subvert human pride. Brunner calls on Kierkegaard here in appreciation of his extensive treatment of the incarnation as more than an intellectual impossibility as well as the necessity of faith to accept it as truth.

Thirdly, Brunner agrees with Kierkegaard that human reason will exhaust itself in trying to render the paradox logically comprehensible. "When witness is borne to revelation a doubt is raised as to the all-sufficiency of reason, and it raises it at this vital point by the assertion that God, the true and living God, cannot be known through the reason."[38] The role of reason in theological thinking again demands attention. While Kierkegaard and Brunner may employ distinct vocabulary as philosopher and dogmatician, they both undeniably show two things by their own example and affirmation: reason is required to know truth; but it is not reason that apprehends God, who is the truth. Faith bows before the paradox as truth in the absence of intellectual mastery of it.

The following statements on which Brunner and Kierkegaard are both consistent further clarify the impact of sin on human understanding. "The Word of God is the fact," Brunner writes—a fact given to human beings from God, not something that we possess in ourselves to be recollected.[39] Though Brunner does not adopt from Kierkegaard exact terminology on this point, two elements of the latter's thought are discernible. The first is that, if we possessed the divine word within ourselves, God's work in Christ would be redundant. *PF* instead insists that the incarnation is essential to human existence because it is only through the incarnation that we become rightly related to the eternal.

The second element refers to Kierkegaard's explanation of sin's blinding effect. Brunner explains: "This is the fundamental idea in Kierkegaard's book, the *Brocken* [*Fragments*], the point at which sin is recognized as an entity for the theory of knowledge: If man is a sinner then he is not in the truth, then he cannot know the truth, he cannot even know that he is not

---

37. Ibid., 43.
38. Ibid., 42.
39. Ibid., 203.

Part III: Transformed Being

in the truth."[40] In so far as "the moment" is the critical issue in *PF*, we have only just begun to address its significance for the knower. Assuming that the god has come and that the paradox does exist, what is the moment when the learner comes to understand the paradox as the truth? Faith has been mentioned in our treatment of *SD* as the condition necessary for the individual to respond positively to the paradox. It remains to identify what exactly faith is and when it takes place. The god's advent to give both the condition and the truth is surely significant for all people of all times.

Here again we find in Kierkegaard a theme already discovered in Brunner: faith renders the believer contemporary with the incarnation and authenticates belief despite the temporal disparity with the historical event of Jesus Christ. This is the point at which the disciple, be he first- or second-hand, believes in "a historical point of departure for his eternal consciousness, for he is indeed contemporary with the historical event that . . . intends to be the condition for his eternal happiness."[41] Kierkegaard interprets this positive, subjective response to the god-become-servant in these terms: "It occurs when the understanding and the paradox happily encounter each other in the moment, when the understanding steps aside and the paradox gives itself, and the third something, the something in which this occurs (for it does not occur through the understanding, which is discharged, or through the paradox, which gives itself—consequently in something), is that happy passion to which we shall now give a name, although for us it is not a matter of the name. We shall call it *faith*."[42] Herein lies the importance of the moment, when the learner recognizes that the teacher is not merely the occasion for his apprehension of the truth but that the teacher *is* the truth. Moreover, the teacher is none other than the god himself.[43]

Kierkegaard is pressed to clarify that the learner's realization of faith is not the same as Socratic knowledge. He argues that there exists an essential difference between knowledge of the eternal, which cannot accommodate the historical, and historical knowledge, which cannot accommodate the eternal. At this point the reader can hear something of Lessing's distinction between eternal truths and truths of experience, and it is here that the paradox challenges idealism most defiantly. If the paradox is true, then the

---

40. Ibid., 204, n1.
41. Kierkegaard, *PF*, 58.
42. Ibid., 59.
43. Ibid., 55–62.

eternal encounters the temporal in such a way that the historical becomes more than accidental.

The most critical test of the paradox lies at this juncture. It is not only that the eternal has entered time in the god's advent as a human servant, as if this were not absurd enough. It is also the contradiction that the human being "receives the condition in the moment, and, since it is a condition for the understanding of eternal truth, it is *eo ipso* the eternal condition."[44] The giving of the eternal condition transpires in the moment and thus is considered historical because it is only as an historical moment that the human being can receive that which only the god possesses. Furthermore it is only because the god enters time as a human being that the gift can be given. "But then is faith just as paradoxical as the paradox?" Kierkegaard asks. "Quite so. How else could it have its object in the paradox and be happy in its relation to it?"[45]

We thus see that the critical element for understanding the teacher as the god is the divine offering and the individual's reception of the condition in faith. "Faith is not an act of will, for it is always the case that all human willing is efficacious only within the condition . . . But if I do not possess the condition (and we assume this in order not to go back to the Socratic), then all my willing is of no avail, even though, once the condition is given, that which was valid for the Socratic is again valid."[46] It is a mistake to discern passivity here. On the contrary, Kierkegaard undeniably holds to working out one's faith in fear and trembling.[47] His argument is that there is a condition, obtainable only as a gift from God, which is necessary for the exercise of faith.

Receiving this condition is the moment when the learner becomes a follower of Christ and becomes rightly related to the eternal. It is evident, then, that historical contemporaneity with the god-man is not essential for faith, for the condition is not dependent upon a physical encounter with Christ. Because he remains eternal the god is free to give the condition as and when he pleases. Kierkegaard further states that it is not temporal

44. Ibid., 62.
45. Ibid., 65.
46. Ibid., 62–63.
47. Kierkegaard's text *Fear and Trembling* is in reference to Phil 2:12, though it is an exposition of Genesis 22 and Abraham's working out his faith in the event of the binding of Isaac. I have not treated this particular volume here because its focus is on moral philosophy and the relationship between faith and ethics which, while it is relevant to this chapter, is not at its center.

Part III: Transformed Being

proximity that determines greater or lesser contemporaneity, for one can be non-contemporary from the view of faith even while being temporally proximate, and one can be contemporary by faith while being temporally distant. As a result, we see that immediate contemporaneity with the event of the god-man is only the occasion for one to receive the condition, not the stipulation.

Kierkegaard's definition of contemporaneity is one of the more obvious contributions to our treatment of Brunner. Brunner himself discusses the contemporariness of the believer with Christ in Kierkegaardian terms when he contends that it is revelation of Jesus Christ that leads to the "illumination" of the believer's mind so that the believer can indeed recognize this human being, Jesus, as the Christ. It is in this moment that the believer thereby becomes "contemporary" with Jesus in the same sense that the apostles were. Brunner connects this contemporaneity with the witness of the Holy Spirit in the believer who is the seal of what is referred to in *PF* as the condition of faith.[48]

Brunner concurs with Kierkegaard that the testimony of the first generation serves as an occasion for subsequent learners to become disciples. Although Kierkegaard addresses the issue of first-hand contemporaneity with Christ, it is not his purpose to treat the specific issue of any qualitative significance between their witness and another's. What matters most to him and to Brunner is that, whether for the first or the four-hundred-and-first generation, it is only ever the god himself who gives the condition of faith.

Concluding Unscientific Postscript

We turn our attention now to what is perhaps Kierkegaard's most famed volume, *Concluding Unscientific Postscript*. This lengthy oeuvre takes its place in this chapter for the convergence it expresses between the individual, despairing subject in *Sickness unto Death* and the message of the Christian faith philosophically expressed in *PF*.[49] The result is Kierkegaard's preoccupation in *Postscript* of the process of becoming and remaining a Christian. The key question he addresses in these pages, which every human being

---

48. Brunner, *Revelation and Reason*, 170. In n10 on the same page Brunner make reference to "*Philosophical Fragments*, ch. 4, and *Training in Christianity*, ch. 4."

49. *CUP* is not a literal convergence of *SD* and *PF*, as *SD* was not published until 1849, with *PF* and *CUP* preceding it.

must answer when confronted with the paradox of the Christian faith, is, What is *my* relationship to this truth?

This subjective concern of personal response to the Christian faith is often transmuted into an objective one, both inside the church as well as outside of it. The question thus becomes, Is Christianity true? This is the issue that Kierkegaard identified in *PF* to which *CUP* is the postscript. "Can a historical point of departure be given for an eternal consciousness; how can such a point of departure be of more than historical interest; can an eternal happiness be built on historical knowledge?"[50] Kierkegaard laid this investigation to rest in *PF* by outlining a response in non-theological terms. Although he adds a brief sequel to it in part 1 of *CUP*, part 2 deals more extensively with the subjective corollary of the objective issue, which is "simply stated" by his pseudonym as "How can I, Johannes Climacus, share in the happiness that Christianity promises?"[51] Our present focus falls on two themes uniquely expressed in *CUP* that are especially relevant to Brunner's work: faith as paradoxical-religiousness and truth as subjectivity.

Faith as Paradoxical-Religiousness

It was established in *Sickness Unto Death* that the absolute end of the human person is his own eternal happiness. The speculative point of view that dominates modernity's interpretation and presentation of the Christian faith ignores this personal end. Though Western religion of recent centuries is based on the presupposition that "everyone" is a Christian, Kierkegaard asserts that this actually ignores the knower's eternal happiness that is at the heart of the Christian faith.

The historical moment was presented in *PF* as the beginning of the Christian's transformation from despair to happiness, a theme that is developed further throughout *CUP*. The central issue here is the subjective relation between the knower and Christianity. "Christianity cannot be observed objectively," Kierkegaard argues, "precisely because it wants to lead the subject to the ultimate point of his subjectivity, and when the subject is thus properly positioned, he cannot tie his eternal happiness to speculative thought."[52] The problem is not in establishing the truth of Christianity as objective; this cannot be done because of the nature of history, as we will

50. Kierkegaard, *PF*, 1.
51. Kierkegaard, *CUP*, 17.
52. Ibid., 57.

soon see. The difficulty lies instead in the misunderstanding of the relation between the subject and the truth.

Christianity, as Kierkegaard understands it, focuses on personal existence before God and this can only take place in subjective becoming. It requires inwardness and transformation, not abstract speculation. The church's appeal to two thousand years of religion as "proof" for the truth of Christianity has exacerbated a mistaken interpretation. For this reason Kierkegaard regards the question of the *what* of Christianity as misguided. The answer to the question of the truth of Christianity can only be offered in terms of the *how* of the individual's response of faith. He explains that the issue is "not to decide *what* Christianity is but *whether I* am a Christian."[53] Before we approach a discussion of the *how* of faith, though, we need to address the nature and role of history. The first reason for this is that an historical event is at the heart of the incarnation paradox. The second is Kierkegaard's dialogue with numerous philosophical voices, particularly that of Lessing.

We have already stated that the temporal-eternal dialectic is precisely the offense of Christianity: we cannot reach beyond our temporal existence to attain the eternal, so the eternal one enters history in order that we might exist in the fullness of our design. To know the eternal in the temporal is a paradox that cannot be comprehended in any other way. Kierkegaard concludes that we cannot know the eternal God in the fullness of his eternal being; we can only know him in the *incognito* of his historic event. He thus summarizes the heart of Christianity as the message that "that the eternal truth" has become an historical person in such a way that he is actually "indistinguishable" from all other humans as a person in time and space.[54] This is the absurdity of the paradox to which the gospels testify. Our present focus is on the role of the historical event at the heart of the story and its status as truth. Notwithstanding the certainty that faith affords the Christian,[55] the uncertainty of the paradox is based on the view that history is communicated only through approximation.

---

53. Ibid., 607 (emphasis mine).

54. Ibid., 210.

55. Kierkegaard recognizes a kind of certainty to faith, even though it is not the certainty of modern qualifications. For example, the Christian acknowledges speculative thought "with suspicion, lest it trick him out of the certitude of faith (which at every moment has within itself the infinite dialectic of uncertainty) into indifferent objective knowledge." Ibid., 55.

Here Kierkegaard reminds us of Lessing's rejection of historical realities as agents of eternal truths, for how can something absolute like eternal happiness be contingent upon something as accidental as an historical individual? Kierkegaard maintains that the Christian story does not seek to objectively communicate truth thereby rejecting Lessing's conclusion that eternal truths cannot be communicated through historical events. Establishing the objective certainty of the Christian story is not Kierkegaard's primary concern in *CUP*. Instead, the more pressing need is to respond in faith to the Christianity his readers otherwise take for granted. In this way his priority remains the subjective relation of the knower to the incarnation.

Even though for Lessing there is no direct correlation between experiential truth and eternal truth of reason, he does not deny the potential reliability of historical reports as attesting to actual events. What he does reject is that such historical statements can communicate truth as *sub specie aeterni*. According to Kierkegaard, Lessing does not negate the validity of belief in miracles and prophecies for those who are contemporary to these events, but he holds that those who come after these events do not believe as the first witnesses did. The import of Lessing's reasoning is this: that which is true religiously must be true universally because it is not possible to have revelation of religious truth in particular events of history. He argues that the nature of the historical and the nature of the eternal are such that a leap is required across "the ugly broad ditch" that lies between them. Because the historical is contingent, no contingent truth can accurately communicate eternal reality. Lessing's verdict is that the witness of the New Testament cannot be accepted as communicating eternal truths apart from such a jump, making the events recorded therein an insufficient basis for knowledge.[56]

Modernity's pursuit of eternal truth *á la* Lessing hurtles toward the prize of producing measurable, conclusive systems of universals that stand over and above historical contingencies. It is a most seductive aim and Kierkegaard sardonically admits, "I am as willing as anyone to fall down in worship before the system if I could only catch a glimpse of it. So far I have not succeeded, and although I do have young legs, I am almost worn out by running from Herod to Pilate."[57] Both Lessing and the modern systematician refer to a continual striving after an incomplete truth-system. Though there is clearly a striving in the Christian life, it is not towards a system but

---

56. Ibid., 96–103.
57. Ibid., 107.

towards becoming fully oneself before God in suffering. Kierkegaard insists that the truth of the Christian story evades objective calculation because it originates in the life and death of the God-man, not in philosophical rumination. Christianity also shows up the heretofore futile attempt of a universal "system," disclosing the vanity and impotence of the systematician's quest pursued in ignorance of his own existence.

The point that Kierkegaard establishes in this contradistinction is that, while "a logical system can be given," "a system of existence [*Tilværelsens System*] cannot be given."[58] With Hegel in mind Kierkegaard continues: "In a logical system, nothing may be incorporated that has a relation to existence, that is not indifferent to existence. The infinite advantage that the logical, by being the objective, possesses over all other thinking is in turn, subjectively viewed, restricted by its being a hypothesis, simply because it is indifferent to existence understood as actuality."[59] In other words, logical systems disregard existence because they do not allow for the movement from non-being to being that is characteristic of all life.

What is the conclusion? Kierkegaard asserts that all logical systems are indifferent to existence. They cannot accommodate the process of becoming, the dialectic of negative and positive, the movement from non-being to being, the temporal-eternal tension. It is for this reason that a system of existence is impossible, ridiculous, and laughable. There is no person who could arrive at a final conclusion because he himself is in the process of becoming. He cannot abstract himself into eternal categories by which to posit a definitive set of truths.

A serious problem results. The reflection of the person who ignores his own existence becomes abstracted in such a way that his thinking becomes fundamentally dissociated from reality and he becomes "absentminded." Herein lies Kierkegaard's critique of modern speculative thought. It has "forgotten in a kind of world-historical absentmindedness . . . what it means that we, you and I and he, are human beings, each one on his own."[60] Existence is subsumed by objective reflection, thus ignoring the differentiation that existence creates between the knower and that which is known. Kierkegaard insists that this space between the subject and object, between thought and being, must be respected if we are accurately to

---

58. Ibid., 109, 118.
59. Ibid., 110.
60. Ibid., 120–21.

perceive reality. The historical, personal existence of the knower is the fixed boundary to the object-subject relation.

This brings us back to the paradox of the incarnation. Is knowledge of God possible? What happens when we encounter the eternal God in our temporal existence? Kierkegaard not only maintains that such encounter can happen, he further explains the absolute difference between the god and the human individual as the contingency of human existence on the absolute existence of God. We could hardly credit Kierkegaard with originality on this point given that it is a central tenet of the Christian faith since the apostles, who understood that it is in Christ in whom "we live and move and have our being" (Acts 17:28). His particular concern is how we pursue our eternal happiness based on this contingency. The mirage of self-sufficiency in which most people live reflects their absolute difference from God, as well as their indifference towards him. This is the problem of sin that must be addressed if one is to know the paradox of the eternal god in time. The condition that rectifies the problem, says Kierkegaard, is offered in the life, death, and resurrection of Jesus Christ.

How does transformation of the individual's sinful nature happen? Here we are dealing with what Kierkegaard labels as the various stages of personal maturation, from the aesthetic to the ethical to ethico-religiousness, culminating in paradoxical-religiousness.[61] It is in this final stage that the individual ventures everything in order to be absolutely committed to his eternal happiness. Kierkegaard's next question is, Why do so few people attempt this venture and even fewer actually succeed? Lessing's shadow looms large over the answer. Idealism views the historical as an approximation, which, for moderns utterly committed to pursuing the truth as objective, is an insult to our intelligence. Even at the expense of self-awareness, we much prefer to possess truth in a system, as an owner his bird, caged in the lounge to be admired by all the Sunday visitors.

The absurdity of Christianity becomes clearer when it is recognized apart from and as incompatible with any logical system, whether philosophical or doctrinal. It *is* a contradiction that the individual should venture his eternal happiness on a singular historical event. Nevertheless, such is the invitation of the Christian faith and, within the context of dialectical human existence, it is the only way to know God. It follows that the relationship of the knower to this paradox is of an entirely different nature than

---

61. Kierkegaard treats these stages in prodigious length, but the particulars are not the focus of the present study which is why they are not expanded on here.

that of speculative thought. It is a relation of faith in which truth is subjectivity. Kierkegaard writes, "Faith is the contradiction between the infinite passion of inwardness and the objective uncertainty." This is the only way to exist before God as oneself. "If I am able to apprehend God objectively, I do not have faith; but because I cannot do this, I must have faith."[62] The invitation of the gospel is to venture not only one's intellect but also one's being and becoming on the veracity of God's revelation.

What impact does faith have on our understanding of God's redemptive activity in the world? Most importantly faith does not cajole us into the mindless parroting of doctrine. Instead, the goal of faith is to lead us into the transformation of our personal existence before God. This indicates a second kind of paradox in Kierkegaard's outline. He explains that "the eternal, essential truth, that is, the truth that is related essentially to the existing person by pertaining essentially to what it means to exist . . . is a paradox. Nevertheless, the eternal, essential truth is itself not at all a paradox, but it is a paradox by being related to an existing person."[63] The paradoxical nature of the truth resides not just in the mystery of God becoming human but also in its relationship to the knower.

This is the venture that Kierkegaard calls the "existence-contradiction" which is "an existence-communication."[64] The knower's relation to the truth of the incarnation is necessarily subjective. It is not an aberration of an objective relation, for an objective relation to the reality of the incarnation is impossible. One must believe that God entered time and belief is at odds with objective certainty. We have already seen how thinking is considered higher than being for the speculative enterprise. A speculative thinker "does not base his relation to the eternal on his existing in time," and he altogether dissociates his subjective passion from objective apprehension of the truth. Faith, in contrast, results in a "paradoxical accentuation of existing" in which the knower, "at the peak of his subjective passion (in his concern for an eternal happiness)," bases his commitment to eternal happiness on the historical, which he can know only approximately.[65]

Kierkegaard emphasizes a complementary element to this treatment of the non-systematic and subjective nature of faith. He suggests that it is only as an individual that one responds to the paradox. There is no recourse

---

62. Ibid., 204.
63. Ibid., 205.
64. Ibid., 379–80.
65. Ibid., 574–76.

to another person's decision about the god-man nor to any prefabricated religious position nor to any philosophical "-ism." Existence is ultimately personal being. Because the paradox concerns existence, it is only as an individual that the knower can respond. "The pathway comes into existence for the single individual and closes up behind him." We are not to attempt to travel roads others have taken, because every road to becoming a religious subject is strictly individual. "If the subjective individual himself has not worked himself through and out of his objectivity, all appeal to another individuality will be only a misunderstanding," concludes Kierkegaard.[66] What results from such a faith relationship with the paradox is true individuality, or in the words of *SD*, to exist as oneself before God.

Truth as Subjectivity

It is becoming clear why Kierkegaard's burning question about Christianity for his time is not its objective veracity but the relationship of the individual to its paradox. One of the problems with a speculative method is that it requires the knower to remain unaffected by his knowledge. It views the thinker as something accidental and insists that he exist apart from the process of becoming, apart from himself as a temporal-eternal being. In this way objective thinking renders the knower indifferent to that which he seeks to know. This indifference is contradictory to his passionate concern for his eternal happiness that characterizes human existence.

Such a dispassionate pursuit of knowledge that abstracts reflection from existence creates a logical impossibility. So-called "pure thinking" is comical in Kierkegaard's view, for how can a person purport to understand anything if he does not know the one object to which is he is most closely related? Kierkegaard posits that "to conclude existence from thinking is, then, a contradiction, because thinking does just the opposite and takes existence away from the actual and thinks it by annulling it, by transposing it into possibility."[67] This is the gross delusion of *cogito ergo sum*: it requires the knower to abstract himself from existence, which is the very thing that his knowing is meant to explain.

In contrast Kierkegaard insists that only the particular exists; the abstract remains un-actualized. Because the Christian faith is preoccupied with this specific existence of the individual before God, the subject's

---

66. Ibid., 66–67.
67. Ibid., 317.

relationship to Christianity cannot be objective. "The decision rests in the subject," Kierkegaard argues; "the appropriation is the paradoxical inwardness that is specifically different from all other inwardness. Being a Christian is defined not by the 'what' of Christianity but by the 'how' of the Christian. This 'how' can fit only one thing, the absolute paradox."[68] Subjectivity, or inwardness, is the only way for the paradox to be understood. Truth becomes appropriation, thus transforming the knower in the actuality of his being.

This is the uniqueness of the subjective thinker who balances "imagination, feeling, and dialectics in impassioned existence-inwardness."[69] It is as a subjective person that the individual exists before God in his dialectical particularity. Roberts's summary of the role of feelings in Kierkegaard's presentation of Christianity is constructive and consistent with the thesis of *CUP*. He writes,

> Christianity, whatever else it may be, is a set of emotions. It is love of God and neighbor, grief about one's own waywardness, joy in the merciful salvation of our God, gratitude, hope, and peace. To be a Christian is to have these and other emotions, and so if it happens that I do not love God and my neighbor, I do not find my sins abhorrent and find joy in my redemption, if I am not grateful, hopeful, and at peace with God and myself, then it follows quite clearly that I am not a Christian, though I was born into a Christian family and reared in the bosom of the Church, am baptized and confirmed and willing in good conscience to affirm the articles of the Creed.[70]

Kierkegaard identifies the "medium" in which thinking, imagination, and feeling are held in tension as subjective existence, and it is the subjective thinker who attends to this dialectic of the intellectual and emotional. "The subjective thinker, therefore, has also esthetic passion and ethical passion, whereby concretion is gained. All existence-issues are passionate, because existence, if one becomes conscious of it, involves passion." Unlike the speculative thinker, his purpose is "to *understand himself in existence*."[71] Thus, the goal of the Christian in Kierkegaardian terms is to know and to be himself before God. It is in direct opposition to the spirit of the age, which

---

68. Ibid., 610–11.
69. Ibid., 350.
70. Roberts, "Kierkegaard on Becoming an 'Individual,'" 133–34.
71. Kierkegaard, *CUP*, 350–51.

compels the individual to lose himself in the crowd in order to avoid the harsh wind of despair that cuts to the soul.

This dialectical inwardness retains a special significance for Christianity. It is required for what Kierkegaard describes as the two tasks of faith: (1) "to watch for and at every moment to make the discovery of improbability, the paradox" in order to (2) "hold it fast with the passion of inwardness."[72] Speculative thought is incapable of affirming the illogic of the paradox; only subjectivity can recognize the truth of the eternal God coming to us as a human being. It is for this reason that Christianity cannot be known apart from the inwardness of subjectivity. Kierkegaard continues: "Christianity is spirit; spirit is inwardness; inwardness is subjectivity; subjectivity is essentially passion, and at its maximum an infinite, personally interested passion for one's eternal happiness."[73] When subjectivity is discredited and replaced by the frigid demands of objectivity, passion is forced out along with any interest in one's eternal happiness. The requirement of decision vis-à-vis the truth is made redundant and personal responsibility is avoided. This is the catastrophe that speculative thought makes of faith.

Brunner's Echo

As with *SD* and *PF*, reflections of *CUP* are readily visible in Brunner's work. The ridiculousness of objective thought unveiled in *CUP* is mirrored, for example, in *Man in Revolt*, where Brunner writes, "The thinker who starts his process of thought from the ultimate principles of the *ratio*, transforms the real dialectic of historical reality into a merely logical sham dialectic of concepts."[74] Both Brunner and Kierkegaard argue that queries about revelation can only be asked from within the Christian faith as a believer because theology cannot be done apart from this understanding of revelation that is appropriated by faith.[75] We are once again reminded of Kierkegaard's insistence that the the question is not, What is the Christian faith? but, What is *my relationship* to the Christian faith?

Kierkegaard has shown that, when truth is pursued objectively, speculative results lead away from the knowledge of faith. Religious and philosophical systems may offer the means of quantifying knowledge,

---

72. Ibid., 233.
73. Ibid., 33.
74. Brunner, *Man in Revolt*, 438. See reference in Kierkegaard, *CUP*, n1.
75. Brunner, *Theology of Crisis*, 37–38.

but they leave the knower ignorant of his own existence. This is not true knowing. Brunner corroborates Kierkegaard's conclusion when he rejects all "-isms" as presenting a distorted view of human existence; all "-isms," that is, save existentialism, which he suggests succeeds in presenting "a penetrating view of man which has no rival."[76] This illustrates in a different manner how Brunner directly builds on Kierkegaard's material, specifically regarding speculative systems that are divorced from existence. Because the aesthetic does not require ethical expression, it remains in the conceptual realm. Such ideals can be believed without the knower's behavior being affected, as Kierkegaard puts it, "in the living room" of his life.[77] Persons who remain Christians in the same sense that they are Realists or Idealists or Communists do not have to change how they live as long as they recite the right discourse. Kierkegaard describes this as aesthetic existence.

Brunner agrees that truly religious being requires transformation that both the aesthetic and the ethico-religious avoid. Again in *Man in Revolt* he writes in Kierkegaardian terms: "The pre-Christian human being is not personal in the same sense as the post-Christian human being, because he does not know of personal being in the same way, just as he has not a fully historical existence because he is not aware of the historical in the same full sense."[78] It is only in relation to God in Jesus that we are aware of the temporal-eternal dialectic of our humanity. Encounter with the historical Christ confronts us with our sin and our responsibility for it, and generates a new awareness of existence that leads to personal decision for or against the God-man.

Kierkegaard speaks of this finite-infinite tension as lived in the immediacy of existence through the contradiction between absolute and relative ends. Faith is to remain absolutely orientated towards one's eternal happiness in the immediacy of existence. Although he agrees with this view of faith's relationship with the temporal-eternal dialectic, Brunner's conclusion is not as categorically rigid. He states in *Dogmatics III*, "It is therefore wrong to describe faith as in itself the 'right,' the truly human mode of man's existence. Of course, just by reason of the tension between 'now

---

76. Brunner, *Man in Revolt*, 47.

77. This phrase refers to a long and compelling—even convicting—passage in Kierkegaard, *CUP*, 464 and following, which addresses the unique expression of each Christian's "*essential* expression of existential pathos" (133). It is not pursuing world-significance (another valuable subject) but in being absolutely orientated in hidden inwardness towards one's eternal happiness that leads to true knowing and true being.

78. Brunner, *Man in Revolt*, 456.

already' and 'not yet,' faith is the most inward form of existence that we know (Kierkegaard)."[79] The difference with Kierkegaard's understanding of faith is one of emphasis and not of substance, for Brunner's focus here is the eschatological hope that faith one day will be sight. In this particular context Brunner is dealing with the present reality of faith that is as concerned about the future realization of God's love. As far as faith's expression in the present is concerned, however, Brunner remains solely focused on the paradox of the divine incognito.

In another place Brunner reiterates the particular Kierkegaardian understanding of faith that we have explored in these pages. *The Divine Imperative* records this observation: "When Kierkegaard ventures to make the statement: 'the subject is the truth' . . . he always implies that the objective correlate of 'existential' faith is the 'paradox,' the 'foolishness of the Cross.'"[80] The paradox of the eternal entering time is the counterpart to the inwardness of faith. The historical event of Jesus Christ remains the foundation for personal existence before God.

A question ensues. How is theology to speak about the significance of the paradox for existence, as this reference would suggest? This is one of the difficulties with which Brunner's methodology seeks to come to terms. While we leave a more extensive treatment of the question for the conclusion of this chapter, here I record Brunner's appreciation of Kierkegaard towards this end, noted in *Revelation and Reason*. "But just as the mystery of the Incarnation is followed by our theological reflection upon it, in order that we may understand it and not confuse it with something else, so it is with the relation between revelation and reason in faith. We will allow the mystery—in all reverence—to remain a mystery: but that does not exempt us from the necessity of making an effort to understand as much of it as we can, in order that we may learn what it means to meet man with the Gospel exactly where he is, and not to try to find him where he is not."[81]

Whether in nineteenth century Denmark or twentieth century Switzerland or twenty-first century North America, there remains the need for a renewed understanding of what it means to be Christian. From a faith perspective, modernity has misled us with its logicians, systematicians, and objective theologians alike. Brunner's evaluation is plain when he claims,

---

79. Brunner, *Dogmatics III*, 343.

80. Brunner, *Divine Imperative*, 591.

81. Brunner, *Revelation and Reason*, 415. See n7 reference to Kierkegaard, *CUP*, 187.

Part III: Transformed Being

"The last redoubt of the enemy of faith . . . is born from our claim that reason is the measure of all truth," reason that is "spoiled by rationalism."[82] It is not logic or systems or doctrine that makes the gospel truly good news, but the ever-living presence of Jesus Christ whom we meet in the subjectivity of personal existence.

PART TWO: IMPORT FOR THEOLOGY

We have considered how the fullness of human existence is realized when, "in relating itself to itself and in willing to be itself, the self rests transparently in the power that established it."[83] We have also explored how every expression of human being falls short of this resting, resulting in despair. The landscape surveyed from the precipice of sin is bleak, for "what error needs most is always the last thing it thinks of."[84] Idealism's perspective, as Kierkegaard has argued, remains ignorant of this painful predicament for it does not recognize the impact of sin on the mind. Yet from a Christian viewpoint, knowledge comes only through the subjectivity of faith. The only person who can escape despair's distortion of reality, says Kierkegaard, is the Christian who has been cured of despair. How does this reversal of despair occur, and what are its effects for one's knowledge of one's self and of God?

Rejection of Speculative Thought in the Christian Faith

At the heart of Kierkegaard's epistemology lies faith. Intellectual comprehension on its own is not reliable when it comes to knowing the self because at the heart of Christian anthropology is paradox and offense. Paradox escapes logical resolution, offense irritates human pride, and both are thus repelled by a mind in despair. That which is beyond comprehending must be believed, for who can seize with human mind that he is known and loved by God? To suggest the opposite is not only ridiculous, it is unethical.[85]

Herein lies the scandal of human existence, of sin, and of Christianity according to Kierkegaard, "that as an individual human being a person

---

82. Brunner, *Theology of Crisis*, 43, 44.
83. Kierkegaard, *SD*, 14, 131.
84. Ibid., 92.
85. Ibid., 99.

is directly before God and consequently, as a corollary, that a person's sin should be of concern to God." This too-good-to-be-believed paradox "is Christianity's weapon against all speculation."[86] On the one hand, speculation that takes this truth into account is no longer speculation but is faith. On the other hand, speculation that disregards this truth veers off into conjecture.

The Knowledge of Faith

The individual is the point at which speculation must desist and the particular paradox of existence must take over. Kierkegaard argues that the weight and import of sin lies in its existence in an individual sinner. Speculation does not accommodate the individual, though, which requires us to ignore both the sin and the sinner and to speak only in generalities. Because it is thus antipodal to Christianity's point of departure, Kierkegaard affords no space for conjecture that distracts from revelation. In other words,

> speculation, which talks itself out of paradoxes, snips off a little bit from both sides and thereby gets along more easily—it does not make sin quite so positive—but nevertheless cannot get it through its head that sin is to be completely forgotten. But Christianity, which was the first to discover the paradoxes, is as paradoxical on this point as possible; it seems to be working against itself by establishing sin so securely as a position that now it seems to be utterly impossible to eliminate it again—and then it is this very Christianity that by means of the Atonement wants to eliminate sin as completely as if it were drowned in the sea.[87]

The absurdity of grace remains the measure of what it means to be human. "*Ne quid nimis* [nothing too much]" as the golden rule of human wisdom leads away from faith.[88] As a measure of mediocrity, this rule hedges its bets by avoiding offense and guaranteeing knowledge through dispassionate theories about the mass human. In contrast, Kierkegaard asserts that Christianity does just the opposite in its insistence on the particulars of what it means to be human and therefore on offense. This offense is the cost of being one's self, not in despair but at rest in the loving power of God. For Kierkegaard at least it is not too dear a price to pay for overcoming the

---

86. Ibid., 83.
87. Ibid., 100.
88. Ibid., 86.

sickness unto death. No conjecture, no matter how fantastic, can raise the individual to the same heights as God's favor in Christ. The fact that *I exist before God* is the message of the Christian faith that no objective expression can convey.

Two Ramifications

The consequences of such statements are far-reaching and require serious consideration. Though not unique to Kierkegaard or Brunner, two implications draw our attention to their reflection in the latter's work already treated: the rejection of all proofs for the divine being[89] and the rejection of the doctrine of infallibility.

Kierkegaard is categorical in his rejection of all proofs for the divine being. It is better to "mock God outright," he says, than to "demonstrate the existence of God." For how can we demonstrate the existence of that which already exists unless we ignore that being's existence, in which case why would we want to prove it?[90] We are immediately reminded that Kierkegaard countenances no discourse about the god that strays from "the moment." In a similar tone Brunner also rejects attempts to prove the divine being for even to suggest this enterprise is to fall away from faith.[91] To abandon belief for the structural security of logic is foolishness, for what could be more absurd than the creature objectively "proving" his creator's existence?

We encounter an equally penetrating response from both men to the question of the nature of Scripture. Brunner's view has significant parallels with Kierkegaard's critique of speculative philosophy. As discussed in our brief overview of demythologization, the objective researcher pursues the "greatest historical reliability" of the Bible as a way of getting close to the objective truth of the story.[92] Though this is Kierkegaard's phrase, it is entirely apropos in reference to Brunner's analysis of the subject. Brunner's warning now rings in our ears in Kierkegaardian overtones: when intellectual analysis is dissociated from faith, we pursue constructs of our own

---

89. As Brunner posits in *Dogmatics I*, when faith refers to the existence of God it is based on his revelation and there is no need for a "proof" of divine being; *Dogmatics I*, 149–50.

90. Kierkegaard, *CUP*, 545.

91. Brunner, *Dogmatics III*, 264; see also Kierkegaard, *PF*, 31.

92. Kierkegaard, *CUP*, 24.

making, not the paradox of the incarnation. As a result, faith becomes a hazard in the pursuit of certainty instead of the very key to knowing God and one's self in relation to him.

In the length and breadth of their respective writings their terminology on this subject differs. Brunner readily speaks of revelation, for example, whereas the term is present only implicitly in Kierkegaard. That said, what is significant is that both retain the historical event of Jesus Christ as the center around which theological thinking must revolve. It is this event that transforms our human existence and that enables personal encounter with God (in Brunnerian terms) and the passionate pursuit of one's absolute happiness before God (in Kierkegaardian language).

The nature of the biblical witness to the incarnation naturally requires attention. Recognizing the human element of Scripture, both men affirm the necessity of the response of faith to Christ as part and parcel of divine revelation. Kierkegaard reiterates the danger of idealism's rejection of the subjectivity of historical account. He contends "that even with the most stupendous learning and perseverance . . . one would never arrive at anything more than an approximation, and that there is an essential misrelation between that and a personal, infinite interestedness in one's own eternal happiness."[93] The eternal enters time so that our despair might be transformed, and there is nothing more subjective than personal transformation to which the gospels testify.

Kierkegaard's difficulty with "critical theological scholarship" is that it seeks to foster faith in the Bible. He warns about the risk of founding one's eternal happiness on the doctrine of infallibility, which could result in the loss of faith's subjectivity; for when something is considered uncertain about the Scriptures, as suggested in Luther's rejection of the book of James, the doctrine is falsified and one's happiness is compromised. When we rely on doctrine to protect faith, we relinquish the subjective pursuit of eternal happiness in exchange for objective certainty. Sadly, though, this is no certainty at all because it is exactly the existential concern that is the goal of God's work in Christ, not the demands of objectivity.[94]

We offer Kierkegaard the final word on the rejection of speculative thought for faith. "For whose sake is the demonstration [of certainty] conducted?" he asks. "Faith does not need it, indeed, must even consider it its enemy . . . When faith begins to cease to be faith, then the demonstration

---

93. Ibid., 24.
94. Ibid., 27.

is made necessary in order to enjoy general esteem from unbelief." What results when certainty takes over? It is ridiculous to present oneself as absolutely and objectively convinced of the veracity of an approximation. Kierkegaard cautions that when one does profess such certainty, "zealotism ensues. Every iota is of infinite value for the infinitely interested passion. The fault inheres not in the infinitely interested passion but in this, that its object has become an approximation-object."[95] This remonstrance resonates with Brunner's position on the doctrine of infallibility, reflecting Kierkegaard's suspicion of that position that would declare absolute certainty about the paradox that is only knowable by faith.

Implications for Dogmatics

The rejection of proofs for the divine being and of the doctrine of infallibility are two readily perceived consequences of truth as the subjectivity of personal encounter. There are more far-reaching ramifications for theological methodology, however, two of which draw our attention now.

Content and Communication

If the paradox escapes definition, and if at the very moment we think we have explained it we cease to understand it, what is the proper use of theological language? How does the mystery of revelation affect the goal of believing thinking and the task of communicating that thinking? What light do the preceding pages shed on Brunner's methodology? I posited in chapter 2 that theological language that eclipses the narrative of Scripture eventually leads into the hinterland of speculation, distracting from the historical event of Jesus Christ.

An analysis of theological semantics might be tempting, though such a study is neither Brunner's nor Kierkegaard's concern. Nevertheless there is one element of communication dynamics on which Kierkegaard comments. He maintains that one of the distinctives of "the subjective existing thinker" is that he "is aware of the dialectic of communication."[96] If truth is inwardness, the subjective thinker is focused on existing in his reflection specifically for himself, without concern for its impact on others. He

---

95. Ibid., 30–31.
96. Ibid., 72.

"invests everything in the process of becoming and omits the result . . . partly because he as existing is continually in the process of becoming, as is every human being who has not permitted himself to be tricked into becoming objective, into inhumanly becoming speculative thought." The objective thinker, on the other hand, is interested in that which is common with all humanity—replication, repetition, and even cheating "by copying and reeling off the results and answers."[97] Subjective understanding of his personal existence distracts from the quest for objectivity.

There is no such thing as direct communication of subjective knowledge according to Kierkegaard. Subjectivity is secretive by nature whereas objective knowing seeks the kind of certainty requiring public accord. In this matter we discover a difference between subjective and objective reflection that is present both in the thinking itself and in its communication. He comments, "wherever the subjective is of importance in knowledge and appropriation is therefore the main point, communication is a work of art; it is doubly reflected, and its first form is the subtlety that the subjective individuals must be held devoutly apart from one another and must not run coagulatingly together in objectivity."[98]

Kierkegaard explains that this reality has to do with the complexity of the "duplexity [*Dobbelthed*] of thought-existence." Communication takes place in the immediacy of existence between the speaker and the listener. Even in this directness, however, the thought-existence cannot be communicated as it is because correlation between the words spoken and those heard is only approximate. Given the intricacy of this "double-reflection," the religious thinker "readily perceives that direct communication is a fraud toward God . . . , a fraud toward himself . . . , a fraud toward another human being . . . , a fraud that brings him into contradiction with his entire thought." Objective thinking, on the other hand, is unconcerned with subjectivity, inwardness, and appropriation. It is "aware only of itself and is therefore no communication, at least no artistic communication, inasmuch as it would always be required to think of the receiver and to pay attention to the form of the communication in relation to the receiver's misunderstanding."[99] This is direct communication and it disregards the double-thinking of subjectivity.

---

97. Ibid., 73.
98. Ibid., 79.
99. Ibid., 74–76.

Part III: Transformed Being

Why cannot subjective knowledge of faith be communicated directly? We recall that the goal of paradoxical-religiousness is not mastery of the object but appropriation of the paradox. That which the subject knows transforms him in a manner that is unique to his personal being. We return full circle to Kierkegaard's insistence in *PF*, that it is *how* one becomes and remains a Christian that matters. We come to see that, insofar as the *how* is individual, it "remains a secret for everyone who is not through himself doubly reflected in the same way, but that this is the essential form of truth means that this cannot be said in any other way." To insist on the direct communication of the paradox of faith is "obtuseness."[100]

What has been outlined so far possesses significant implications for dogmatics. Kierkegaard's examination of this double-reflection is visible in Brunner's identification of the difference between first-person language of prayer and third-person language of dogmatics. At first glance we are treading ground already deeply furrowed by historical theology for it is readily recognized that there is a difference between devotional discourse and proclamation, catechesis, or polemics. The particular significance for this study is that the subjective language of faith in the knower must be the starting point (in the apostolic witness) and the overriding concern (in the personal affirmation of *Kyrios Christos*) of dogmatics, no matter what else transpires in the academic middle. For Brunner, truth as encounter is the boundary to theological thinking. Therefore, what is inconsistent with the subjectivity of faith does not belong to theology. The conclusion drawn here is one that has been repeated throughout these pages: all theological reflection must be centered on the historical event of God's self-revelation. In practice this intends every topic of research to find its source and its resolution in God's intervention in human history, or to be left as mystery. This also means that our questions, no matter how personal they feel, must be rooted in God's salvation story as well.

Let us return to the subject of the Trinity to flesh out an example. In worship of Father, Son, and Spirit a person might naturally be led to meditate on the Trinity. According to Kierkegaard, and also Brunner, the person is in the realm of wonder that properly belongs to the subjectivity of faith as he worships the one who is completely other. It is therefore possible to marvel at the mystery of the Trinity without falling into conjecture about how the divine persons interrelate.[101] In contrast, speculative theol-

---

100. Ibid., 79.

101. Karen Kilby suggests this in a thought-provoking manner in "Aquinas, the

ogy disregards the boundary that mystery creates in order to theorize the conversations, emotions, and qualities of the intra-triune life. The results of such reflection might be fascinating and possibly even up-building for some when applied as a model for the self, community, or the church. Yet the difficulty is that such speculation runs the risk of eclipsing what God has revealed to us in Christ. If Brunner and Kierkegaard are right, the point at which we transcend the historical moment is the point at which we must temper our objective explanations and return to the subjectivity of faith.

This is precisely the kind of thinking that is not only slightly misguided but risks becoming antithetical to the love of God. Objective reflection in which the thinker's personal existence is not implicated ignores the purposes of believing thinking. Brunner responds to this kind of theology by insisting that categories that lead away from salvation history into the realm of *sub specie aeterni* must be rejected. In this way the good news can be preserved that we exist before God in freedom, not in despair. The kind of transformation that theology has in view results in the intimate language of the heart. Prayer is the I-Thou language of personal encounter. It occurs and can only occur in total subjectivity. There is nothing objective about listening to God in the Holy Spirit and, as Kierkegaard so insightfully states, the moment the focus of our passion becomes objective we no longer love.[102] It is one's passion for one's absolute happiness that compels and motivates and moves one to venture everything in personal encounter.

The jump from the I-Thou encounter of total subjectivity to the language used to talk about faith is a necessary one because it takes into consideration the double-reflection Kierkegaard identifies. This transition is reflected in the apostles' accounts of first-hand encounter with the Godman. The passion of their personal experiences with Christ comes through in their narratives but it is clear that we are separated from these events by culture, language, and centuries. This distance must be recognized. Still, as Brunner has argued, we trust that because God is with us by his Spirit through the same faith as the apostles we do experience him in our own stories. Here is where Kierkegaard's insistence on the individual path of each person with God applies. Because the apostolic testimony is the means by which we know the incarnation, it is invaluable as the way of personal encounter with Christ. If we have rightly understood Brunner, the same

---

Trinity and the Limits of Understanding."

102. For a powerful example of this, see Kierkegaard, *CUP*, 131–32.

holds true for all theological language that is consistent with faith; it is the tool used by the church to foster the subjective knowledge of faith.

The Object–Subject Relation

This brings us back to Kierkegaard's insistence in *CUP* that the dialectical temporal-eternal existence of the knower is the fixed boundary to the object-subject relation. How does this compare with Brunner's rejection of the object-subject antithesis, which had badly damaged theology in his day? For Brunner, this permeates much of dogmatics to its detriment. For Kierkegaard, it distorts our understanding of what it means to become and to remain a Christian. Kierkegaard rejects the equation of Christianity with doctrine insofar as the former is concerned with existence and its subjectivity and the latter with objective "knowing about." Christianity's validity lies in uniqueness as an "existence-contradiction" that requires personal commitment; it requires one to *be* a Christian.[103] In this light, as far as the object-subject relation is concerned, what is urgently required is a renewed understanding of truth as interlaced with our passionate pursuit of absolute happiness. We recall from chapter 2 that the particular context of Brunner's corrective appeal was to reject from dogmatics theoretical interrogations foreign to Scripture. He tied it in with personal existence by exhorting against willful speculation that leads away from ethical application of the gospel. Kierkegaard's warning about the seductive lure of pure thinking that ignores the highs and lows of personal existence can be heard here with little effort.

It is not the danger of the singular doctrine careening away from revelation that most concerns Brunner; it is the influence of the object-subject antithesis. "*The Biblical understanding of truth cannot be grasped through the Object-Subject antithesis*," he argues; "*on the contrary it is falsified through it* . . . [so] that where the heart of faith is concerned—the relation between God's Word and faith, between Christ and faith—the Object-Subject correlation must be replaced by one of an entirely different kind."[104] The objectivism that he describes offers a system by which to master God's word and to exploit the divine–human encounter according to the subject's whim. What results from the fundamental mishandling of the divine address is a distortion of the word of God. Instead of persevering in a perpetual attentiveness

---

103. Ibid., 379–80.
104. Brunner, *Encounter*, 13–14.

to the Holy Spirit who makes the written word revelation, the church has fashioned its own tools by which to handle Scripture. Thus, in Brunner's view, theologians, pastors, and the layperson alike come to regard doctrine identified by ecclesial authority as synonymous with the word of God. As we have observed, this view of faith against which Brunner militates is Kierkegaard's Jericho as well.

In this regard, is it possible to parallel Brunner's definition of "truth as encounter" with Kierkegaard's description of "truth as subjectivity"? It is fair to suggest that, in Kierkegaard's interpretation, the power by which the god transforms the learner in hidden inwardness is the word of God about which Brunner writes. There is similar evidence in Brunner's understanding that encounter means the I-Thou interface between God and the learner in such a way that the learner is, in Kierkegaardian terms, transformed in his very existence. We conclude, then, that the concern of both thinkers is (a) accurate knowledge of the self in I-Thou relationship with God, in such a manner that (b) one's knowledge of God corresponds to God's self-revelation in Christ.

Conclusion

The thorny issue of what qualifies as speculation and what counts as legitimate theological language faithful to the historical event of Jesus Christ must be wrestled to the ground. One approach to this question, suggested by Brunner himself, is to consider the possibility of a Christian philosophy. Is such an enterprise feasible while staying within the limits of the apostolic witness that Brunner sets for theological thinking? What might Kierkegaard contribute to an understanding of the relationship between revelation and reason? How would a Christian philosophy discuss the historical reality and the existential power of the paradox on an individual level, without falling into conjecture?

Brunner's commentary on philosophy and theological anthropology in *Man in Revolt* is the text that suggests the possibility of a Christian philosophy. Though extensive, his comments are worth citing.

> Rational ideas about the being of man are always, secretly, theological ideas, however formal they may seem to be, namely, ideas of a reason which is set free from God, and therefore one which regards man from a legalistic point of view, that is, from the point of view of reason which misunderstands . . . Even the *formal*

concepts of every philosophical ontology are positions of sinful reason, from which, it is true, not *reason* but *sin* must be eliminated. From the standpoint of methodology this means: we always have already a philosophical ontology of some kind before we have faith; but it would be a hopeless undertaking to try to create the right philosophical ontology without faith. Rather, the right ontology of the being of man arises—approximately—through the critical sifting of rational concepts from the standpoint of faith; that means, through a fundamentally Christian philosophy.[105]

In the same stream of consciousness Brunner casts a backward glance to, among others, Kierkegaard as a *Christian* philosopher and Buber as a *biblical* thinker.[106] His purpose in this paragraph is to expose the false conclusion that there exists a neutral ontology. Though there might exist for certain topics something of a neutral philosophy, such objectivity does not apply to the elemental concept of being. Brunner goes on to defend a kind of dialectical relationship between philosophy and theology, between reason and faith-thinking, that is along the same lines as the relationship between law and gospel. Just as the gospel does not negate or ignore the law, so belief does not eliminate reason. Furthermore, as the gospel has come in Christ and the law is no longer lord, reason likewise submits to faith. Brunner's contention is that Christian belief about what it means to be human, for example, is not necessarily incompatible with reasoned reflection on the same subject. The dialectical tension applies to the entire discipline of Christian theology, made distinct from a passionless, objective study of religion because of the role of faith.

The existentialist influence on Brunner's thinking is irrefutable, yet this is not necessarily a compromising feature, for we can see that Brunner keeps his eye fixed on the purpose of dogmatics. Tillich's judgment is fair when he says, "Brunner develops a theological epistemology which seems to me both Biblical and existentialist and, most important, adequate to the

---

105. Brunner, *Man in Revolt*, 545–46.

106. Buber's influence on Brunner is widely recognized and needs little extrapolation as the source of, among other elements, his I–Thou language; see especially Buber, *I and Thou*. For further discussion of Brunner's use of Buber, see Hynson, "Theological Encounter: Brunner and Buber." There are other philosophical influences beside Kierkegaard and Buber who are also reflected in Brunner; Kant and Hegel among them. However, the space restrictions of this present study as well as Bruner's emphasis on personal encounter mean that only Buber receives mention here. For a broader study of Kant and Schelling alongside Kierkegaard, see Kosch, *Freedom and Reason in Kant, Schelling and Kierkegaard*.

subject matter with which theology has to deal."[107] I have tried to show that Brunner's faithfulness to the apostolic witness as the criterion for believing thinking is the control that commands his work, even more than an existentialist tendency. The similarity between "truth as encounter" and "truth as subjectivity" reaffirms what was suggested in previous chapters as the dynamic, personal, and passionate knowledge of faith. This is the nature of revelation and this is the character of Christian truth to which both Scripture and personal encounter testify.

One final note must be made in reference to Kierkegaard's influence on Brunner. Regarding the task of believing thinking, Brunner boldly judges "that no other thinker has ever worked out the contrast between the Christian Faith and all the 'immanental' possibilities of thought with such clarity and intensity as [Kierkegaard] has done. Kierkegaard is incomparably the greatest Apologist or 'eristic' thinker of the Christian Faith within the sphere of Protestantism."[108] Given Brunner's appreciation of this unique second task of theology, this is high praise indeed.

107. Kegley and Bretall, *Theology of Brunner*, 99.
108. Brunner, *Dogmatics I*, 100.

7

Conclusion

"This, then, is conversion: that we seek first the Kingdom of God; that God's desire, namely, service to our neighbor, becomes our chief concern. But you cannot convert yourself; God alone can do it."

—Brunner, *Our Faith*, 85

The goal of this book has been to outline and evaluate Emil Brunner's approach to the "doing" of theology. As with many investigative projects, there have been interests and subjects along the way that have caught my attention that rightfully deserve further study but for which we have no room here. These final pages will conclude by briefly positing two contributions to theological method and three suggestions for the life and work of the church. Because Brunner saw himself as a servant of the church and understood theology to be a responsibility of the church, it is apropos that we finish by considering the import of his example both for the occupation and existence of the church.

There is one matter, though, that requires attention first, which is the question of weaknesses, both real and potential, in Brunner's theological schema. McGrath helpfully (and, I hasten to add, even-handedly, which is not the case with all of Brunner's critics) summarizes several, proposing that these factors might have assisted in the decline of Brunner's influence and

Conclusion

publicity.[1] Briefly noted, they begin with a tendency towards truncated biblical exposition where more fulsome treatment of scriptural foundations is necessary. This tends to be coupled with an opaque and at times complex writing style in some of his major works, rendering accurate digestion of his writing a more challenging task than it might be under a more fluid pen. Also, at times in his work, Brunner tends towards categorical dismissal or condemnation of another's theology.[2] To my mind this is especially unfortunate because he is in equal measure moderate and accommodating of different views in other parts of his theology, and also because this was not a feature of his engagement with Barth though it seems to have been characteristic of Barth's dismissal of Brunner on the same occasion. Finally, Brunner at times has been accused of speaking out of both sides of his mouth, as it were, of saying simultaneously both "yes" and "no." McGrath offers a different interpretation of this impression as it concerns his apologetic objectives in particular.

> Some portray Brunner as offering an unconditional or uncritical affirmation of secular viewpoints and methods. It is impossible to maintain this position. Brunner's opposition to what he regarded as Barth's monolithic "No" was not its polemical inversion—an equally uncritical "Yes"—but a theologically constructed and grounded framework of evaluation, which enabled discerning judgements to be made concerning what was to be affirmed, and what to be rejected. *Brunner's vision* of "eristic theology"—whether it is to be referred to by that clumsy term or not—*allows the Christian community to engage in critical dialogue with culture, rather than withdrawing into its own linguistic and theological ghetto*.[3]

If Brunner's work is not without fault, then why make a plea for its relevance and fecundity for theology almost half a century after his death? It must be noted that, as with many theologians when read on their own terms, Brunner does not neatly fit into one box. And, as with all theologians, he was a person of his time and place—a time and place that has an especially unique position in modern history due to its wars and their subsequent impact on Western culture. His response to and engagement in and around the German-speaking context of World War Two and the decades

---

1. McGrath, *Reappraisal*, 225–28.

2. His short shrift treatment of Schleiermacher in *Die Mystik und das Wort* is a well-known example.

3. McGrath, *Reappraisal*, 74 (emphasis mine).

following has been found wanting by some (Barth included); but by others he is credited with playing an important role in the ecclesial response to the war as well as subsequent crises, both on the European continent and on the North American one.[4] With this in mind we can appreciate Brunner's view of the individual's place in history: "That which seems most insignificant may suddenly emerge in its eternal significance, and the 'drama of world history' (Kierkegaard) may prove to be merely blind confusion. We are not standing upon a tower whence we can survey all that is happening in the world. But what we can and ought to do is this: to stand faithfully at our post, and to do what is commanded us, whether it be 'great' or 'small,' knowing that God's standards are very different from ours."[5] In my view, this is the best kind of theology—one that calls the church to faithfulness to Jesus Christ *hic et nunc*. It is fair to assert that this was Brunner's personal objective in his work as a theologian, pastor, and scholar, as well as his goal for the church of which he was a part. The following suggestions together affirm that this remains a trustworthy aim for us as well.

BRUNNER'S RELEVANCE FOR THEOLOGICAL METHODOLOGY

At least two points can be made on this subject. Firstly Brunner's theology reinforces the need for and the benefit of limiting our theological investigation, and certainly our theological conclusions, to that which is affirmed by the apostolic witness. Why are such limits necessary? They are necessary in order to remain faithful to the revelation that God has given us in Christ and to its primary source. That primary source—Scripture, though lengthy, is itself finite. Its limits should determine the theologian's boundaries insofar as the subjects that Scripture addresses are the subjects theology properly undertakes. As Deuteronomy 29:29 says, "the secret things belong to the Lord our God," and it is right and good that such things remain known to God alone. Even so, Deuteronomy's author continues, "the things that are *revealed* belong to us and to our children forever." *These* things, contained within Scripture, form the proper subject of theology.[6] It is this kind of

---

4. For example, McGrath traces with notable precision the impact of Brunner's theology in response to events such as the Great Depression and the resistance of the Confessing Church; see *Reappraisal*, 66 and context.

5. Brunner, *Divine Imperative*, 287.

6. Although Kilby's work on different topics does not make reference to Brunner

humility on behalf of the theologian that facilitates the kind of knowing of God that dogmatics seeks.

It is fair to ask, then, whether the limitations such as Brunner suggests render redundant the actual task of theology in the form of dogmatics or systematics. I am not positing, however, the end to theological research, writing, or conversation, lest I convict myself (and Brunner for that matter) by the work of my own hands. The work of theology for the purpose of faith is second only to the proclamation of the church. In this light dogmatics is and will remain necessary as the truths of faith require translation for each new generation.

What I am proposing is that Brunner offers a model for dogmatics that both informs and forms faith by following the contours of the biblical witness. In this way I see Brunner offering a path for believing thinking that leads to a kind of humble theology that does not limit faith by presuming to dispel all mystery or by powerfully explaining every spiritual reality, but, by its very boundaried nature, fosters faith in a manner consistent with the testimony of God to himself. Towards this end we recall Brunner's understanding of the purpose of theology: to critique the church's language according to the primary witness to God's self-revelation in Christ found in Scripture. In *The Divine–Human Encounter* he posits, "The task of theology is to elaborate what is formal and at the same time to place it in such a relation with the central contents of the Biblical revelation that it becomes clear how this structural 'form' is determined by the 'matter' and the 'matter' by the 'form.'"[7] Otherwise put, it is the theologian's job to critique the church's formal language according to God's self-disclosure in Scripture, which is the material basis of doctrine, and this, for the purpose of proclaiming Jesus Christ to every generation.

A second point germane to theological methodology relates to the kind of knowing that preoccupies theology. The bifurcation between so-called academic and creedal knowledge that has come to dominate the discipline in modernity is unhelpful if one considers the purpose of theology to be to know God. I propose that Brunner's example, though not entirely unique, offers a practicable middle way.

---

himself, it is a recent example of the kind of boundaries to the theological task that are consistent with Brunner's approach. See Kilby, "Aquinas, the Trinity and the Limits of Understanding;" also Kilby, "Is an Apophatic Trinitarianism Possible?"

7. Brunner, *Encounter*, 30.

In his book *Faith's Knowledge* Paul Tyson helpfully outlines some of the presuppositions of modern scholarship that have impacted significantly the pursuit of "knowing." He summarizes four options: "the separation of faith from reason (to the exclusion of faith);" "the separation of nature from divinity (to the exclusion of divinity);" "the isolation of facts from values (to the relativization of all values);" and "the objectivity of research and the autonomy of discrete spheres of scholarly expertise."[8] For us the question then becomes, What happens within theology when these are the only possibilities for the pursuit of knowledge? Tyson's observation is that "it is expected that scholars must (and can) shelve their metaphysical perspectives, their personal interests, and their moral and religious commitments when they are doing proper academic work." The danger with this "shelving," Tyson goes on to argue, is that, for the theologian, "many of these normal academic assumptions must actually restrict what truth can be known rather than facilitate the knowledge of truth."[9]

Brunner's methodology is consistent with Tyson's evaluation in the sense that Tyson sees God himself as the foundation for knowing. Brunner states it thusly: "Dogmatic thinking is not only thinking about the Faith, it is believing thinking." Without faith theology becomes the general science of religion and ceases to be theology.[10] For both Brunner and Tyson, *knowing God* is theology's apriority.

BRUNNER'S RELEVANCE FOR THE CHURCH

With these elements in mind, I conclude with three concrete points of relevance that Brunner's work offers us for the doing of theology and the being of the church today. The first is his reminder that dogmatics is at the service of proclamation. "The one truth of Christ is refracted in the manifold doctrines of the Apostles; but it is the task of the Church—which has to proclaim the truth of Christ, and thus also has to teach—to seek continually for the one Light of Truth within these refractions. Dogmatics is the science which enables the Church to accomplish this task."[11] We consequently are reminded that the goal of systematic theology is to ensure that our exegesis, catechesis, and polemics are concordant with God's revelation in Christ. In

---

8. Tyson, *Faith's Knowledge*, 85.
9. Ibid., 86.
10. Brunner, *Dogmatics I*, 5.
11. Ibid., 13.

other words, we "go therefore and make disciples of all nations" by retelling the story of salvation history. This is the primary task given to the church, to which theological thinking remains ancillary. Dogmatics must never become master of, nor replace, proclamation.

The second contribution is Brunner's insistence that God is the Lord of revelation. Our experience of God in I-Thou encounter must be assessed according to who God reveals himself to be in the God-man. Personal experience never stands alone; God's word in Scripture must critique it. Hilary of Poitiers's reflections are apropos. "He is the best student who does not read his thoughts into the book but lets it reveal its own; who draws from its sense, and does not impart his own into it, nor force upon its words a meaning which he had determined was the right one before he had opened its pages. Since then we are to discourse of the things of God, let us assume that God has full knowledge of Himself, and bow with humble reverence to his words. For He whom we can only know through his own utterances is the fitting witness concerning Himself."[12] The apostolic witness is the first and last port of call as we seek to hear God's "own utterances" to us today. He continues by his Spirit to be Lord of his self-unveiling as we meet him in the personal encounter of faith through prayer, worship, and the life of the church.

A final point of relevance is Brunner's interpretation of proclamation which extends well beyond the Sunday sermon to include a "proclaiming *existence* . . . not a mere matter of uttering words, but of passing on the life in which God has communicated Himself."[13] Central to this concept is the work of the Holy Spirit effecting on-going revelation, but it also includes the role that we as believers play in this event. The historical element of revelation is not only that it took place at specific points in the past, but also that it continues to occur in the particularities of *our* human story. This leads us to ask, what is it that we, as believers first and theologians second, ought to be spending our time on?[14] In such a manner, we, alongside Brunner, seek to maintain the interconnection between orthodoxy and orthopraxis.

To state it in another way, if our work is to be consistent with the gospel itself, it has as much to do with who we are as it does with what

---

12. From 'On the Trinity,' in Schaff, ed., *Nicene and Post-Nicene Fathers*, vol. 9, Book I, par. 18.

13. Brunner, *Dogmatics III*, 4.

14. We are reminded that the question, "What ought we to do?" is one that drives *The Divine Imperative*. See Brunner, *Divine Imperative*, 9.

we proclaim.[15] Examples from Scripture are too plentiful for exhaustive citation. It is clear, though, throughout the Bible that true religion and right theology are tested by the care of the people of God for the stranger, the orphan, and the widow—the "little ones" of society—as well as our commitment to justice and the common good. Personal encounter that leads to true knowledge of God results in recognizing Christ's Lordship over all aspects of personal and communal life. Furthermore, that Lordship binds one into a broader believing community that is determined as much by its engagement as salt and light in the world as by its creedal affirmations.

Where does this leave us as theologians, as church people, as students of theology, and as seekers of God himself? I suggest that Brunner's conviction that God continues to will his self-disclosure in a manner consistent with the historical event of Jesus Christ is good news for church and culture alike: Emmanuel, God is *still* with us. The twenty-first century West, as much as any time or place in human history, needs the people of God not only to study and to preach but also to practice "a real religion of revelation, in which God confronts the human 'I' as 'Thou,' . . . in which from beyond human possibilities God Himself discloses Himself to man."[16] With such an end in view, it is my hope that this study helps to establish Brunner's model of bounded theology as a valuable example for our believing thinking and transformed being today.

---

15. A fuller exposition of this point can be found in Brown, "The Personal Imperative of Revelation."

16. Brunner, *Divine Imperative*, 50.

Bibliography

Baillie, John. *Our Knowledge of God*. London: Oxford University Press, 1939.
Barth, Karl. *Church Dogmatics*. I/1, *The Doctrine of the Word of God*. Translated by G. W. Bromiley. Edinburgh: T. & T. Clark, 1975.
———. *Church Dogmatics*. I/2, *The Doctrine of the Word of God*. Translated by G. W. Bromiley and T. F. Torrance. Edinburgh: T. & T. Clark, 1963.
———. *Church Dogmatics*, II/1. *The Doctrine of God*. Translated by T. H. L. Parker, W. B. Johnston, Harold Knight, and J. L. M. Haire. Edinburgh: T. & T. Clark, 1957.
———. *Dogmatics in Outline*. Translated by G.T. Thomson. London: SCM, 1949.
Bartsch, Hans-Werner, ed. *Kerygma and Myth: A Theological Debate, Volume II*. Translated by Reginald H. Fuller. London: SPCK, 1962.
"The Holy Bible (English Standard Version)." Wheaton, IL: Crossway, 2001.
Brown, Cynthia Bennett. "The Personal Imperative of Revelation: Emil Brunner, Dogmatics and Theological Existence." *Scottish Journal of Theology* 65 (2012) 421–34.
Brown, James. *Subject and Object in Theology: The Croall Lectures, 1953*. London: SCM, 1955.
Brunner, Emil. *Dogmatics*. Vol. 1, *The Christian Doctrine of God*. Translated by Olive Wyon. 1949. Reprinted, Eugene, OR: Wipf & Stock, 2014.
———. *Dogmatics*. Vol. 2, *The Christian Doctrine of Creation and Redemption*. Translated by Olive Wyon. 1952. Reprinted, Eugene, OR: Wipf & Stock, 2014.
———. *Dogmatics*. Vol. 3, *The Christian Doctrine of the Church, Faith, and the Consummation*. Translated by David Cairns with T. H. L. Parker. 1960. Reprinted, Eugene, OR: Wipf & Stock, 2014.
———. "The Christian Understanding of Man." In *The Christian Understanding of Man* by T. E. Jessop et al., 141–77. Church, Community, and State 2. London: Allen & Unwin, 1938.
———. *The Divine-Human Encounter*. Translated by Amandus W. Loos. London: SCM, 1944.
———. *The Divine Imperative: A Study in Christian Ethics*. Translated by Olive Wyon. London: Lutterworth, 1937.
———. *Eternal Hope*. Translated by Harold Knight. London: Lutterworth, 1954.
———. *Faith, Hope, and Love*. The Earl Lectures 1955. Philadelphia: Westminster, 1955.
———. *I Believe in the Living God*. Translated by John Holden. London: Lutterworth, 1961.
———. *Justice and the Social Order*. Translated by Mary Hottinger. London: Lutterworth, 1945.

———. *Man in Revolt: A Christian Anthropology*. Translated by Olive Wyon. London: Lutterworth, 1939.

———. *The Mediator*. Translated by Olive Wyon. London: Lutterworth, 1934.

———. "The New Barth: Observations on Karl Barth's Doctrine of Man." *Scottish Journal of Theology* 4 (1951) 123–35.

———. *Our Faith*. Translated by John W. Rilling. London: SCM, 1949.

———. *The Philosophy of Religion from the Standpoint of Protestant Theology*. Translated by A. J. D. Farrer and Bertram Lee Woolf. London: Nicholson & Watson, 1937.

———. *Revelation and Reason*. Translated by Olive Wyon. London: SCM, 1947.

———. *The Scandal of Christianity*. Robertson Lectures 1948. London: SCM, 1951.

———. "The Significance of the Old Testament for Our Christian Faith." In *The Old Testament and Christian Faith: A Theological Discussion*, edited by Bernhard W. Anderson, 243–64. New York: Herder & Herder, 1969.

———. *The Theology of Crisis*. Swander Lectures 1928. London: Scribners, 1929.

———. *Truth as Encounter*. Translated by David Cairns and T. H. L. Parker. London: SCM, 1964.

———. *The Word and the World*. London: SCM, 1931.

Brunner, Emil, and Karl Barth. *Natural Theology*. Translated by Peter Fraenkel. 1946. Reprinted, Eugene, OR: Wipf & Stock, 2002.

Buber, Martin. *I and Thou*. Translated by Walter Kaufmann. Edinburgh: T. & T. Clark, 1970.

Burnier, Edouard. "Protestant Theology in Wartime Switzerland." *Theology Today* 4 (1947) 59–79.

Calvin, John. *Institutes of the Christian Religion*. Translated by Henry Beveridge. Grand Rapids: Eerdmans, 1997.

Crites, Stephen. *In the Twilight of Christendom: Hegel vs. Kierkegaard on Faith and History*. AAR Studies in Religion. Chambersburg, PA: American Academy of Religion, 1972.

Dorrien, Gary. *The Barthian Revolt in Modern Theology: Theology without Weapons*. Louisville: Westminster John Knox, 2000.

Dyck, Arthur J. "Moral Requiredness: Bridging the Gap between 'Ought' and 'Is'—Part II." *Journal of Religious Ethics*, Spring 9 (1981) 131–50.

"Emil Brunner and the Wide-Open Spaces." *Christian Century* 80 (1963) 255.

Fergusson, David. *Bultmann*. 1992. Reprinted, Outstanding Christian Thinkers. London: Continuum, 2000.

Gibson, David, and Daniel Strange, eds. *Engaging with Barth: Contemporary Evangelical Critiques*. Nottingham, UK: Apollos, 2008.

Grenz, Stanley J., and Roger E. Olson. *Twentieth-Century Theology: God and the World in a Transitional Age*. Downers Grove, IL: InterVarsity, 1992.

Hart, John W. *Karl Barth vs. Emil Brunner: The Formation and Dissolution of a Theological Alliance, 1916–1936*. Issues in Systematic Theology 6. New York: Lang, 2001.

Hebblethwaite, Brian. *The Christian Hope*. Oxford: Oxford University Press, 2010.

Heideman, Eugene Paul. "The Relation of Revelation and Reason in E. Brunner and H. Bavinck." PhD diss., Utrecht University, 1959.

Henry, Carl F. H., ed. *Christian Faith and Modern Theology*. Grand Rapids: Baker, 1964.

Humphrey, J. Edward. *Emil Brunner*. Makers of the Modern Theological Mind. Waco, TX: Word, 1976.

Hynson, Leon O. "Theological Encounter: Brunner and Buber." *Journal of Ecumenical Studies* 12 (1975) 349–66.

Jehle, Frank. *Emil Brunner: Theologe im 20. Jahrhundert.* Zurich: Theologischer Verlag, 2006.
Jewett, Paul King. *Emil Brunner's Concept of Revelation.* London: James Clarke, 1954.
Johnson, Keith L. *Karl Barth and the Analogia Entis.* London: T. & T. Clark, 2010.
Johnson, Wendell Gordon. "Soteriology as a Function of Epistemology in the Thought of Emil Brunner." PhD diss., University of Michigan, 1989.
Kegley, Charles W., and Robert W. Bretall, eds. *The Theology of Emil Brunner.* New York: Macmillian, 1962.
Kierkegaard, Søren. *Concluding Unscientific Postscript to Philosophical Fragments: Volume I.* Translated by Howard V. Hong and Edna H. Hong. Kierkegaard's Writings 12. Princeton: Princeton University Press, 1992.
———. *Philosophical Fragments, Johannes Climacus.* Translated by Howard V. Hong and Edna H. Hong. Kierkegaard's Writings 7. Princeton: Princeton University Press, 1985.
———. *The Sickness Unto Death: A Christian Psychological Exposition for Upbuilding and Awakening.* Translated by Howard V. Hong and Edna H. Hong. Kierkegaard's Writings 19. Princeton: Princeton University Press, 1980.
Kilby, Karen. "Aquinas, the Trinity and the Limits of Understanding." *International Journal of Systematic Theology* 7 (2005) 414–27.
———. "Is an Apophatic Trinitarianism Possible?" *International Journal of Systematic Theology* 12 (2009) 65–77.
Kosch, Michelle. *Freedom and Reason in Kant, Schelling and Kierkegaard.* Oxford: Oxford University Press, 2006.
Law, David R. "How Christian Is Kierkegaard's God?" *Scottish Journal of Theology* 48 (1995) 285–314.
Lovin, Robin W. *Christian Faith and Public Choices: The Social Ethics of Barth, Brunner, and Bonhoeffer.* Philadelphia: Fortress, 1984.
McEnhill, Peter, and George Newlands. *Fifty Key Christian Thinkers.* Abingdon, UK: Routledge, 2004.
McGrath, Alister E. *Emil Brunner: A Reappraisal.* Chichester, UK: Wiley-Blackwell, 2014.
McKim, Mark G. "Brunner the Ecumenist: Emil Brunner as a Vox Media of Protestant Theology." *Calvin Theological Journal* 32 (1997) 91–104.
Moltmann, Jürgen. *The Crucified God: The Cross of Christ as the Foundation and Criticism of Christian Theology.* Translated by R. A. Wilson and John Bowden. London: SCM, 1974.
———. *The Trinity and the Kingdom: The Doctrine of God.* Translated by Margaret Kohl. Minneapolis: Fortress, 1993.
Nelson, J. Robert. "Emil Brunner—the Final Encounter." *Christian Century* 83 (1967) 486.
O'Donovan, Joan E. "Man in the Image of God: The Disagreement between Barth and Brunner Reconsidered." *Scottish Journal of Theology* 39 (1986) 433–59.
Reymond, Robert. *Contending for the Faith.* Rossshire, UK: Mentor, 2005.
Roberts, Robert. "Kierkegaard on Becoming an 'Individual.'" *Scottish Journal of Theology* 31 (1978) 133–52.
Schaff, Philip, ed. *Nicene and Post-Nicene Fathers.* Vol. 9. Grand Rapids: Christian Classics Ethereal Library, 1898.
Schrotenboer, Paul G. *A New Apologetics: An Analysis and Appraisal of the Eristic Theology of Emil Brunner.* Kampen: Kok, 1955.

BIBLIOGRAPHY

Schwarz, Hans. *Theology in a Global Context: The Last Two Hundred Years*. Grand Rapids: Eerdmans, 2005.

Smith, Joseph J. "Emil Brunner's Theology of Revelation." *Heythrop Journal* 6 (1965) 5–26.

Tyson, Paul. *Faith's Knowledge: Explorations into the Theory and Application of Theological Epistemology*. Eugene, OR: Pickwick Publications, 2013.

Van Til, Cornelius. *The New Modernism: An Appraisal of the Theology of Barth and Brunner*. London: James Clarke, 1946.

Williams, Daniel D. "Brunner and Barth on Philosophy." *Journal of Religion* 27 (1947) 241–54.

Williams, Stephen N. *Revelation and Reconciliation: A Window on Modernity*. Cambridge: Cambridge University Press, 1995.